ADVANCE PRAISE FOR Video Journalism

"*Video Journalism* is an important contribution to understanding the role of new video technologies in journalism: small cameras, electronic editing and communication, easier access to people and events, and professional realignments with news media institutions. Mary Angela Bock's lucid account of ethnographic fieldwork consists not only of many compelling stories and a wealth of new conceptions she has employed to make sense of them, but it is also committed to keep video journalists' bodies in the images they are creating. This book is important not only to journalists seeking to understand their new environment but also to sociologists, communication scholars, and students looking for templates of exciting inquiries."—*Klaus Krippendorff, The Annenberg School for Communication, University of Pennsylvania*

"Everyone who is chair of a journalism and communication department today hears from employers that they want us to produce 'one-woman bands': graduates who can tell powerful stories in words and images across all media platforms and using many technologies. Mary Angela Bock has written the first major book documenting and explaining the rise of this 'all-in-one' worker in the visual news industry. Anyone who wants to understand how we got here and where we are going in visual journalism—from a news director at a local station to a doctoral student studying changes in newsroom practice and culture—will now have to start by consulting this excellent book."—*David D. Perlmutter, Director of the School of Journalism and Mass Communication, and Professor and Starch Faculty Fellow, College of Liberal Arts and Sciences, The University of Iowa*

"Theoretically sophisticated yet immersed in concrete professional practice, *Video Journalism* provides a timely, in-depth exposition of developments in video news making and the challenges they pose for the conventional practices of news organizations. Journalism scholarship has long paid too little attention to the visual aspects of news. *Video Journalism* not only draws attention to the crucial role of images in news but explores how mobile video technologies and new paradigms of independent news work are changing news production practices across media formats—for newspapers, cable and satellite news services, and local TV."—*Michael Griffin, Visiting Professor of Media and Cultural Studies, Macalester College, and Chair of the Visual Communication Studies Division, International Communication Association (ICA)*

"Video journalists have changed television news but just how they've done so has rarely been studied. Mary Angela Bock's thorough examination of the video journalist (VJ) revolution shows how this trend has affected both the process of newsgathering and the product that goes on the air, sometimes in worrisome ways."—*Deborah Potter, NewsLab*

Video Journalism

Mass Communication and Journalism

Lee B. Becker
GENERAL EDITOR

Vol. 6

This book is part of the Peter Lang Media and Communication list.
Every volume is peer reviewed and meets
the highest quality standards for content and production.

PETER LANG
New York • Washington, D.C./Baltimore • Bern
Frankfurt • Berlin • Brussels • Vienna • Oxford

Mary Angela Bock

Video Journalism

Beyond the One-Man Band

PETER LANG
New York • Washington, D.C./Baltimore • Bern
Frankfurt • Berlin • Brussels • Vienna • Oxford

Library of Congress Cataloging-in-Publication Data

Bock, Mary Angela.
Video journalism: beyond the one-man band / Mary Angela Bock.
p. cm. — (Mass communication and journalism; v. 6)
Includes bibliographical references and index.
1. Video journalism. 2. Digital video. 3. Online journalism.
4. Journalism—Authorship. 5. Reporters and reporting.
6. Journalism—Technological innovations. I. Title.
PN4784.V54B63 070.4'9—dc23 2012005679
ISBN 978-1-4331-1454-0 (hardcover)
ISBN 978-1-4331-1453-3 (paperback)
ISBN 978-1-4539-0905-8 (e-book)
ISSN 2153-2761

Bibliographic information published by **Die Deutsche Nationalbibliothek**.
Die Deutsche Nationalbibliothek lists this publication in the "Deutsche Nationalbibliografie"; detailed bibliographic data is available on the Internet at http://dnb.d-nb.de/.

Front cover concept by Rosie Carlson
Author photo on back cover by Emily Carlson

The paper in this book meets the guidelines for permanence and durability of the Committee on Production Guidelines for Book Longevity of the Council of Library Resources.

29 Broadway, 18th floor, New York, NY 10006
www.peterlang.com

Printed in the United States of America

For David,
who made it possible.

Table of Contents

List of Figures & Tables

Preface

More years ago than I'd like to admit, I was an assignment editor for WPVI-TV, home at the time to the nation's top-rated newscast. The job of an assignment editor is to dispatch photographers and reporters to news stories—simple enough. But combining the list of scheduled events with breaking news, being able to navigate a photographer who is driving and can't stop to examine a map, using (at that time) a two-way radio while listening to the chatter on police scanners turns the job into a daily pressure-cooker. One day I was anxiously trying to help a photographer find his way through one of the suburbs of Bucks County, Pennsylvania, one of many areas around Philadelphia where boundaries make little sense and nothing runs according to the compass. My voice on the two-way became more and more shrill as I asked him repeatedly, "have you entered Bristol Township?"

He'd had quite enough of my fretfulness and barked back on the radio: "Look, I don't have a map! It's not like the street changes color when I cross the border!" Little did he know how strongly his words would echo, much later, when I was in graduate school reading Michel DeCerteau's *Walking In the City*. The city is not a map. A map is not a city. We use our bodies to live in the world, and our senses are all we have for understanding it. In turn, our bodily senses inform the way we talk about the world.

News photographers don't generally quote DeCerteau, but they exemplify his argument. Their work is a special blend of technology, the body, and the world around us. What I've written in this book will likely strike most photographic journalists as patently obvious and deliriously dull. But the connection between bodily practice and the construction of news images is often overlooked in news scholarship, and one I believe must be explored more carefully if we are to truly understand visual forms of communication. All too often, we in the academy work as though our world is a map. It is not. Our world is hot, dry, cold and wet. We experience real pain, we get tired, we carry heavy objects, and our hearts race when we are afraid or in love. Where we stand, what we see, and how we feel inform our constructions of the world—our intellectual maps. We must never forget, though, that our maps are not the city, and the street doesn't change color when we cross the border.

Acknowledgments

I started this research in 2007, but the project's roots go back much further than that—to the days when I was a student at Drake University in the 1980s, helping to produce and write a student news show. It was then that I realized I could easily do without the many volunteers who wanted to report and anchor, as long as I had colleagues who were willing to shoot video. Without video, I had a radio show. During my career as a reporter, assignment editor, and field producer in local television news, my appreciation for the men and women who could manage technology under pressure, respond to quick changes in the field, and come back to the station with compelling images only grew further.

Consequently this book is in part dedicated to all the video journalists who've helped me create compelling stories, who've saved the day when I got them to a scene late, who've managed to make what's called in newsroom vernacular "chicken salad" for stories without obvious visual appeal. It's for those who taught me when to shut up in an interview, who've shared tears with me at the scenes of tragedy, and who've occasionally put their camera down when it was clearly more important to respond as a human being than to shoot someone in grief.

This book is also dedicated to Dr. Klaus Krippendorff, whose brilliant insight is rivaled only by his kindness and patience. My scholarship and writing skills improved under his guidance. It's a rare graduate student who can say they've never left a meeting with their advisor feeling diminished; I am one of them. I am further grateful to the other members of my dissertation committee, Dr. Michael Delli Carpini and Dr. Barbie Zelizer, for their keen insight and amazing breadth of knowledge, which elevated this work to a level far beyond my singular abilities. My colleagues at the Annenberg School, faculty, staff, and my fellow students also enriched my work and my life as my research took shape.

This project would not have been possible without the help, time, and consideration of the BBC, the *Gannett Corporation*, *The New York Times*, the *Philadelphia Daily News* and *Inquirer*, *News12 the Bronx*, *Our City, Our Voices*, and the multitude of other institutions that allowed me to observe their operations. A grant from the Annenberg School's Center for Global Communication Studies, spearheaded by Dr. Monroe Price, made my travel to England possible. The BBC assisted me with transportation when plans went awry. Dozens of individual journalists gave generously of their time so that I could gather information. As I warned them in my IRB-consent form, all I can do in return is express my appreciation.

I am forever indebted to Dannette Bock, who used her considerable talent, patience, and eye for detail to format this book. Finally, David, Rosie, and Emily: thank you for listening to me whine about my research summer after summer, for patiently nodding when I droned on about social constructivism, and for celebrating with me as each chapter was completed. Your love provided the energy I needed to finish. Thank you.

Chapter One:
Video Journalism & Its Origins

"Are you a journalist? Or just a photographer?"
—questions posed repeatedly to a former photo journalist

Decades before he went to Congress, former comedian Al Franken[1] performed a sketch from downtown Des Moines, Iowa, with a fake satellite dish attached to his head, a camera and deck attached to his body, and a microphone in his hand. He declared himself to be the world's first self-contained live television journalist. The size of the equipment and the cumbersome way it was attached to him made for a hilarious sketch. Today, a one-person live television unit is no longer a joke. With smaller, lighter cameras and editing equipment and wireless internet technology, one person can carry everything necessary to gather, edit, and transmit video news in a backpack. They have come to be known as *video journalists*, or *VJs*. Dozens of such video journalists, working in the UK and the US, for newspapers and television, in small markets and large, took part in the research for this book. They are changing the way we watch the news.

To understand how this is possible, it helps to know a little about what video journalism is and its history. This means looking a bit not only at its technological history, but the way journalism itself has historically treated images, and the sometimes rocky relationship between journalism's literary tradition and the mass appeal of pictures. Because video journalism unites word and image, writer and photographer, it is helpful to unpack these concepts to better analyze how this new form of newsgathering is changing video storytelling. The rest of this chapter presents these foundational concepts and starts, simply enough, with an attempt to define the subject at hand.

Exactly What Is Video Journalism?

So-called "one-man bands" have long existed in the documentary filmmaking world (less so, of course, during the mid-20th century when sound required a separate recorder and technician). In television news, solo video newsgathering or documentary filmmaking tended to be the exception until the 1970s—again, given the constraints of separate camera and sound-recording systems (Baddeley, 1973). Generally, single-person units were more often found in smaller markets where young reporters would shoot, write, and edit solo with the goal of eventually working their way into larger markets where they'd work as part of a team with a video-photographer[2] and (much longer ago) sound technicians who carried and controlled microphones. Large market and network teams might also include field producers to write, negotiate with officials, or gather information. The norm for conventional television newsgathering in the United States generally involves cameras that weigh considerably more than the cameras used by those who call themselves "MMJs" (multimedia journalists), "BPJs" (backpack journalists), "SoloJos" (solo journalists), "Mojos" (mobile journalists [Martyn, 2009], or, most simply and with the phrase that will be used throughout this book, video journalists, or VJs.

Digital technology and the convergence of news platforms are changing the business models for both conventional television and newspapers and, similarly, the means by which news images are gathered. Now, as more newspapers are posting video to their websites, staff photographers are being asked to (if not forced to) learn how to use video cameras, microphones, tripods, and video edit systems. Cameras are many pounds lighter and easier to manipulate, and wireless internet technology makes it possible to transmit images untethered. Broadband internet connections allow for the transmission of high-quality video at speeds impossible only a few years ago. The emergence of video journalism as a distinct form is not only a result of changes in camera size, therefore, but also in computer technology. Increasingly clear video playback systems on broadband, user-friendly digital editing, and wireless transmission are among the key factors that have influenced the development of this nascent form of newsgathering.

The popularization of the term *video journalism* to describe solo newsgathering with a small camera can be traced to a former network television producer, Michael Rosenblum, who used it to title a course he taught at Columbia University as an adjunct in the late 1980s (M. Rosenblum, personal communication, June 23, 2008). Inspired by the smaller "Hi8" cameras available at the time, and the ease with which one person could operate, Rosenblum established a short-lived international news network using only

VJs (M. Rosenblum, 2008; M. Rosenblum, n.d.). Video News International (VNI) eventually became New York Times Television and later folded when the *New York Times* established a video journalism unit within its overall newsgathering operation. Both reviled and revered[3] for his incendiary message that conventional television news is a bloated system that presents an uninteresting product, Rosenblum nonetheless attracted converts across the world, consulting with the Voice of America, the BBC, and numerous television stations in the US. David Dunkley Gyimah, a former Rosenblum student, now teaches video journalism in Britain (Gyimah, 2007). A VNI colleague, Dirck Halstead, is a leader in teaching print photographers how to produce video stories with his annual "Platypus" workshops (Halstead, 2008). The influence of Rosenblum's consulting will be detailed in later chapters, as will his arguments about video storytelling, which, while not necessarily unique, played a considerable role in the early development of video journalism worldwide.

Today, the phrase video journalist is common among news workers even though its practice and product are unevenly defined. *News Photographer*, the professional trade magazine for the National Press Photographers Association, started using the phrase regularly in 2005, and in 2006, the organization announced a new category for (solo) video journalists to its annual Best of Photojournalism contest (Murray, 2006). Many television executives, however, continue to use the term one-man band, with all the negative connotations that goes with the term.

Currently, it is hard to find a media organization or market that is not adopting some form of video journalism, with widely varying routines and styles of presentation. While the practice remains uneven and news workers may argue over the title, two features stand out: first, one person is responsible for shooting and producing a VJ story and second, a dependence on digital technologies, including cameras, editing software, and transmission. In the course of my research, I've developed the following working definition:

> ***Video Journalism*** is the practice of video news production whereby one person shoots, writes, and edits news stories, using digital technologies, to be disseminated via broadcasting or broadband internet.

Note that this definition does not include mention of video journalism's artifact, the way the word journalism is used to describe both an activity and a product. One of the driving forces behind this project is the question of whether or not video journalism's process is unique. So for now, the definition focuses only on the unique, distinct aspects of the process.

Video journalism is a natural outgrowth of media *convergence*, a term that's on the verge of overuse by scholars and practitioners alike, and requires clarification such as that provided by Rich Gordon (2003). Gordon traces the history of the word's modern application to the early 1980s when media leaders started to recognize the impact of computer networks, and Ithiel de Sola Pool (1983) wrote *The Technologies of Freedom* in which he described "the convergence of modes." Gordon identified three primary facets of convergence, namely technology, organization, and presentation. Video journalism is a product and manifestation of all three of these facets. Technological convergence is represented by more than internet websites and smaller cameras; it is also manifest in the user-friendly editing software and broadband access which make is feasible for one person to set up their own live coverage.[4] Organizationally, convergence represents both changes in ownership as corporations merge and unite properties once considered print or television, as well as in organizational structure by adjusting managerial, workflow, and organizational tactics as when a news organization shifts from a nightly printing-press deadline to adjust to the internet's 24-hour, immediate news cycle. Gordon's third facet, presentation (or story-telling), is of particular interest, for convergence has the potential to change the way news stories are told. In a sense, video journalists are the very embodiment of convergence: working in converged organizations, with converged technology, and incorporating multiple work-roles, the convergence of what were once journalistic specializations (Boczkowski, 2004; Deuze, 2004).

Not surprisingly, the way VJs are deployed by news organizations varies according to a news organization's historic form of exhibition, and largely according to what Altheide and Snow (1979) described as the "media logic" of various institutions. Newspapers are adopting the form differently than local television or direct-to-the-web news operations. VJs may not always work in the field entirely alone; in some instances, two VJs are sent out, each with their own equipment, to collaborate or assist one another in the field. They may or may not narrate their own stories—something that is largely unsettled and debated by its practitioners. They may cover part of a story, and then work with a technician to transmit a taped portion live during a newscast. So the distinguishing features of the working definition posed here, namely that one person shoots, writes, and edits alone, provides a useful, albeit negotiable, starting point.

Why Video Journalism?

The pressure for newsrooms to adopt video journalism is often on par with organizational survival. Newspapers are losing traditional readers at an alarming rate, with a Harris Poll in 2007 finding that only two in five adults regularly read a newspaper (Harris International, 2007). The Pew Foundation similarly found most people unconcerned with the prospect of losing their local newspaper (Pew, 2009). The economic challenges that started in 2008 were especially hard on news organizations with revenue declines that compelled furloughs, layoffs, and the shuttering of many a newsroom across the US (Carr, 2007; Saba, 2008; Sass, 2008, 2010a; Stelter & Carter, 2010). By 2010, Pew reported that, on average, newspaper staffs were 30% smaller than they were in 2000 (Pew, 2011). As more and more institutions struggle to adopt convergence strategies, old-model organizations are likely to continue to suffer. One bright spot for traditional media? The growth in revenue from internet users downloading news videos (Sass, 2010b). In 2008, WUSA, an ABC-affiliated station in Washington, D.C., announced to its staff that all of its reporters would begin shooting their own stories as "backpack" journalists or they could take a severance package.

No matter how it is deployed, the technology of video journalism is changing job descriptions and expectations. Journalists are being asked to think technically, visually, and narratively. Photographers are writing far more than captions; they're writing scripts. Writers are being asked to learn technical skills, such as using a video camera and editing software, employing visual composition and lighting. Sound is essential for the construction of video stories and all VJs, whether working for TV stations, newspapers, or independently, must collect and work with sound in the form of interviews and what's called *NATSOT*[5] to construct a narrative that is understandable from start to finish. The narrative skill required for video journalism, something taken for granted among textual journalists, takes on a different form when it is integrated with moving images and sound. It is not enough in these pages to address the nature of images and alpha-numeric text—video journalism is further complicated by its incorporation of all matter of sound, a facet essential to understanding its process and the stories that result.

Video Journalism's Family Tree

A bit of history is useful for understanding the relationship between technology and storytelling, process and product. Video journalism's roots reach back centuries to the *camera obscura* of the Renaissance: darkened rooms whose small windows cast inverted images onto a wall, enabling artists to sketch more realistic pictures. This was the beginning of technological experimentation to accurately record a visual scene and, in the process, create seemingly realistic representations. The history of photo journalism, as it branches into documentary film and in turn branches into television news, can be traced in terms of these two lines. Human users have employed camera technology as an accurate recorder of the visual world for a variety of purposes: to create art, to answer scientific questions, to record history, to establish journalistic authority, and, most importantly for this exploration, to tell stories.

Technology & Photo Journalism

Photography's invention grew out of a strong artistic impulse in the West to represent reality. The earliest cameras were tools utilized by painters for more accurate depictions. The stunning technological advances announced by Louis Daguerre and William Henry Fox Talbot in 1839 inspired an entirely new branch of artistic endeavors, with still-life and tableau-styled photographs imitating historic paintings (Barsam, 1973; Clarke, 1997; N. Rosenblum, 1997). The mechanical accuracy of their inventions was almost immediately recognized by scientists, governments, historians, social activists, and artists as a means to advance their own purposes (Clarke, 1997; N. Rosenblum, 1997; Scharf, 1974; Sekula, 1986). Journalism, remarkably, was a bit slower to embrace photography for reasons both technical and organizational (Barnhurst & Nerone, 2001). The earliest cameras, large and heavy, made field work difficult. Matthew Brady, considered by some to be America's first "photo journalist" struggled to traverse Civil War battlegrounds with equipment that required a horse and wagon (Morrow, 2007). Battle scenes were all but impossible because the cameras needed extensive setup and long exposure times, so the photographs tended to depict not battles but the dead and wounded in their aftermath (Morrow, 2007).

Illustrated newspapers in the mid-19th century did not print photographs but woodcuts, often very subjectively drawn by skilled artists (Barnhurst & Nerone, 2001). Such illustrations, sometimes based on photographs, were not always technically accurate and sometimes combined elements from more than one view. Not until the invention of the halftone in 1880 were photos themselves occasionally reproduced in newspapers and periodicals—yet, engravings held on for years in part because, as Barnhurst and Nerone (2001) point out, while the illustrations may not have been perfectly accurate, they were considered truthful representations of an overall story. Consider also that early halftones, the printed versions of photographs, were often blurry and less appealing than the illustrations. Consequently, the two forms coexisted for years (Barnhurst & Nerone, 2001; N. Rosenblum, 1997). Nevertheless, towards the end of the 19th century, photography became the norm for journalistic representation, in part due to the lure of what was considered "realistic" and shifts in publication patterns (Barnhurst & Nerone,

2001). This nuanced early confluence of illustrated narrative and photographic documentation constitutes a visual version of what Michael Schudson has identified as contemporary journalism's core activities: information relay and storytelling (Schudson, 1978).

As technologies of photography developed, so too did the use of images to relay information and tell stories. Camera size was merely one consideration. Camera mechanics, such as shutter speeds, darkroom techniques, emulsion types, film formats, and so on, served to change not only *what* photographers could portray but *how*. For example, as early film became more sensitive and required shorter exposure times, photographs of cityscapes became populated; earlier images couldn't capture the movement of people on the streets, so early cityscapes were devoid of the urban bustle of humanity (Brecheen-Kirkton, 1981; Scharf, 1974). Flash powder made possible Jacob Riis' tragic photos of dark, airless New York slums in *How the Other Half Lives* (Carlebach, 1997; N. Rosenblum, 1997). The switch from photographic plates to George Eastman's flexible rolls of film ushered in the era of "candid" shots, produced by professionals and thousands of amateur newcomers. In the early 20th century, news photographers dependent on their 4×5 format "Speed Graphic" cameras developed practices for capturing one, at most two, synecdochic shots on crisp, clear, dependable negatives (Carlebach, 1997).

Eventually, a camera arrived with a combination of mechanics, format, and size that could replace the Speed Graphic, Leica's® 35-millimeter camera. Developed from a device used by movie-makers to check lighting setups, this lightweight, small, maneuverable camera, which used the same film as cinematic cameras, eventually became the choice of photo journalists—though not without a fight (Carlebach, 1997; Leica Corporation, n.d.). Longtime users of the Speed Graphic resisted the quick-snapping shooting style afforded by the Leica®. Frank Scherschel and Stanley Kalish, two of the era's leading photo editors advised "...what we believe is needed in picture coverage...of big stories such as disasters, fires, and crimes is a little more thinking and a little less picture snapping" (1940, p. 261 quoted in Carlebach).[6] The action sequences it made possible, along with Henri Cartier-Bresson's popularization of the idea of the "decisive moment," eventually granted victory to the Leica® (Brecheen-Kirkton, 1981; Carlebach, 1997; N. Rosenblum, 1997). The vituperous resistance by longtime Speed Graphic users is echoing, decades later, in the debate among conventional television photographers over the adoption of the smaller, lighter video cameras at television stations. An understanding of everyday photographic practice helps in the interpretation of such intense resistance to change. Photographers develop intense loyalty to certain pieces of equipment, in part because the camera becomes a part of their body. A news photographer and her equipment operate much as a marksman and his pistol, a chef with her knife, or a musician at his keyboard. After years of successfully working in tandem, one doesn't easily dump a good dance partner.

Yet the processes of photo journalism are rooted in more than camera technology. Advances in the mechanics of publication and exhibition, as well as changes in social and organizational demands, changed the ways images were used and claimed by journalism. For instance, more sophisticated darkroom techniques in the early 20th century ushered in the yellow press' use of photographic collage—manipulations, really—using photographs to create illustrations (Carlebach, 1997). The invention of wire photo between the two World Wars allowed newspapers to use internationally transmitted (and therefore judged to be more current and newsworthy) images on the front pages, making the images more relevant to the stories of the day (Zelizer, 1995). Even paper stock is a consideration: *Life* and *Look* magazines were only possible when production of pictorial magazines could be profitable (Carlebach, 1997). While newspapers had already been publishing sets of photographs, the pictorials gave the documentary-style still-photographer greater prestige, refining the photo "essay" as a distinct media form (Barnhurst & Nerone, 2001; Rothstein, 1956). Yet even within this prestigious realm, photo journalists generally did not control the story; this remained the territory of magazine writers and editors, journalism's textual workers (Lutz & Collins, 1993; Morris, 2002).

In 1946, news photographers started fighting against what they perceived as professional marginalization, forming their own advocacy and standards organization, the National Press Photographers Association (NPPA). An editorial in their first newsletter proclaimed: "With this issue is born a voice, one that has been mute much too long!" (NPPA, 2005). Setting forth a code of ethics, a series of national contests, and a concerted effort to improve the public image of photo journalists, the NPPA became the premier trade organization for print and eventually television news photographers (Cookman, 1985). In response to the sea change represented by video and multimedia journalism, the National Press Photography Association board in 2008 considered changing the name of its organization to The Society of Visual Journalists (NPPA, 2008). The measure was postponed so a consultant could research the matter and remains unresolved at this writing.

Branching Out: Documentary Film

Not many years after Eadweard Muybridge[7] used a series of still images to settle a bet about a racehorse's gait, inventors in America and in Europe found a way to recreate his efforts more efficiently with flexible film flowing through one camera (Barnouw, 1974; N. Rosenblum, 1997). Again, the mechanics of the early cameras influenced its application and the types of films created. Thomas Edison's Vitascope was enormous and heavy, better suited for filming fictional stories; whereas the five-kilogram, hand-cranked *Cinematographe* developed by the Lumière brothers in France proved to be perfect for documentary-style storytelling (Barnouw, 1974; Barsam, 1973). The *Cinematographe*, as Barnouw writes, "made *documentary* film a reality—on a world-wide basis, with sensational suddenness" (p. 5). The first projects of the Lumières' studio depicted ordinary life: of people disembarking a boat, military processions, or families at play—what the Lumières called *actualités* (Barnouw, 1974; Barsam, 1973). It wasn't long before the film cameras were trained on news events, such as the opening of the Kiel Canal by Kaiser Wilhelm II in 1895 or the Derby at Epsom Downs in 1896 (Barnouw, 1974; Barsam, 1973). Nor did it take long for political leaders to seize upon film as a means of spreading their messages and enhancing their visibility, both literally and metaphorically, and soon ceremonial occasions were filmed for mass distribution (though they were often reenactments). By 1900, this newsreel genre was in full flower, and its form would eventually be adapted to early television news.

The development of documentary filmmaking around the world was subject to political and economic realities. In the US, government funding was available for films that advanced the cause of the New Deal farm program during the depression or the military during World War II (Barnouw, 1974). John Grierson championed documentary film as a populist medium, also funded by the government (Aitken, 1998). In the US after World War II, the development of television changed the market for documentary; socially-conscious films were shut down during the Red Scare and large industrial corporations such as Shell Oil took over funding for educational and nature documentaries, which were often shown in schools, not commercial cinemas (Barnouw, 1974). Independent documentary production continued, but with a limited market and audience, until a renaissance led by activist Michael Moore with his scathing account of General Motors' labor practices, *Roger & Me*, in 1989.

Today's documentary filmmakers usually work independently of news organizations, often choosing their own topics and employing an individual, albeit nonfictional, presentational style. In popular debate, filmmakers and journalists will use the words *subjective* and *objective*, but such terms are of limited value as discourse cannot be adequately categorized using this binary. Some documentarians eschew the title of journalist even as they practice what might be called "journalistic acts," by conducting interviews, researching facts, and constructing nonfictional narratives. They may or may not work alone. A documentary filmmaker might never actually carry a camera but will instead direct another professional to do so. Finally, documentary *film* might be a misnomer today as videotape becomes the medium of choice; documentarians continue to work within a cinematic paradigm, something that overlaps with but is not entirely shared by television news.

Television News & Documentary Film

Early in the 20th century, documentary film and news film started to diverge in form. Newsreels were shot serialized and produced by large media corporations such as MGM, Time-Life, and 20th Century Fox (Barnouw, 1974; Bliss, 1991). For a while, documentaries and newsreels existed side by side on network television, with the CBS documentary unit headed by Edward R. Murrow, a tremendous source of prestige—and financial strain (Bliss, 1991). The apex of the network television's relationship with documentary film may be marked by the Thanksgiving Day airing of Murrow's *Harvest of Shame* in 1960 (Barnouw, 1974). The powerful exposition of the living conditions of America's migrant workers was narrated by Murrow before he'd left CBS to head the US Information Agency. In the decades that followed, network documentary production tended to be practiced as a public service obligation, with tamer, more advertiser-friendly styles (Barnouw, 1974).[8] Dissenting voices migrated to independent filmmaking, where the documentary enjoyed a tremendous resurgence in the new century (Barnouw, 1974; McEnteer, 2006). The gap between individual, in-depth, and more opinionated documentaries widened as television news developed its own short, seemingly objective, and almost staccato style, marked by its brevity and authoritative third person narrative (Bliss, 1991; Tuchman, 1978). During this era, news, particularly local news, became a profit center: cheap to produce, popular with the public, and with only three major networks, even a station trailing in the ratings could be highly profitable.

Until the late 1970s, television coverage employed film cameras. At first, heavy 35mm cameras were favored for their high-quality images, but later the 16mm Arriflex became the most popular choice (Fang, 1972). Early cameras were silent, requiring a separate machine for recording sound, though eventually synchronized audiotape was married to the film into a single sound-camera system. During this time, it was not uncommon for a news-film photographer to work with a technician who would be in charge gathering and monitoring the microphones, recorder, and other sound equipment (Fang, 1972). A major market or network television crew, therefore, might consist of a reporter, photographer, sound-technician, and possibly a field producer to assist (Lewis, 1984).

Image-based stories for television news developed according to two basic categories: one, often called the *voice-over*, displayed video and was narrated by an anchor-reader live (or seemingly live) from the studio (Boyd, 1993; Mayeux, 1991); and the other, commonly called a *package*, is a self-contained story usually narrated by a correspondent, though occasionally using only the recorded audio of interview subjects and *natural sound* (NATSOT) (Boyd, 1993; Mayeux, 1991). Adopting the newsreel style (and indeed, in the earliest days, simply buying clips from newsreel producers) meant that certain subjects were easier to cover than others, with the easy ones tending toward ribbon-cuttings, fashion shows, accidents, fires, and, of course, crime. In spite of Murrow's warning that ideas can't always be put into pictures, what was considered news became not a matter of the important issues of the day necessarily, but instead, what could be filmed (Bliss, 1991).

The arrival of videotape and electronic newsgathering (ENG) in the 1970s gradually put darkroom technicians out of work (or reassigned them), while speeding up the process of creating TV news. The earliest video camera systems were portable, though not by today's standards. A *minicam* developed by CBS and Norelco® was the lightest of its kind at the time and weighed 32 pounds with its tape deck and batteries attached (Fang, 1972). This faster camera system, requiring fewer people to operate, arrived at about the same time television executives around the US discovered something that would dramatically change the local news landscape—local news could be profitable (Kaniss, 1991). Ensuring profitability meant working for ratings, which fostered a system by which dramatic, visual stories could be covered easily (a form of *media logic*, to use Altheide's term), rendering television news more dependent on official sources than their print counterparts (Altheide & Snow, 1979; Kaniss, 1991).

Advances in ENG technology led to the use of microwave trucks that could transmit video images live from a scene, adding even greater immediacy to the story and greater pressure for speed on the part of reporters, photographers, and tape editors. Live capabilities allowed for reporters to present events as they unfolded, even before the "facts" were established from official sources, with far more flexibility than before, and the audience could watch the narrative unfold in real time (Livingston & Bennett, 2007;

Scannell, 2004). Scholars who examined those stories, though, found that "liveness" didn't necessarily add information to stories, nor did the ease of taped newsgathering foster greater story depth (Slattery, Hakanen, & Doremus, 1996).

Unlike their brethren in the documentary filmmaking world, video news photographers working in what might be simultaneously considered the golden age and the cultural nadir for local television news, usually did not control the presentation of their work.[9] While they might collaborate with a correspondent or field producer, they did not write or voice their stories. Their secondary status as journalists is well summarized by this advice from a textbook for television reporters from 1984:

> For the reporter, the most intimate working relationship will be with his *[sic]* camera crew. The reporter has to establish authority over the editorial content of the story and yet at the same time develop with crew members a sense of shared commitment to the excellence of the final story. (Lewis, 1984, p. 162)

Television's emphasis on personality highlighted the work of the reporter; stories became, in the words of one video consultant,[10] stories of "the adventures of the reporter—and oh, by the way, we shot some footage too." These pieces are written in a conventional expository and seemingly objective reporting style, obscuring the photographer's role. In television news, the reporter will sign off "from the scene," or an anchor may narrate live footage with a royal "we," but generally the photographer's identity is omitted from the presentation. Now that more reporters and photographers are doing the same jobs, it seems possible that this could change.

History & Storytelling

Changes in camera technology have affected the types of images produced, the stories told, the ways individual photographers work, and the way journalistic institutions operate. They are also changing the way individuals who have relationships with journalism (politicians, for example, or corporate leaders) attempt to influence their own representations. Finally, as cameras have evolved, the way photography is regarded and the rhetorical strategies used to invoke its truth value have also evolved according to the need of these various stakeholders.

Video journalism owes its heritage to still photography, documentary film, and television news: all of which have intertwined and have influenced each other since photography's invention in 1839. The practice of video and still photography is less disparate than current (albeit disintegrating) institutional separations imply, and the contemporary reality of web-based journalism only serves to highlight the way these boundaries are not inevitable but have been constructed for the sake of institutional convenience. Series of still photographs formed the basis for early motion pictures. What was perhaps the most popular news camera in history, the Leica®, was an invention of necessity for cinematographers who needed to check light levels for movie sets. Even the software for editing video on computers continues to employ film-based vocabulary, calling storage files "bins," a nod to the days when film was developed and dried over bins filled with chemicals.

The stories told with images have changed as technology and the media logic of news organizations have developed. If photographic images were merely mirrors of reality, the stories created with such images would have remained stable as technology changed, but this is not the case. Changes in camera, darkroom, film tape, and ENG technologies have inspired changes in what types of stories are covered and how, whether because flash powder allowed someone to work at night or a microwave truck made immediate coverage of a forest fire possible. It is logical, therefore, to ask whether the smaller video cameras, user-friendly editing software, and broadband internet connections—even something as seemingly innocuous as the flip screen viewfinder—may similarly change the stories that are presented in news. My research indicates that the answer is yes.

Images, Their Creators & Journalistic Legitimacy

In order to understand how video journalism might affect the storytelling process, it is necessary to understand how images have been used in the construction of journalistic truth. Journalism has long treated images and those involved with their creation and use with ambivalence (Becker, 2003; Zelizer, 2005, 2006). In semiotic terms, photographs are *indexical* because they are tangible recordings of physical space in time. This indexicality of photographs has long been held up as a source of legitimacy for journalism, even though their use is often inconsistent and their publication often derided as a form of low culture (Carlebach, 1997; Stam, 2000b; Zelizer, 1990a, 1995, 1998, 2005, 2007). Pictures have historically been treated as culturally "lower" than text: associated with tabloid journalism (Becker, 2003), beneath the dignity of a literary endeavor (Zelizer 1995)—and the people who made those pictures have been granted a lower status within news institutions (Carlebach, 1997). One sociologist's ethnography of television photographers even suggested that his subjects occasionally deserved the stereotypical label of "media animal" (Lindekugel, 1994). In contrast, the *camera* has status within journalism as an instrument of truth, a tool that gathers and disseminates indisputable facts, thereby imbuing stories with what is claimed to be unimpeachable authority (Becker, 2003; Dona Schwartz, 1992, 1999; Zelizer, 2004, 2005, 2006). Such paradoxical thinking continues to this day, with news photography held up as a reflection of real events and yet secondary to "serious" journalism (Becker, 2003).

Faith in photography's ability to deliver visual truth continues in spite of scholarship highlighting its constructed nature and even professional admissions to its subjective elements (Dona Schwartz, 1992). A photographer's choices regarding composition, lighting, perspective, distance, darkroom enhancements, and other constructive techniques that alter the nature of an image seem not to sway the overall faith in the camera as a perfect recording device. It may be the case, as Bruce Cumings (1992) observed, that the strength of reality's presence, particularly for film and video, is simply so seductive that a viewer's sense of skepticism is overpowered:

> The seeming transparency of the medium and the presumed objectivity of the camera's eye disarms the critical faculties or drowns them in the fascinating flow of images. (p. 42)

The authority of images as reflections of undisputed "reality" stems from three elements: technology, witnessing, and journalistic contextualization. Each of these elements is a social construction born of human discourse, which attaches meaning to what is essentially merely a mechanical record of light waves. At the same time, each of these three elements is detrimental to the status of photographers and an understanding of their role in creating images: anonymity, physicality, and a separation from context. The way video journalism combines the work of text and image production strikes squarely at these three tensions.

Technology as Credibility

The belief that the "camera doesn't lie" has been ingrained in modern culture—in spite of evidence, very early in the history of photography, that in human hands, photographic technologies may be used to distort reality as well as accurately reflect it. Scholarship of photographic construction similarly has not significantly undermined the faith in a camera-recorded reality. The technology itself is indeed accurate, far more accurate than memory-centered accounting or hand-drawn illustration. Indeed, since cameras were invented by painters who wanted to create more realistic art, they have from the very beginning been tools that were invented, developed, and refined by humans with specific purposes in mind (Clarke, 1997). From the very beginning, they have been tools invented, developed, and refined by humans with specific purposes in mind.

Images as Indexical Artifacts. Once introduced in the mid-19th century, cameras were quickly put to use for purposes of memory work, particularly portraiture, and for evidentiary work by scientists, historians, police agents, and other power-wielding institutions (Clarke, 1997; Dona Schwartz, 1992; Tagg, 1999). Faith in the perfection of photographic representation was nearly unshakable. This early assessment from the *London Quarterly Review* in 1857 (Eastlake, 1857/1980) is typical in its perception of photography as visual truth:

> [Photography] is the sworn witness of everything presented to her view. What are her unerring records in the service of mechanics, engineering, geology, and natural history, but facts of the most sterling and stubborn kind? (p. 65)

The introduction of the film camera a few decades later was no less perceived as realism on the screen. One of the first screenings of a film, Louis Lumière's *Arrival of a Train* in 1895, depicted a train entering a station, prompting startled members of the audience to duck or leave their chairs they were so seduced by the presence of its moving image (Barnouw, 1974). As sound was introduced, and later color, to both still and moving images, their verisimilitude was magnified. Our faith in the indexical power of photographic images seems difficult to shake; its reproduction of a scene creates a sense of presence that overpowers our knowledge that photographs are artifacts: not part of nature but of culture.

Photographic Anonymity. At the same time the camera's accuracy is promoted, the identity of individual photographers is occluded. It must be: to acknowledge the human being using a camera would be to acknowledge the individual, human, decision-making inherent in the creation of a photograph (Dona Schwartz, 1992, 1999). Relative anonymity has been part of the tradition of photo journalism since its inception. Many of the photographs credited to Matthew Brady, for instance, were not created by Brady but by members of his studio, and the early documentary films popularized by the Lumière brothers were shot by unnamed, uncredited employees (Barnouw, 1974; Morrow, 2007). It might be that anonymity is part of the profession's attraction (Archebald, 1986; Quart, 2008). The consequence of remaining hidden is not merely a matter of professional status, but of journalistic responsibility, as Barnhurst and Nerone (2001) point out in their analysis of the historic shift from artistic illustrations to photography:

> As a result of its marriage with realism, press photography embraced a notion of reportage that required the effacement of authorship. If photographers simply operate the machinery revealing reality, they cannot be held accountable for what the

> camera exposes...Thus, the realist regime effectively removed any clear lines of responsibility, hiding news work in what has been called the fog of documentary force. (p. 138)

Journalism has long dealt with the paradox between the technical accuracy of photography and the subjective role of the witness by imposing anonymity on its practitioners, thereby hiding the infinite number of choices made by humans in the process of image creation. Video journalism disturbs this ruse. Television reporters who've always worked under a spotlight and newspaper writers who fight for credits and bylines are being asked to operate cameras for their own stories. Newspaper photographers who've worked in relative anonymity are struggling with whether to add their own recorded voice track to web stories. Video journalism opens up myriad possibilities for ways a journalist might or might not be seen by an audience.

Witnessing as Testimony

Photo journalism's indexical authority is stronger still when combined with a second source claimed by journalists and documentarians—proximity. Physical proximity and its active partner, witnessing, lend journalism the power of truthful testimony. But the terms, and their practices, are subject to inconsistent employment by journalists. Also—as any photographer who has waited in the rain, hiked through a field, or run from gunfire in pursuit of a story knows—bodily proximity has its price.

Proximity, Photography & the Body. Proximity in photography can be thought of as technological witnessing. Zelizer identified "eye-witnessing" as a "key word" for journalists, using Raymond Williams' definition of key word as a marker that helps shape the culture in which that community (in this case, journalism) resides (Zelizer, 2007). But as a key word, Zelizer found it to be applied inconsistently, sometimes marking mediated witnessing by viewers or outsourced to citizen contributors or with the deployment of (seemingly) autonomous cameras. "It remains unclear to what journalists refer when they make claims of eye-witnessing," she concludes, "the technology of newsgathering, the person, or the report that they produce" (2007, p. 425).[11]

This slippery nature of the term within the larger community of journalism notwithstanding, the actual acts of photo journalism do constitute acts of witnessing—in person and in real time and space. In a typology set forth by John Durham Peters (2001), photo journalists are witnesses in the "paradigm case" in that they work in real time and space (p. 720). Peters helpfully situates forms of witnessing in time and space, with its purest form requiring presence in both. Witnessing might also take place in space but separated by time at a historic site, for instance, or in time separated by space as with live television coverage, or separated by both time and space as is typical for most television coverage. Peters notes that witnessing "raises questions of truth and experience, presence and absence, death and pain, seeing and saying, and the trustworthiness of perception in short, fundamental questions of communication" (2001, p. 707). He dissects the conceptualization of witnessing put forth by John Ellis, Susan Sontag, and others who have explored how greater visual exposure to the world has not granted the public greater power or will to respond (Ellis, 1992; Rentschler, 2004; Sontag, 2003; Zelizer, 1998). Peters' analysis addresses the body's role in this type of witnessing to the point of pain and survival. He focuses, though, on survivors as witnesses: persons who survive genocide or war. Consider the statements "I was there" for an historic event and "I saw it on television." As Peters asserts, "There's no comparison in the authority of cultural capital of the two statements!" (p. 718). In this paradigm form, witnessing is a combined act of bodily presence and textual telling.

With construction of news images in the purest quadrant, a photographer, to apply Peters' words, is "a privileged possessor and *producer* of knowledge in an extraordinary, often forensic, setting in which speech and truth are policed in multiple ways" (p. 709). Paradigm witnessing carries with it a moral imperative to honestly speak, whereas second-hand, or mediated witnessing, does not (Ellis, 1992; Sontag, 2003, 2004; Taylor, 1998; Zelizer, 1998).

Proximity & the Body. Proximity and the occasional bodily risk involved with photographic witnessing is vaunted as a source of legitimacy, one that lends photo journalists a heroic "cowboy" image, while at the same time lowering their professional status. They are trained, professional witnesses who not only "put their bodies on the line," to use Peters' words (p. 713), but they do so every day, are paid to do this, and do so in routine, ritualistic ways. Such witnessing carries with it the responsibility of working as intermediaries of reality, a responsibility that cannot be as consistently claimed by reporters, editors, and writers.[12] With the exception of the sort of convenience store or bank surveillance video that makes its way onto television newscasts (which still reflect human purpose in the deployment of a camera), the vast majority of images that are published, edited into a film, or broadcast involve a human being who was present in time and space, carrying with her all the moral responsibility imbued in the act of bearing witness.

The essential relationship between body and camera, time and space, is what separates the work of news photographers from that of other journalists. Reporters and writers may obtain information about a story remotely, via interviews with witnesses, by talking to individuals on the phone, or even, as suggested above, by viewing surveillance video (Moeller, 1989; Morris, 2002). "I have to be there," explains one of the photo journalists who helped with my research and who called herself the newspaper's "ambassador." It is perfectly possible to write a news story by sitting at a desk and using a telephone and it is not at all uncommon. Some of the very best investigative reporting is based entirely on desk work: reading hundreds of documents and phoning sources. Even television correspondents who are sent to cover major events may not physically witness that event—they might watch a video feed from a remote location if a debate is too crowded, or use videotape collected earlier to perform a live report from a location far away from a disaster (Lang, 2004). To collect the images on that tape, however, requires a photographer-body to be physically present at a moment in time and space: to select an actual or anticipated subject, to carry the camera to an optimal location, to monitor a viewfinder, or to physically hold a camera in relationship to the subject. Video journalism can never be "phoned in."

The physicality of camera work has cultivated a sense of machismo for many photo journalists, male and female, as well as a rivalry between writers and photographers. Susan Moeller's (1989) *Shooting War* describes the difference between the body work involved with photography vis à vis reportage in her historical account of individual photographers on the battlefields of Vietnam:

> Fewer writers, but most photographers, had to leave the safety of the Saigon cafés to go out into that danger to get stories…To record a napalm drop, an officer recalled, "[Larry] Burrows conned the T-28 pilot into flying so low that we actually went through part of that fireball after he made his picture." (p. 381)

Such exploits feed the mystique of wartime news photography and the tension between textual and visual journalists. The mystique that comes in the face of danger is balanced by the actual practice of photo journalism, which requires skill, creativity, planning, and thought, of course—but also muscle, movement, and a willingness to get dirty. "Great pictures are made with your knees" is the mantra of one newspaper photographer and university instructor.[13] Another instructor, a video workshop leader, jokes that if one of his students returns from a story with clean pants it means some shots were missed. Good photographs and video require bending, kneeling, walking, running, climbing, and sweating.

Such activities are avoided by civilized/literary society, which elevates itself above corporeal sounds, movements, and excretions (Douglas, 2002; Elias, 1978; Levine, 1988). Because a photo journalist constantly uses his body to carry equipment, to run to the scene, to bend, climb, kneel, or hide in the weeds, he is relegated to a lower level on the professional ladder than his writing-reporting colleagues. Marvin (2006, p. 70) notes in regard to textual professions, "Much cultural energy is devoted to concealing this absolute reliance of the textual class on its bodily substratum and to eliminating opportunities for it to move against the textual class." In the professional realm, textual work is valued more highly; the PhDs, writers, and financial analysts of the world rank above those who build roads, clean offices, or otherwise work with their bodies (Boyer, 2005; Marvin, 2004, 2006). The division of labor in newsrooms is similarly hierarchical. Even in organizations devoted to photo journalism, the writers, bloggers, and "pundits" have a higher status within their organization than the photographic staff (Lutz & Collins, 1993).

Again, video journalism lands right in the middle of this tension. Text-based workers may balk at the physical demands of shooting video when their newspaper editor hands them a camera. Lifelong photographers who suddenly start producing video stories may find their status in an organization changing or threatening the status quo. Reporters who once collected interviews by phone might be required to travel for on-camera interviews instead, slowing down their usual routines. The men and women who helped with my research rarely complained about having to carry a camera, but they nonetheless found their daily routines to be dramatically changed by the physical demands of video journalism.

Images & Context

Any image is, essentially, a decontextualized moment in space and time. By choosing a position and instant for making an image, a photographer creates an artifact that pulls that moment out of its original context. News images are then recontextualized into a production—whether printed page, website, or video program—and surrounded by language in the form of text or the spoken word, which allows the viewer to interpret them. News images rely on language for their authority and meaning: they cannot "speak" for themselves. Language might be direct, as with a caption that is connected to a photograph or with a spoken script that describes a video scene, or it might be indirectly discursive, tapping into the viewer's awareness of an image's cultural purpose, i.e., a truthful representation of events. Whether direct or indirect, language surrounding images recontextualizes them according to the purposes of their presenters, and this can happen repeatedly. Consider, for instance, the way Joe Rosenthal's photograph of the raising of the flag on Iwo Jima was originally recontextualized in newspapers in the US, then repeatedly recontextualized and appropriated by artists, movie-makers, cartoonists, and satirists according to their purposes (Helmers & Hill, 2004; Spratt, Peterson, & Lagos, 2005). That trope was repeated after the attacks of September 11th when Thomas Franklin of *The Bergen Record* photographed firefighters hoisting a flag in the wreckage of the World Trade Center towers.

Relationship with Text. Every image is an image of something and its meaning changes as it is presented in various contexts: we have to learn to interpret their meaning (Gergen & Gergen, 1991). As Zelizer (2006, p. 5) writes: "Using indexicality or referential force as a springboard, photographs operate by activating connotative meanings that are most effectively suited to *the contexts* into which they travel" (italics added). For both still and moving images, the relationship of pictures to words and the uneven, often inconsistent ways in which this occurs has been well-established by visual scholars (Barnhurst, 1994; Becker, 2003; Sekula, 1984; Tagg, 1999). In an analysis of the way photos are used by serious and tabloid newspapers, image scholar Karin Becker (2003) writes:

> Photographs attain meaning only in relation to the settings in which they are encountered. These settings include…the historically constructed discourses in which specific topics and styles of photography are linked to particular tasks or patterns of practices. The photograph's setting also includes the concrete, specific place it appears in and how it is presented. In the newspaper, photographs have no meaning independent of their relationship to the words, graphic elements, and other factors in the display which surround and penetrate them. (p. 302)

Everything Becker describes in the ways photographs derive meaning is the result of the socially driven news production process. In newspapers, a photograph's meaning is recontextualized with words, such as a caption, or by way of other graphic cues, such as its placement on the page. For television, image-meaning is derived from narration, placement in a program, and the manner in which it is edited and contextualized in relation to *other* pieces of video. News images are placed into very carefully constructed "shows," or presentations, which emphasize certain parts of their meaning and occlude others (Hartley, 1982, 1992; Tuchman, 1978; Vidal-Beneyto & Dahlgren, 1987).

Photographs are constructed at multiple levels, starting before a human being triggers a camera shutter. Decisions about where to point that camera, how to manipulate it in relation to a scene, what lens to use, and so on, are human decisions made according to practical circumstances and convention. The artifact created by the camera is further constructed by humans using computer software to crop, enhance, or deceptively manipulate an image. The image is further constructed as it is presented or exhibited within a particular context; it might be assigned meaning as a personal snapshot on a social networking site like *Facebook*, printed out for someone's grandmother, printed in a newspaper with a caption, or edited into a filmic narrative. This list is not exhaustive—every moment of an image's existence is ruled by human intervention; its meaning is interpreted and assigned according to social conventions and pre-existing understandings.

Video's meaning is similarly constructed by its recontextualization in relation to other images. John Corner points out, "The moving image… almost always and quite quickly becomes the edited image" (Corner, 1999, p. 27). Editing can define and change an image's meaning. Consider the Kuleshov effect: Soviet filmmaker Lev Kuleshov tricked an audience by inter-cutting the same expressionless face of an actor into different cinematic stories. While the shots of the actor were exactly the same, the audience was impressed by his talent as an actor (Messaris, 1994). Messaris rightly asserts that a juxtaposition between video and audio in which the visuals "say" what the words do not is an especially effective form of visual rhetoric (Messaris, 1997, 2001). Even as journalism holds up images as having unimpeachable technological authority, practices of recontextualization undermine that claim.

Recontextualization & Journalism. While recontextualization is a key component in constructing the authority of images in news, photographers generally are not part of the process. One researcher has even hypothesized that this anonymity motivates some photographers (Archebald, 1986). (Indeed, I have found this to be the case with many, though not all, of the photographers I have interviewed.)

In print organizations, reporters will write the stories, photo editors choose and crop them, and page editors place them. Photographers are often required to write captions, but captions might be edited, eliminated or re-written according to the overall presentation. Even for image-centric magazines such as *National Geographic* and *Life,* while there is collaboration, in the end there has existed a Weberian division of labor in which writers provide the words and photographers provide the pictures (Bissell, 2000; Lutz & Collins, 1993; Morris, 2002). Generally, the division has also been hierarchical in spite of the special skills required for each occupation (Lindekugel, 1994; Moeller, 1989). As Susan Moeller (1989, pp. 273–274) succinctly observed regarding combat journalists, "These writers believed that if photographers did not write, they could not think."

Moreover, language that could recontextualize an image according to the photographer's experience and provide transparency for the viewer is rarely presented. It is rare for a news image's contextualizing language to include information about how the photograph was taken, even though this information would assert the photographer's authority as witness. Information about the choices a photographer had, the choices taken, the freedoms and constraints that existed for a photographer at that particular moment of witnessing, is generally missing. In this way, journalism's recontextualization of an image serves to assert the production's claim to authority while subsuming the photographer's status. The authority of the camera's technology occludes the authority of the witnessing photographers' human experience.

The situation is similar for documentary film and television. It is possible for filmmakers to shoot their own work, but just as often, a director will hire photographers and instruct them on what and how to shoot.[14] The person who conceives of the overall storyline, the film's auteur in cinematic argot, is ultimately in charge of the product, and has often not operated the camera. An excellent illustration of the way text leads the way of documentary photography comes from the production methods of Frederick Wiseman, the "controlling artist" behind *Titicut Follies*. While shooting inside the hospital for the criminally insane, he did not carry the camera—he carried the sound-recorder—directing the photographer's attention by pointing a microphone toward the scenes he chose (Barnouw, 1974, p. 246).

Video-photographers working for television news organizations traditionally have worked with reporters, writers, producers, and, in larger markets, videotape editors (Lewis, 1984). It is the reporter who might insert him- or herself into the story with a standup, or "piece to camera," a short presentation in which they appear before the camera as part of the story (Boyd, 1993; Lewis, 1984). In medium to smaller markets, photographers generally edit their own video stories, but they do so according to scripts written by others (Boyd, 1993; Lindekugel, 1994). This is just one more way journalism has tended to use images as a way to bolster its authority. Images (and their creators) are necessary, even desirable, but remain auxiliary and inferior to the written text and its creators.[15]

Authors & Narrators

Authoritative claims based in technology, witnessing, and contextualization are all part of what makes a news story. Additionally, because news accounts are presented as *stories*, they incorporate the structural elements of narrative. Already scholars have noted that filmic and television news accounts have a more distinct narrative structure than traditional inverted pyramid textual news accounts. Television news' use of narrative has been criticized as its weakness—especially its emphasis on conflict and colorful characters at the cost of less interesting but perhaps more important and complicated issues of public interest. Narratives are built with a beginning, middle, and end. They have characters, settings, plots, complications, and resolutions. They also—and this is what is critical to any exploration of video journalism—require authors and narrators. Someone must *write* the story and someone must *tell* the story. That "someone" may be the same human being, but with video journalism and other forms of media, this is not necessarily the case.

In the simplest of terms, authors write stories and narrators tell them, but as with most social processes, news is not so simple, for journalistic stories are passed along through various actors (who have different stakes in the process and value the information differently), converted to texts, produced with images, published, and so on. The terms *author* and *narrator*, therefore, are complex social and cultural constructions that must be examined in detail in order to understand the development of video journalism as a storytelling form.

News Images & Authorship

Michel Foucault (1977) conceptualized authorship as a culturally regulated construction and the author's name "functional in that it serves as a means of classification" (p. 122). Foucault identifies three discursive functions of the "author," namely as a legal-economic classification, a mark of literary authenticity, and the assignation of a realistic dimension of the person who created a text. Significant to the discussion of news images, Foucault found a division in the second function, for authorial anonymity served to enhance the credibility of scientific and mathematical truthfulness historically. Sociologist Pierre Bourdieu arrived at a similar conclusion: that authorship is a discursive construction—something continually negotiated and contested within fields—and subject to political/economic pressure (Bourdieu, 1993).

Yet within journalism generally, and photo journalism specifically, "authorship" has not been constructed consistently (Zelizer, 1990a, 1990b, 2007). The presumption of photography's indexicality is buttressed by the hiding of its practitioners. True, professional norms call for a news photographer to be identified with a "credit" much like a reportorial byline, but this norm was slow to develop and remains inconsistently followed (National Press Photographers Association, n.d.). For instance, The International Press Telecommunications Council (for wire services) has a system in place for embedding a credit and other information into images, yet publications in print and on the web might still credit a photographic *agency* but not a human being (Graulich, 2007). The human role in the construction of news is unevenly acknowledged by journalistic organizations. Textual journalism applies bylines more frequently, but again, not necessarily consistently, with norms varying from organization to organization, publication to publication. The growth of the byline norm can be traced with the ascent of interpretive journalism, accenting its denotation of witnessing and interpretation (Schudson, 1978). In television news, the question becomes further confused. When Zelizer pointedly asked "Where is the author in TV news?" the answer, essentially, was "everywhere and anywhere"—reflecting what is convenient for television journalists for their claims to authority (Zelizer, 1990b).

Authorship is also a central theoretical question for film scholars who developed the concept of the film auteur in France following World War II, in part an effort to legitimize cinema as art (Stam, 2000a). Auteur theory, which generally attributes a film's authorship to its *director,* was widely applied to fiction films, some of which were distinguished by an identifiable, distinct style and "vision," connoting an aspect of higher culture and equating the creation of a film with the writing of a novel. For documentary filmmakers, the auteur theory is helpful in that it points to the work of the person who conceives of the overall work, weaving words, images, music, and movement into a coherent narrative. Contemporary documentary filmmakers might not call themselves auteur*s*, yet might still be known for a distinct style and point of view, as well as allowing themselves to be seen and known by the audience. The disadvantage of auteur theory is its occlusion of the extensive collaboration often required of filmmaking (Stam, 2000a). Why should directors have auteur status and not producers or scriptwriters? What of the film's photographer? When is she the auteur and when is she not? Contemporary documentary filmmaker Michael Moore has appeared in his films holding a camera, yet this means another photographer was present to record the scene. Here, as with other collaborative systems, a documentary photographer might be composing the film, or might be simply a "camera operator" taking direction from a creator, making a film without the title of filmmaker.

What is important about auteur theory, for the purposes of understanding video journalism, is its acknowledgment of the filmmaker as creator, a notion that contrasts with journalism's usually hidden photographers and videographers. Unlike photo journalists, who have developed ethical codes to assert their objectivity and truthfulness, documentary filmmakers generally endeavor to create a filmic argument (Hampe, 1997). "I make movies because I want to influence others," writes Swedish documentary filmmaker Stefan Jarl (1998). "There is no such thing as an accurate and objective documentary" (p. 149–150). Dale Bell (1995), whose film on the Woodstock music festival won an Academy Award in 1971, considers his creation to be a "truer" representation than its journalistic counterparts:

> We knew we did not want to produce "news coverage." Let the news teams do that! We wanted to produce something which would last, which would be different, and would truly represent the seminal role that music and their lyrics played in the life of the generation of the sixties. (p. 77)

This perspective, while common among documentary filmmakers and those who consider themselves citizen journalists, contradicts the stated and central goal of conventional (more commonly known as "mainstream") journalists, who assert their authority by way of the norm of objectivity (Schudson, 2001; Tuchman, 1972). In contrast with conventional television news photographers who work for profit-making corporations, documentarians have worked largely outside of the mainstream media. The growth of cable television and other outlets for such independent productions is one factor behind the current revival of their counter-cultural discourse. Michael Moore, Morgan Spurlock (*Supersize Me*), and Robert Greenwald (*Outfoxed*) were able to find audiences without help from the television networks.

While the anonymity of conventional television photographers and other photo journalists contributes to the presentation of their images as objective facts, documentary photographers and filmmakers traditionally are more likely to impose their own point of view or style on a subject. Indeed, documentary tradition is a persuasive one and many of the earliest works, both still and cinematic, were intended as tools for social change (McEnteer, 2006). At the same time, it is important to also note that many filmmakers produce documentaries without carrying their own camera—their role as auteur does not necessarily extend to the photographic work. Even those who narrate their movies in the first person do not necessarily carry their own camera. Nevertheless, their persona is injected into their films and their scripts; modern documentaries are often marked by the distinct, subjective point of view of an auteur.

Video journalism, with its blending of the writer and photography roles, exists in the intersection of the auteur, the bylined reporter, and the anonymous photographer. Film scholar Dai Vaughn (1995) notes,

> Once we have accepted that there is no purely technical criterion for realism—no gimmick of presentation which can guarantee authenticity—then we are forced to recognize that we must rely upon the integrity of the artist for its creation and upon the judgment of the viewer for its proof. (p. 58)

When we uncover the "hidden" authors—what narratologists might call the "implied narrators" of photographs or video stories—we lose one form of understanding but gain another. We lose the ability to consider the image an objective representation of a world "out there," but gain a more transparent understanding of who created the image, how it was created, and (perhaps most importantly) what was omitted, ignored, or cut out—the alternatives not chosen in the creation of that image.

Video & Narration

The matter is further complicated in filmic presentation by the dual roles of a script's writer-narrator and oral-narrator. Conventional documentary and television is often marked by a separation of the two roles, but video journalism blends them. Therefore, it is necessary to explore not only the nature of authorship, but narration and its relationship between authorship, narration, and news images.

Narration is a multi-layered concept that on its face would seem much simpler for video stories. The embodied, heard narrator for video stories is not entirely a construction in the minds of writers and readers, as is the case with printed texts. The images of a television video news story are nearly always accompanied by a human voice, or voices (the exception being montage videos edited with natural sound or music to convey a narrative). Generally, though, until now, such video news and filmic documentaries have been collaborative efforts, so the originator of the story, the person who writes and composes a narrative, may *not* be the audible voice of the story. It may be someone else entirely who happens to have vocal talent (or has a connection to the producer, or is a known celebrity). Other formats, which rely on sound and interview clips only, may not have one embodied narrator, only an implied author-narrator, with the quotes of many voices edited together.

How, and indeed *whether*, to vocally narrate has long been the subject of debate among documentary filmmakers who have experimented with a variety of formats. The most declarative style, which film scholar Bill

Nichols (1991) labels *expository*, is typical of conventional television news, with an authoritative, declarative voice-over image that illustrates the script and sound bites[16] from subjects in support of the filmmaker's overarching argument (Kochberg, 2002; Nichols, 1991, 2001). The expository format utilizes an all-knowing (and seemingly objective) "voice of God" narrative track shaped by logic and problem-solving, using quotes, or sound bites, from subjects without granting those outside voices control of the narrative. Nichols (1991) locates authority in expository documentary largely within the narrator's script:

> The voices of others are woven into a textual logic that subsumes and orchestrates them. They retain little responsibility for making the argument, but are used to support it, or provide evidence or substantiation for what the commentary addresses. The voice of authority resides with the text itself rather than with those recruited to it. (p. 37)

Television news-film follows these conventions for narration in part because its predictability allows for systematic and predictable production (Tuchman, 1978). In his analysis of television news discourse, Peter Dahlgren (1987) notes its "particular manner of speech" is a

> ...matter of factual and self-assured, with little or no trace of self-doubt, emotionality, or uncertainty about the material it presents. It conveys seriousness and, where appropriate, urgency and even light touches of irony. News talk is confident talk, secure in its professionalism. (p. 42)

Ultimately, such a format is not only a predictable system for television journalists, but it is efficient for its audience: there is no vacillation or self-doubt on the part of the speaking narrator; it is the privilege of journalism to declare "That's the way it is."

Occasionally, television news programs will adopt one of Nichols' other narrative forms, in particular the *observationalist* style, which eliminates the objective voice of God third-person narrator, editing together quotes (sound bites) from news subjects in order to construct a coherent narrative. Such pieces are commonly called *NATPAKs* for their use of natural sound incorporated into a story-package. Observationalist style involves an absence of voiced-over narrative, an absence of interviews with subjects, an absence of direct address to the audience, and editing that emphasizes real time and spatial realism. It is less declarative and invites the audience to a larger role in the interpretation of meaning. Its use in journalistic contexts has come under fire for that very reason, a decision that "can turn even the most compelling footage into a mish-mash," in the words of one critic in the *Columbia Journalism Review* (Massing, 2009).

Video journalists, particularly those who have previously worked as still-photographers for newspaper organizations, often use the observationalist style with their videos and web slide shows. Years of working to "let the pictures tell the story," coupled with the professional culture that values photographic anonymity, inspire a less intrusive and declarative narrative style. Video journalism offers the possibility that the vocal narration might be recorded by the photographer, the same person who shot the rest of the story, but does not require it. The impact of a shift in work style on the narrative structure of audio visual news and the debates over the journalistic merit of these various styles motivated my research—in the end, is there anything truly "special" about video journalism?

VJ Technologies & Their Affordances

The preceding pages revealed that changes in technology have often made a difference in the way news stories are structured and told. Similarly, video journalism's technologies might also be expected to have an impact on journalistic narrative. Smaller, lighter cameras, flip screens, user-friendly software, and wireless internet connections all have the potential to change journalistic practice in the field. Each of these technological developments has a corporeal impact, whether by way of coordination with the photographer's body, the way it allows the photographer to interact with the environment and the viewer's sense of time and location, and, of course, the potential for changing the way narratives are constructed. The difference between a video camera and a $2,000 paperweight is in the way human beings use them. What's important is the way journalists adopt, adapt, and make use of these technologies.

Camera Size & Weight

The first small video camera, the Hi8, is what inspired Michael Rosenblum to establish the first all-VJ news operation, Video News International, in 1992. Today's video cameras are even smaller and lighter. Amateur video cameras can fit into one hand—even cell phones can record short clips. The shrinking of broadcast quality cameras has been limited not by the video electronics but by the other components, particularly optics and sound-recording inputs, which allow for professional-grade imaging. The lens is perhaps the heaviest item on the newer cameras, and may be what limits any further reduction in video camera weight—any smaller or lighter and the optical quality could suffer.

Today's professional-grade cameras are far smaller and lighter than ever. The Canon XL series and the Sony Z1 (the requisite camera for BBC VJs) weigh between five and eight pounds, about one-fifth or one-sixth of a conventional broadcast-quality video camera. The actual weight will depend on what's added on, such as microphones, lights, and the lens. The lighter cameras are a far cry from the first ENG[17] equipment introduced in the 1970s, when the full ensemble of camera and tape deck weighed 80 pounds (Medoff, Fink, & Tanquary, 2007). Many newspaper photographers who are asked to work as VJS are working with cameras that do double-duty as high-end still cameras that can record short video clips.

The weight reduction makes it possible for many more individuals to operate a video camera, most notably women whose average upper body strength is lower than that of the average man. Smaller, lighter-weight cameras are also easier to conceal, easier to hold overhead or in awkward positions, and less imposing for the subjects of video interviews—though they are also harder to hold steady with one's body. If a user isn't careful, the resulting image might be shaky or even move in time with their breathing. Heavier cameras sit more solidly (albeit occasionally painfully) on a person's shoulder. Tripods and other steadying systems, therefore, become more critical to the process when VJs use smaller, lighter equipment.

The Flip Screen

Video journalists often rely heavily on a camera feature known as the flip screen viewfinder. A video-photographer who uses a television camera with a conventional eye piece works with her face partially covered—imagine trying to communicate with her. Her face is vulnerable to accidental or intentional injury if his camera is pushed or bumped.

In contrast, *Figures 1.1* and *1.2* (shown on the next page) depict a Sony Z1 camera and its flip screen. On the left, notice how Paul Myles, chief of the BBC's Nations & Regions video training programs, uses the camera much lower against his body to talk to me. He can check the screen and maintain better eye contact with an interview subject. In the second photo, Paul has turned the camera onto himself, allowing me to view the flip screen. Because the screen can be turned 180 degrees, VJs are able to see themselves as they shoot a standup (or piece to camera), maintain eye contact with sources, or manipulate the camera into unusual angles.

Figures 1.1 and *1.2*. Paul Myles demonstrates the advantages of the flip screen. In *Figure 1.1*, he is able to talk to me while recording my picture. In *Figure 1.2*, he turns the camera onto himself, allowing me to see what is in the viewfinder.

Editing Software

Video journalism's "double whammy" boost, as one former veteran of Video News International called it, came with the introduction of laptop video editing software. As recently as the 1990s, video editing was accomplished with a system called *tape to tape*. Editing equipment consisted of a player on one side, a player/recorder on the other, and a console in the middle with controls for both. The equipment could cover a full-sized desk. To construct a story, an editor would electronically mark the receiving tape to record sections from the tape recorded in the field. The process started with the recording of an audio track, usually using NATSOT (natural sound), sound bite, and recordings of the reporter's voice. Then, *B-ROLL*[18] (illustrative video) would be recorded onto the receiving tape in appropriate spots. Tapes played back in real time and they recorded in real time.

The best editors often have advanced kinesthetic, if not musical, intelligence for marking in-cues and out-cues in a rhythm that appropriately match the story's script and human speech. Because the tape players operate in real time and with physical tape, material could not be added into or pulled from the middle, only tacked on to the end of a receiving tape side. Changing the middle of a story whose audio track has been recorded the first time would require a complete re-recording from the point of change. Finally, since physical videotape is separated into *tracks* for audio and visual information, it has limited space so the number of layers for audio, video, and unseen information (i.e., a time-code or roll-cue tone) is finite.

Digital editing can be done outside real time. The software uses two boxes to help editors distinguish the source tape from the receiving tape, on the same computer screen, along with something called a timeline, which is a visual representation of the video and audio "layers" in the resulting story. Editing in a digital environment is more like cutting and pasting with word processing software: sections can be added and subtracted from the middle. The material is not being manipulated on physical tapes but in a computer code. Physical tape might be a source that is converted into a digital file, and a physical tape might be used to then record a file from the digital system—but physical tape does not move back and forth in a player in a digital environment. In fact, the story itself is *not* being created during this part of the process. The software essentially writes the program that dictates to the computer what to cut and paste later into a "rendered" file.

The result is a much more flexible system that allows for far more layers of sound and video—and a system that can be harder to learn. This changed dramatically in the 1990s when Apple® introduced Final Cut Pro®, a more user-friendly software program for video editing. Final Cut Pro®, coupled with the portable Macintosh® laptop series, which was designed for easier manipulation of visual material, made digital editing far more accessible.

TIME:	00:00	00:10	00:40	01:00
Video	Wide shot of Governor	Head shot	Band playing	Wide shot of campaign party
Graphics	Today, Harrisburg	Governor Rita Bluster		Fred Bennett
Narration	The Governor was happy			This is Fred Bennett reporting
Sound Bites		"I'm so glad I won."		
Music	(low)	(low)	(high)	(low)
NATSOT	(low)	(low)	(low)	(fade out)

Figure 1.3: Schematic of a video story. Editing software generally does not display the text of what is said or descriptions of the visuals; it displays sound volume levels and markers for shot changes. The information was added here for clarity.

Wireless & Broadband Technologies

A longtime VJ from a large television station, [KQ], rarely visits his own newsroom and instead works entirely out of a news van that he drives home at the end of the day. [KQ] can do so thanks to the final technological piece of the video journalism puzzle, one that has developed outside the world of video production yet continues to make a difference for video journalists: wireless broadband internet access. Where at one time video on the web resembled shaky and intermittent films of the Lumière brothers, with today's connections, video on the web is essentially comparable to watching conventional television. More than half of American adults have broadband access in the United States, and fully a third of online internet users have used a WiFi connection (Horrigan, 2008). One provider, AT&T, has more than 20,000 hotspots in the United States, and reported more than ten million users in the first quarter of 2009 alone (more than triple in the first quarter of 2008 (Churchill, 2009). The significance of this dramatic growth has made it possible not only for journalists to send video information across the internet, but to actually broadcast *live* on the internet by way of VOIP (voice over the internet protocol) services, such as *Skype* (Tompkins, 2009). Wireless technology is not simply useful in terms of transmitting stories. For VJs in the field, simple wireless microphones can free them from a location, allowing them to move around a scene, change position, and still ask questions of their subjects while collecting quality audio.

What Impact Might These Have?

These four technological developments and their somatic properties create both opportunities and challenges for journalists working with video. They are the force behind video journalism's growth and are influencing its development. Together, they have the potential to change the news we watch because of two distinguishing features.

Expansion: The Spread to New Users. The first is primarily a matter of economics. The price of entry for video journalism practice is far lower than ever before. In the 1980s, the price of a broadcast-quality television camera, deck, and editing equipment was nearly as high as a modest house in the US. Today, a similar kit that delivers video of acceptable broadcast quality[19] can be purchased for several thousand dollars. Nonprofit organizations and nonprofessionals can now create videos, and news organizations can equip far more employees. In the fall of 2009, CNN announced a $1.99 application for the iPhone that allows users to send news stories and video to the network and participate as citizen journalists (Blair, 2009). Beyond the economic factors, though, lighter cameras, accessible software, the flip screen, and wireless internet also make it much easier for anyone to shoot video stories and share them in the public sphere.

Singularity: One Person Does It All. The second influence is a matter of technological affordance. The combined new technologies allow for greater flexibility in the field and make it far easier for one person to work alone. Smaller cameras can be more easily manipulated in the field and video files can be e-mailed instantly. Every new generation of film and video camera has made it increasingly possible for one strong and intrepid person to work alone, but the latest technology has done so quite dramatically, and it is no longer necessary to be particularly strong or, for that matter, intrepid. The ability to put an entire kit into a backpack, including the technologies of editing and transmission, makes it possible for one person working alone to shoot, write, edit, and relay their work in real time. Such autonomy has both advantages and disadvantages. A single video journalist might be deployed more quickly and flexibly, thereby enhancing access to locations or individuals, but at the price of newsroom collaboration and camaraderie.

New Narrative Possibilities. Together, expansion and singularity pose the possibility that video news stories might be presented in different ways. Until now, local television news has set the standard for video narrative. Critics within and outside the local news industry have long complained of its overemphasis on highly visual stories, crime and disaster, and personality-driven, expository presentation (Epstein, 1973; Kaniss, 1991; McManus, 1994). Video journalism, especially when exhibited on the web and not tied to a chronologically fixed program, presents the opportunity to experiment with new formats. Rosenblum encourages his trainees to develop a more observational style, one that lets the story "tell itself." *YouTube* is replete with nonprofessionals using video to commit "journalistic acts" using all sorts of forms: from observational to participatory to poetic. Changing storytelling style is not entirely dependent on technology or access, but a matter of social practice. Some longtime documentarians worked as one-man bands to create compelling observational stories long before cameras shrank and editing went digital. What is different today is that so many more people in a variety of organizations are shooting stories, and so many of them are doing so alone.

Summary: Significant Shifts in Newsgathering

Because video journalism is being adopted by disparate news organizations and with varying goals, it is unclear at this stage how video journalism is developing and whether its form is distinct. In combining the jobs of writer, author, narrator, editor, and photographer, video journalism practice cuts through three traditional sources of authority for images: indexicality, proximity, and contextualization. Because it uses new technological form and combines the job of photographer, author, and speaker, it seems possible that the process of video journalism will yield its own presentational and narrative style. Video journalism's proponents have already made claim to changes in subjects, styles, and voices. These issues formed the central questions of this project, namely, how, if at all, does the *process* of video journalism differ from other types of news-making? And then, how, if at all, does the *product* of video journalism compare with other forms of filmic news.

The first question is largely a social one. Based on the way the histories of camera technology and journalism have continually intertwined and informed each other, it is reasonable to expect that smaller video cameras, digital editing systems, and the broadband internet mechanisms might similarly affect both process and product. It is necessary to consider the process according to multiple dimensions, for while an image is created in one particular intersection of time and space, it is created within a system of social conventions, understandings, and practices. A news story is not conceived in a vacuum. Social practices surrounding the actual inception; that is, the interactions between social actors who control access to news events, for example, or those who endeavor to attract camera coverage, must be considered. The work of contextualizing a video story within a news organization—and how it is metaphorically framed, assigned, talked about, and presented—is all dependent upon accepted understandings of what constitutes news and what is considered appropriate journalistic practice. Human beings who are the actual subjects of video stories, such as individuals who consent to an interview, politicians presenting a speech, or victims of a tragic event, also take part in the social process that is news-making, and here too, the interactions might be changed when smaller cameras are wielded by journalists operating alone. The audience, both real and as imagined by journalists, is yet another factor to be considered, for while they don't generally accompany a video journalist in the field, they are always "in mind" as the eventual consumer of the story being created.

The second question, while it overlaps and intertwines with the first, is more a textual matter. What does the product of video journalism look like? Sound like? How do its narratives compare structurally and materially from other filmic representations of news? Does it make a difference when one person shoots, writes, edits, and voices a story in singular fashion rather than as part of a team? Proponents of video journalism, such as Michael Rosenblum and David Dunkley Gyimah, envision a new, utopian video discourse that reflects a greater intimacy with subjects and "ownership" on the part of the VJ (Gyimah, 2007; M. Rosenblum, n.d.). Video journalism's critics see it as merely a way to do the same old thing with fewer people.

The answer is likely to vary according to practitioner, setting, and organization. It will be essential, therefore, to not only study the material produced by video journalists, but to examine the ways it is produced: to see the choices not taken, the positions not held, the shots that got away. For this reason, the people involved in the construction of video journalism and the stories they produce are the object of this study. What they say about their work, coupled with direct observation and the stories they've created, guided me as I sought to understand just how video journalism operates and whether or not its stories are unique. The next chapter presents a brief discussion of my theoretical approach, blending long-established understandings of news as social construct with the brute force, physical reality of what it is to make a photograph in real time and real space.

NOTES:

1. He became a US Senator in 2009.
2. I use the word "photographer" to describe the work of still and video photographers. When a distinction is necessary, I will use the preface still or video. I will not use the phrase "camera man" because this term is not only sexist, but it occludes the subjective, artistic nature of photographic work.
3. One news director for a medium market television station referred to him as "Michael *may-he-rot-in-Hell* Rosenblum."
4. Already in some VJ newsrooms, reporters are using the video feature of *Skype* to transmit live shots, where once such a production more commonly required a reporter, a photographer, and a microwave van technician.
5. Short for "natural sound," this includes the sound of a fire truck's siren, children playing in the background, or cornstalks rustling in a field. Such sound contributes to the viewer's sense of "presence" in place.
6. This classic text on photo editing remains relevant to this day. Kalish's name lives as the eponymous title of a prestigious annual photo-editing workshop.
7. Muybridge was an artistic self-promoter who chose this unusual spelling for his name (Rosenberg, 2010).
8. One notable exception would be the 1971 airing of the CBS-produced *Selling of the Pentagon*, which challenged the US government policy in Vietnam.
9. It is important to distinguish studio camera operators, whose work is controlled by a director, and video news photographers, who work in the field.
10. Personal communication, Dirck Halstead, July 25, 2008.
11. See also (Zelizer, 1990b) for a discussion of television news and the unevenness of claims to authority by way of proximity.

12. One website devoted to local news in California has gone so far as to outsource its writing to workers in India (Glaister, 2007).
13. Personal communication with [LM], one of the project participants. All of the men and women who participated in this project were granted anonymity, and their names have been converted to random initials in brackets.
14. Here is where the term "camera-person" is appropriate: those instances in which the person operating the camera is doing so robotically, or as an extension of the director's body.
15. Informally, television photographers who work with correspondents are frequently referred to not as partners of but as *belonging to* a particular correspondent, as "his cameraman" or "her photographer." One Massachusetts journalist, during the 2008 primary, carefully watched how various candidates fared in his so-called "blue collar" test (Gorenstein, 2008). Would they take time to acknowledge and shake the hand of a television photographer? Or would they respond to the reporter only, treating the photographer as a sort a mindless camera-toting robot? The phrase blue collar is especially telling, indicating the way television photographers and the physical work that they do fits into the professional hierarchy.
16. A discrete video quotation; the sound-on-tape tied to an interview subject.
17. Electronic news gathering using portable videotape cameras and recorders.
18. Illustrative video that depicts scenes, and is not tied to interview sound. It is usually added to an edited story after the audio track is complete. The term is rooted in film practice when playback for a television newscast would require one projector for the interview sound (A-ROLL) alternating with a projector showing the illustrative film (B-ROLL).
19. More on this issue of image quality will be examined later because the debate rages within the photo journalism community over whether a difference is discernable—and whether it matters.

Chapter Two:
A Foundation for Understanding

> *"You put your camera around your neck along with putting on your shoes, and there it is an appendage of the body that shares your life with you."*
>
> —*Dorothea Lange*

Introduction

Now that we have an understanding of how video journalism came to be, we can explore how it ought to be studied. Journalism and its products have been studied by all manner of researchers, such as political scientists concerned about public discourse, sociologists interested in the web of meaning created by professional practices, and rhetorical scholars who want to know how news informs and persuades us. As is often the case with professional territory, strands of scholarship have developed in parallel, often without adequate conversation between specialties. Film scholars do not often contend with television news; journalism's scholars discuss the narrative of news, often without considering literature's contribution to narratology.

No matter what the tradition, researchers tend to bypass the photographer in favor of the image. This is understandable—photographic practice occurs in real time, whereas images on newsprint and videotape can be collected, archived, and reviewed any time. News images have attracted study from a wide variety of useful approaches. They have invited textual analyses, which trace their use and relay, demonstrating the way certain iconic representations or patterns of imagery shape cultural discourse. Historical scholarship has contextualized the interplay between photographer and filmmaker within his or her historical setting and the impact technology has had on the types of material created. Biographical studies have emphasized the role of human intellect, talent, and purpose, as demonstrated by a single, famous photographer. Sociologies of the newsgathering process provide a window to the ways journalists have made decisions, and have located their work into larger political, economic, and social systems. Effects studies have focused on the relationship between images as texts and the viewing audience, finding, perhaps most importantly, that human beings rely heavily on visual information for both cognitive and emotional processing, often more so than on other forms of sensory stimuli. Studies of news images as texts provide a rich understanding of the way they operate denotatively and connotatively. Analyses of news discourse provide insight into the way merely labeling an artifact as "news" imbues it with particular social significance. Narratology contributes a means by which structural analyses may be formulated for the study of the video journalism's products.

In large part, something is missing from most of the research into journalism and images: the human body and its role in constructing news. Even practice theory, which purports to examine norms and routines from the subjective standpoint of actors, generally has not incorporated data regarding the role of the body into its analyses. Feminist theorists contend with the body, but normally to analyze unequal distribution of control or power in given situations, or to discuss social *reactions to* female bodies—not how actual bodies move, work, or function. Narratological theory also points us to the body, but frames it in terms of intangible authorship. Keeping in mind that a photographer *has to be there*, the study of photographic practice demands a body-centered constructive approach, which requires that any study of the social forces involved with news work include careful observation of that work's corporeality.

Video journalists use their bodies to directly witness events; this is one source of authority for their stories. VJs choose where to go and what events to cover; they interface with technology to record events, and create narratives to make sense of those events for others in a social process anchored in time and space. Shifting analytical focus from text to process requires observation of human behavior within their environment and with each other. These two dimensions are related: the individual acting within a body in the world *and* in social interaction—thus, a body-centered constructivist paradigm. In this chapter, I will detail what I mean by "body-centered constructivism," and why this approach is appropriate for this exploration of the process and product of video journalism.

The Body and Constructivism

Constructivism is a liberating way to view the world. It presents possibilities of that which *might* be, of the alternatives we as humans have for shaping our world. Constructivism forces us to acknowledge the degree to which how we talk about the world shapes our actions within it. It is often misunderstood as a form of relativism, or worse, an interesting philosophical exercise with no practical application. But constructivism is far more than a philosophical exercise because it forces us to take responsibility for what we believe we know, which is entirely what we are able, as live creatures (to use Dewey's [1934] phrase) to sense of the world. The body, its senses, and actions are central to constructivist thinking.

Unlike "constructivism," the word "body" is deceptively simple. After all, we all know what our body is—until we start to think about where it begins and ends. If we describe the body as the tangible self, what happens when a person loses a limb? Their body is incomplete, but their self remains intact. If the body is a cell-based machine, how is it possible to act against the id? Social science is not necessarily helpful here, as it applies multiple meanings to the notion of a body. Bryan Turner (1984) lists the social body, the sexual body, the medical body, even bodies of nations. Webster's collegiate dictionary[1] delivers seven categories of definitions for body, starting with "the organized physical substance of an animal or plant either living or dead, as (1) the material part or nature of man" (Webster's New Collegiate Dictionary, 1977, p. 124). The live body is of central importance to constructivism, which, to put it perhaps too plainly, treats the human body as the ultimate communicative medium. It is our connection to the world; we use it to define our material borders; it contains the senses we use to interpret and interact with the physical world.

Those who believe that a world exists outside our experience, which can be responsibly and objectively described, do not need to contend with the body or its senses. As Klaus Krippendorff (2009) explains, objectivists are committed "to the belief that one could describe the world as it exists objectively, without reference to observers, in effect excising the researcher's *bodily involvement* from the descriptions they generate" (p. 172, italics added). Objectivism insists that it is possible to detach our own experience, and engage in discourse about that experience from an external, knowable reality that is *independent* of its observers. Constructivism, on the other hand, asserts that all reality is our own reality, shared socially, perhaps, as Peter Berger and Thomas Luckmann (1967) have described, but one that is always described in language and filtered through human—essentially somatic—experience. Or, to use Krippendorff's (2009) words,

> Constructivism…locates reality neither outside and independent of human observers, nor inside an imagining human mind (as solipsists hold true), but within circular processes—perception and action or conception and construction of things. In other

> words, constructivism locates reality in the *human senses* and in *social practices*, which implicate the use of language. (p. 175 italics added)

Of these two loci for reality, the human senses and social practices, the latter have tended to attract more scholarly attention. Social practices are the habits, conversations, and norms we live by. Through repeated actions over generations they become, as Berger and Luckmann (1967, p. 59) put it, "the way things are done," and so entrenched in society that we forget that once upon a time, things might have been done differently. John Searle elaborates this argument through his philosophy of speech acts and their construction of reality when he explains how an utterance can set off a series of well-understood social practices to create what he calls "institutional facts" (Searle, 1969; 1995; Smith, 2003).

Those who argue against the constructivist paradigm tend to focus on its explanation that language is our means of constructing reality, and interpret this as denying the existence of a tangible reality. They argue that there is more to human experience than language—and they are right. But they misunderstand. When Krippendorff explains that reality is "*not knowable without constructive participation* by its observers" (original italics, 1993b, p. 38), this does not deny that a world outside us exists, but forces us to consider how our observations and our senses allow us to construct knowledge of that world, that what we "know" is limited to what we can sense and speak of. Our senses are the means by which our observations of the world are carried to our mind, and they do so through the body. While we use language to coordinate our understanding of the world, we *experience* that world through our senses. Constructivism does not deny what Searle (1995) calls the "brute facts" of the world; it helps us to understand that we must use language to explain those brute facts, and language is ultimately malleable. Constructivism demands that we take responsibility for our own observations.

The other locus of reality, the human senses, is what is often neglected by both constructivists *and* their detractors. That we live in bodies and use them to interact with one another and the world is a notion so taken for granted as to be ignored—even denigrated—as the rival of higher thinking. In the centuries since Plato elevated spirit over body, and Descartes declared "*Cognito ergo sum*," Western thought has divided human experience between the physical and mental. This division quickly developed into a hierarchy, with thought above bodily experience: the (so-called) rational above emotional, verbal above visual. "Civilization" eschews the body, the physical, and endeavors to deny, hide, and control the body and its elements (Aho, 2002; Boyer, 2005; Cregan, 2006; Hancock & Tyler, 2000). Dewey

(1934, p. 21) observed "Prestige goes to those who use their minds without participation of the body and who act vicariously through control of the bodies and labor of others." Philosopher Theodore Schatzki makes a compelling case for interpreting Wittgenstein's "ways of life" as incorporating mind and body with action, though Wittgenstein's writings do not directly do so: "Bodily doings and sayings, and bodily sensations and feelings, are the medium in which life and mind/action are present in the world" (Schatzki, 1996, p. 41).

Scholarly interest in the body and its role in the social system germinated slowly in the past century. Dewey emphasized the body in his treatise on aesthetics in the 1920s, *Art As Experience*; sociologist Pierre Bourdieu emphasized the importance of the body within its *habitus*, yet rarely included corporeal detail in his studies; Michel Foucault made the body central to his discussions of social control, yet focused more on what was done *to* bodies and not *by* them (Bourdieu, 1980, 2003; Bourdieu & Wacquant, 1992; Cregan, 2006; Dewey, 1934; Foucault, 2001, 1977; Neveu, 2005; Sterne, 2003; Swartz, 1997). The beginning of the 21st century saw a renewed scholarly interest in the body's role in social action and communication, reversing a trend Marvin (2006) noted in which "modernization" was in large part marked by "textualization," i.e., the process of concealing or removing bodies from texts. When we bring the body back into the discussion of language, as George Lakoff and Mark Johnson have done, the strength of the constructivist approach becomes clearer (Johnson, 1987; Lakoff & Johnson, 1980, 1999). They point out that linguistic metaphors are based in bodily sensations and spatial experience: profits are "up," the future is a long way "away," or we "hold" these truths to be self-evident. "Reality" begins and ends with our body's sense of it.

My emphasis on the body and its interaction with the physical world is more than an exercise in armchair philosophy. The body is an integral part of the photographic process. Human beings use technology to materially record parts of the environment they experience through their ears and eyes. Video journalism bridges the Cartesian divide: its practice combines both mind and body, text and image. It cannot be adequately understood without addressing both sides of the divide, and without acknowledging the hierarchical thinking about this divide that has shaped its course. Photography (as well as its associated form, video journalism) produces a tangible artifact through *interaction with the physical world.* It might be possible to bypass the role of the body in the creation of linguistic texts,[2] but not for photographic images. If we are to understand news photography, we are compelled to consider the observers themselves, how they observe with their senses, and their body's role in individual practices (as when it is using a camera) and within social practices (as when covering a news event). By pulling the body back into the discussion of practice, it is possible we gain a more complete understanding of the artifacts video journalists produce.

Photographic Images as a Sensorimotor Metaphor

The body and social interaction are both present in our interpretations of the meaning of images as well. It's true that much of the meaning assigned to a news image is derived from its discursive context, but what is unique about photography is its physical connection to time and space. When a photographer uses his body and a tool known as a camera to interface with the environment, the resulting concrete artifact contains his *perspective*. For this reason, photographs convey orientational information for their viewers. All photographs (especially news photographs for reasons that will be discussed shortly) contain the body-message of "being there," something sensed even more strongly in video's movement and sound. This may be the source of the rationally dismissed yet eternally latent notion that photographs have messages without language. The inherent orientational information contained within a photographic image is seductively simple and generally overlooked. I invite those who are not convinced to indulge me with an exercise. Lie down on your kitchen floor. Do you notice dust in a place you cannot reach with a broom? Scratches in the paint under the table? An old pen you'd forgotten you'd lost under the microwave cart? When we see one scene from reality as recorded by a body-camera entity, we "see" that frame from one particular vantage point—not only with our eyes, but with the *rest of our body as it is attached to our eyes*; we gain positional knowledge. We can better understand the way news images operate when we consider not only the gaze, but the body behind it.

One notable experiment recently illustrated the variable nature of the orientational metaphor by asking a group of people to determine which way was "up" for a series of NASA photographs from space (Burriss & Burriss, 2008). After all, there is no up or down in space, only up or down in relation to our bodies. The experiment used photographs released by NASA: photographs the space agency enhanced with color and assigned a "correct" orientation. When subjects not acquainted with NASA's system were asked to choose the correct orientation for such photographs, not everyone agreed with the NASA version (though men agreed more often than women). We interpret photography corporeally. This positional knowledge connects to the photographer's work: through the photograph, their position is, metaphorically, our position. In practice, their position affects the way a viewer interprets the photograph.

Krippendorff (1993a) identified five elements of metaphor that are helpful in understanding photographs as corporeal metaphors. First, he writes that metaphors "carry explanatory structures from a familiar domain of experience into another domain." The orientational element and embodied nature of a news image make it possible for news images to be interpreted by the audience in an embodied way. That is, the first domain, what a photograph depicts, is interpreted by viewers in their domain. Second, Krippendorff writes that metaphors require seeing some structural similarities between these two domains, however far-fetched these may be. Viewers are able to discern shapes, faces, and scenes according to previous understandings so their understanding of a photograph is largely a matter of recognition, or seeing something they are aware of in photographic form. Structural similarity is hardly far-fetched considering the proxemic information of a news image, which allows us to momentarily "be" in the photographer's body at the ontogenesis of a photograph. We stand in their shoes and behind their eyes—if only for a moment. Krippendorff's third quality of metaphors echoes the work of Lakoff and Johnson (1980, 1999), asserting that metaphors have entailments "for the domain they thereby organize far beyond any initial structural similarity."

Here's where we find the seductive nature of news images and their reflection of reality. For when we are in the photographer's shoes momentarily, we are "there." Instead of understanding that "this is what it was like while I was kneeling in front of the presidential podium using a Nikon SLR and a 17mm lens at one-five-hundredth of a second," (which is, by the way, very much the way photographers might talk about their work to one another) we sense: "…this is what it *was*." The corporeal essence of a news image carries with it such authority that the other details critical to image-making are lost. The scenes a camera has captured are decontextualized, only to be recontextualized *according to social practices*.

Krippendorff's quality four: metaphors organize perceptions and create realities. As metaphors for being there, news images show us a particular form of the world. Their daily display shows the Governor in front of various backgrounds telling us where he's been traveling. We see Congress from a particular angle above the floor and think of it as a working unit. We become accustomed to various editing techniques with news video that show us first the street signs of an intersection where a crime occurred, then the close-up of the bullet on the ground, and we are signaled that this is a murder story. Through all these forms, we travel metaphorically in the photographer's body. Finally, in Krippendorff's typology, the original domain of a "metaphor recedes into the background of un-recognition." As the metaphor recedes, we cease to consider the origins of an image.

Because the mechanism of photography accurately reproduces a particular visual scene, and because we experience it through the photographer's body, an image feels so real that the photographer's role in carrying us there is often forgotten. We feel we are there so completely that the photographer's decisions, work practices, and subjectivity often disappear—unless the photograph is so dramatic or offensive that we are inspired to consider how the image was created.

The corporeal metaphor imbues an image with a sense of presence. We are present before a scene because a photographer was once present in that moment of time and space. Add sound and movement, as with film or video, and this sense of presence is enhanced. For film theorist Robert Stam (2000b, p. 362), the source of television's pleasure is that it "…prosthetically extends human perception…." The sensation can be qualitatively enhanced when images are labeled as "live," but this is a linguistic construction, a discursive act. A live label can be added to a television feed when it isn't live,[3] or programs can be produced in ways that something appears to be happening in real time but is not. Therefore, liveness is not part of the corporeal metaphor being discussed here, even though it may add to a viewer's sense of presence.

When we think of photography and video texts as conveying a sensorimotor metaphor, we are forced to pay more attention to the body's role in their creation and interpretation. To interpret photographic objects merely as texts to be sensed with the eye is to view them as objects with inherently objective qualities. This has implications both for our understanding of the ways photographic materials are constructed and how they're interpreted. Take, for instance, what feminist cinema scholar Laura Mulvey named the "power of the gaze" (Mulvey, 1975). The scopophilic, exploitative nature of the male gaze over the feminine form is derived not just from looking but by metaphorically *trespassing*. Pornography metaphorically delivers unearned intimacy. In another example, Lutz and Collins (1993) suggest that documentary photography constitutes an "intersection" of gazes by photographer, subject, and viewer; these three vectors constitute a spatial-orientational metaphor. Julianne Newton (2001) writes of an "ecology" of the visual and visual creation, implicating the body in visual processes.

Moving images contain even stronger sensorimotor stimuli. As film historian Richard Barsam (1973) notes,

> Previously, paintings and photographs could only preserve a visual memory of movement. They function as the visual equivalent of the past tense; their single, static images are the remembrance of a moment in time and space. Motion pictures also record memories, but they also provide a visual equivalent of the present tense, *a representation of movement itself*. Their kinetic images, which record temporal sequence and make space move, not only confirm the process of human vision, but also alter the spectator's psychological relationship to the visible world as projected on a screen. (italics added, p. 6)

In other words, watching video is more than a visual experience, more even than an audio-visual experience. The sensorimotor metaphor fosters a physical understanding of a film or video story, and is a helpful consideration for any constructive analysis of photography and its practitioners. Understanding the way a VJ works to gain physical access to a scene and uses her body in concert with a camera in relation to a scene allows for a richer understanding of the resulting artifacts of filmic news.

Cameras, Bodies, Agency

When studying photographs as text, it is easy to neglect the process by which they were created. The phrase "the camera's eye" is often invoked as a shorthand term for the role of images in culture, and the mediated ways in which we view the world. For textual analyses, this shorthand may be useful. But when examining the origin of photographs, we must keep in mind that cameras indeed do not have eyes. The use of a camera requires a *human* eye. A camera is a *tool* in the hands of a human agent who decides how it should be used and what its products might mean. Cameras, without humans behind them to examine surveillance video, to snap a family portrait, or to witness atrocities in war-torn regions, are inanimate objects with no agency of their own. I use the word agency to mean the ability to make reasoned choices. Humans make choices about what to do with objects based on the affordances those objects present (Gibson, 1979). A rock, for instance, might be a weapon, a paperweight, or a surface for striking a match.[4] A human actor decides how the rock's attributes might serve an immediate need.

An illustration: some years ago in Pittsburgh, Pennsylvania, a male falcon engaged in a bloody battle against another falcon that had intruded upon his nest (Bauers, 2007). A conservationist, who just happened to log on to her webcam that was trained upon the nest at that very moment, managed to record the scene—unique and historic in the world of raptor science. This event illustrates the essential components of the concept of a photographer as a body with a camera. The camera was trained on the event and it recorded every frame. Yet without human intervention, the images would not have been saved and rendered meaningful. A naturalist—a human being—recognized the significance of the event; the camera merely delivered the scene before it. Without humans to interpret the images, the birds would have fought, the elder would have won, and the natural world would continue.

So while it is true that a camera can operate on its own, the rendering of an image as "meaningful" requires human recognition. Attaching meaning to that image is ultimately a social process, one that is the linguistic and often dialogic result of at least one person behind the lens and another who views its product (Newton, 2001). Even in cases where the photographer is taking pictures for him- or herself, the person takes on socially defined roles of creator and viewer—roles that have been learned from others through language. When we fail to acknowledge the human agency in photographic production, we are more likely to overlook their socially constructed nature, which blinds us to other possible ways of understanding the way they operate.

A human is only a photographer when using a camera. They are, to borrow a phrase, a camera-body.[5] In the company of photographers, it is hard to find examples when they are separated from their equipment; their professional identity is bound with the camera. In professional training, they are encouraged to take it everywhere, even when they are not working. Photographers have been observed holding their cameras up when they fall, protecting their equipment while allowing their physical bodies to suffer; when photographers are in a confrontation, they consider any touch to the camera to be an assault to the body.[6]

A photographer's body is as much a tool as the camera is, in that he uses his body to position the camera in relation to a scene. Recall the advice in Chapter One from [NE], a photo journalist and teacher: "Great pictures are made with your knees." In certain situations, particularly political coverage, photographers might spend hours on their knees in a pit before a dais. In crowded scrums, they can be seen trying to extend the reach of their bodies by carrying small step ladders or special extension posts with shutter controls. The difference between an amateur snapshot and a professional photograph is often evident in the angle a professional will use: they go low, start high, move to the side—there are infinite possibilities for both horizontal and vertical angles (unless constrained by social and geographic limits) from which a photographer may choose for creating an image from the scene before him.

A camera lens also defines the image in both limiting and revealing ways. It does not have peripheral vision, as humans do, and it can only allow one scene at a time to be recorded. A photographer must therefore choose a scene, based on social, cultural, aesthetic, and in the case of news, journalistic understandings, of what needs to be included in that recorded image. Importantly, the act of choosing what to include by necessity also implies a choice of what not to include. The camera may accurately record what is in front of it, but *only* what is in front of it. A human agent makes visual editing decisions before the image is recorded.

The relationship of time and location to photographs is hardly new territory. Photographs capture and hold time for us. Photographers aim to record what Cartier-Bresson (1952) called "decisive moments," with the idea that the best, most emotionally powerful photographs freeze humanity's most powerful, yet fleeting, epiphanies. Remember, though, that Cartier-Bresson would search for the right place to wait for such moments. He anticipated events, and his brilliance was as much about this preparation as the moments he chose to press the shutter. News photographers are called upon to be ready at all times to carry their gear everywhere, and to research their subjects in order to react (Horton, 2001). They must constantly negotiate their peculiar relationship with space; their work is a perpetual struggle to stand in the right place. Ethical principles demand that still photo journalists not change, alter, or doctor their scenes (before and after recording an image), so their only option to create aesthetically pleasing and informational images is to adjust their body in space and make decisions in real time about when to capture what's before them (Henderson, 1988; Dona Schwartz, 1992). The interdependence of photographers with their technology offers its own set of constraints and freedoms. To create an image that can be published or televised requires technical prowess over lenses, exposure, and light. Video-photographers might be tethered to a particular location where microphone output is available, or a cable running back to a microwave van.

What this means is that a photographer's practices must be considered in order to understand the nature of the resulting images. They are actors in the physical environment, interacting with other human beings according to social and organizational norms, practices, and demands. Habituated practices and real and imagined constraints and freedoms (both physically or socially imposed) will influence the work that is done. Photographers, videographers, and VJs will exercise agency with their cameras according to understandings of what is expected from them by their organization and in interactions with external actors. They are able to justify their actions according to institutional rules and regulations, or the cultural norms and expectations of journalism. They may also use those same norms and expectations to deny agency, and offer excuses for their practices.

Now that the digital technologies make it easier than ever to manipulate photographs, it becomes even more important for us to consider the camera-body and the agency of photographers. True, duplicity has been part of photographic practice if not from "day one" of its existence, then perhaps "day two." Whether by moving a Confederate soldier's body to create a more aesthetic composition, or using darkroom techniques that superimpose elements, or faking reenactments in early "documentaries," camera technologies have been continuously employed by their human users to deceive. The introduction of digital photographic software, such as Adobe's Photoshop®, is only the latest tool for duplicity—its danger lying in its ubiquity and facility, not its novelty. While people may distort images, though, faith in the camera itself remains. Its use by the institutions of journalism and documentary film, contextualized as truth, perpetuates this faith. Professional codes and institutional policies condemning manipulation, coupled with very public censuring of manipulation cases (such as *Time Magazine*'s OJ Simpson cover or *National Geographic*'s decision to rearrange the pyramids of Egypt), may have gone far in perpetuating the idea that cameras don't lie but people do. In her discussion of photographic truth in the digital age, Newton (2006) concludes:

> We may not be able to determine Absolute Truth through any means, but we can determine a Reasonable Truth—the best humans can discern, given the limits of individual perception and our means of representing the world. Photography's most significant gifts to humankind are not the means for establishing THE TRUTH, but rather a means for exploring the world in all its complexity. (p. 8)

As established in the preceding discussion of Krippendorff and objectivity, the traditional view of journalism is that "truth" requires accurate correspondence with a somewhere-out-there reality. The optics of a camera, as a determinist mechanism, can record with stunning accuracy the nature of light waves reflected off objects before it. This is not truth; it is optic representation. So, if truth is not possible with a news photograph, what are we left with? Trust. Traditional notions of truth assume access to unmediated reality. Trust is a social concept. By directing attention to the human creators of images, we not only gain an understanding of image-based journalism, but we are better able to understand where trust ought and ought *not* to be placed.

Recontextualization & the Meaning of Images

Constructivism's other locus of reality, social interaction, complicates our exploration, for the meaning of news images is created not merely in conversation but within an interdependent series of institutional practices. As many visual scholars have noted, much of the authoritative power of a news image or video is derived from a system by which human interaction declares that image to be a truthful representation, or a "fact" (Barnhurst, 1994; Newton, 2001; Zelizer, 2005). The essential act of journalism occurs when a reporter declares a set of circumstances to be "a story." As soon as a set of circumstances becomes a story, journalists engage in a series of work practices that record, *narrativize*, and *recontextualize* those circumstances. Human beings are objectified in photographs, tragedies become headlines, and a father's sobs become an "element" in a video story.

The institutional practices of journalism and the understandings that the public and other actors have about journalism are what make a photographic image more than dots on paper. Think of it this way: Suppose you and I were lost in a forest and needed to start a fire to stay warm for the night. I could hand you a rectangular piece of thick paper, you could light it with a match, and we'd soon have a campfire for warmth, cooking, maybe even a signal for rescuers. The meaning of the piece of paper was in its affordance as a bit of kindling. Others might have looked at it and seen a news photo, perhaps even a dramatic, emotional news photo that revealed an important political scene. But in our hour of need, that piece of paper held a different, more important meaning to us. Our use of the artifact, in our language about it, *we* determined what it was. It has no intrinsic meaning. Similarly, a camera lens might afford us the ability to build that fire. A camera might also be used to hold down papers on a breezy day. Humans assign meanings to objects, and use them according to the needs of the moment, often in terms of affordances —that is, what the object can do for us.

In sum, photographs are not facts. They are artifacts: objects made meaningful and useful by human activity. Considered this way, it is possible to apply Krippendorff's (2003, 2006, 2009) argument for a nonsemiotic epistemology of artifacts to news images. For, in spite of the intrinsic indexical nature of photographs—indeed, they do record reflected light (and in the case of videotape, physical sound waves)—the meaning of news images is determined by what we can and do say about them. As artifacts, they are imbued with what Krippendorff describes as "dialogic meaning," that is, their meaning is based on the interactive use of language, the discourse, of human beings. Scholarship of news images often focuses exclusively on their ontology, which assumes a static, objective reality. A useful alternative is what Krippendorff (2006) calls the "onto-genesis" of artifacts, by which "The real becomes manifest in trans-formations, in transitions, translations, rearticulations, and deconstructions" (p. 178). A nonsemiotic approach encourages consideration of the norms, routines, choices, and decisions involved in visual journalism and, concurrently, the choices and decisions *not* taken. That is, by acknowledging the body's involvement with visual journalism, we are better able to explore alternative constructions.

Body-Centered Social Constructivism

The primacy of the body's interface with camera technology in time and space is central to the work of any news photographer. By keeping the body central to this inquiry, it is possible to better understand the process and the decisions made by each participant. The need for basic access to events, for instance, is qualitatively different for photographers than it is for text-based journalists. The types of clothing worn, the equipment they choose to carry, the choices they make in terms of where to go to cover a story, the ways they make claim to space and move within it are body-centered decisions photographers must make as they work each day, and these decisions affect the images they create. The way they use their bodies affects the way they interact with their colleagues within organizations, in the field with other journalists, and with the human subjects they cover.

Ultimately, a body-centered approach to constructivism provides a framework for the study of video journalism. This general framework is not a grand theory, such as structuralism, critical theory, or post-modernism, because to choose a grand theory would be to impose an interpretation on a subject that is in its very early stages of development, bending the project to the subject, rather than letting the subject take its own shape. At the same time, using a general framework allows for some organization of material, some categorization, and some guidance for study. By carefully attending to both dimensions of constructivism, the social interaction and human senses, it is possible to gain a richer understanding of both the process and resulting product of video journalism.

A System of Stakeholders

A news image, therefore, is the product of a multidimensional system, rooted in the world of a human body acting within the physical environment *and* in social interaction with other actors. The creation of an artifact known as a photograph is a concrete, physical act, but ascribing meaning to it is ultimately a social process. The choices of where and when to work, and the decision of when to click the shutter are all dependent on a social process, one that requires at least one person behind the lens, another to view the product, and, in the domain of journalism, the members of a news organization, external intermediaries, professional societies, sources, and so on (Krippendorff, 2003; Newton, 2001; Schudson, 2003; Tuchman, 1978).

As Krippendorff explains, dialogic meaning implies a process—a circular process in fact—with multiple players, actors, or stakeholders in the system by which a news image acquires different meanings as it passes through a sort of bricolage of "other artifacts, people, practices, and events, jointly participating in the constitution of systems of enacted meanings..." (2003, p. 29). The process of creating and assigning meaning to the artifacts we call news images involves a network of photographers, journalists, public relations representatives, subjects, viewers, readers, editors, managers, and others who have an interest or stake in such an image. The process can be conceptualized as a series of passages which often overlap, "gates" in one sense, but not gates in the sense that a discrete fact or meme flows through intact or is blocked, as is the case with traditional gatekeeping theory (Bennett, 1996; Shoemaker, 1991; Sigal, 1973). These passages are better imagined as conduits for dialogue[7] wherein the image (artifact) is initially decontextualized when it is pulled from space and time and then continually recontextualized by human actors. This recontextualization is how an image-artifact's meaning is negotiated, debated, and temporarily assigned. I say temporarily because the materiality of images, even digital images on the web, can exist beyond their preliminary recontextualization and the human beings who originally create, edit, process, and present them. The process of recontextualization is unstable and dynamic. There is also circularity to the process. After all, what constitutes a story in the first place? Prior to collecting material to create news images, journalists have to have preconceptualization of those circumstances in mind. These preconceptualizations are based on discursive patterns that have declared similar situations to be stories. Each story creates another example of what a video news story is and ought to be, thereby setting the stage for the process to begin anew.

How shall this notion of stakeholders in a media production process be understood? Stakeholder theory is commonly used by business scholars when talking about products in a commercial sense, but Krippendorff (2006, pp. 64–65) found it a useful term for discussing the dialogic process for design technology. He notes that stakeholders operate in networks of other stakeholders, all of whom:

- claim their stake in a technology;
- are experts in their own worlds;
- are willing to act in support or opposition to a technological development; and

- are willing to mobilize the resources they command, such as information, expertise, money, time, connections to members of their communities, and the powers of the institutional roles they occupy.

To consider the role of such stakeholders in the newsgathering environment is useful because it allows us to consider the roles of nonjournalists in the production process, and because it forces us to consider the complexity of the network through which an image's meaning evolves. Photo journalists, and by extension video journalists, do stake a claim in technology, are indeed "experts" in their own work worlds, are willing to act in support of or opposition to a technological development, and are willing to mobilize their resources to protect and nourish their stake in the process. So, too, are the actors in other domains of the video journalistic process.

Figure 2.1 (shown on the following page) illustrates the environment in which photo and video journalists work. Note that they work within an overlapping set of social domains, including the news organization with which they are affiliated, the intermediaries, or sources, with whom they interact in the course of covering a story, the scene itself, a physical place and time in which they create images, as well as the real and imagined audience. The thick black arrow represents the process by which a photo/video journalist decontextualizes scenes and subjects, then recontextualizes them for an audience according to the norms, routines, and expectations of the domains in which they operate.

Note that the entire system is located within a larger social framework, or culture, which holds a conception of what news is and ought to be. In the US, Britain, and most of the industrialized world, that conception holds that news is a truthful accounting of current events.

Key to this conception is the idea that many individuals and forces are involved with the construction of a news image's meaning. This operates in concert with the unique aspect of photography as a constructive act: that which sets it apart from other meaning-making activities, namely the photographer's body interacting with technology in the environment. Images are created in the worldly environment, in locations chosen strategically by journalists. Access to those locations must be negotiated with outside stakeholders who might include the subjects themselves or image managers such as public relations officers, media "handlers," and so on—in large part, the officials and sources of Sigal and other gatekeeping theorists (Bennett, 1996; Shoemaker, 1991; Sigal, 1973). Social processes, negotiations, understandings, and forces influence the location, time, and circumstances of the moment—and they also influence the image's recontextualization. But the moment of decontextualization, that is, the point in time and space as it intersects with a camera-body, is a physical moment *that can never be revisited*. This is what sets news photography apart from other forms of journalism. Facts are based in discourse, and can be transmitted through interpersonal or technological devices. A video image is an artifact whose meaning resides in language, is shaped by language, and can be transformed by language, but whose creation requires a human body with a camera—a photographer in concert with the physical environment.

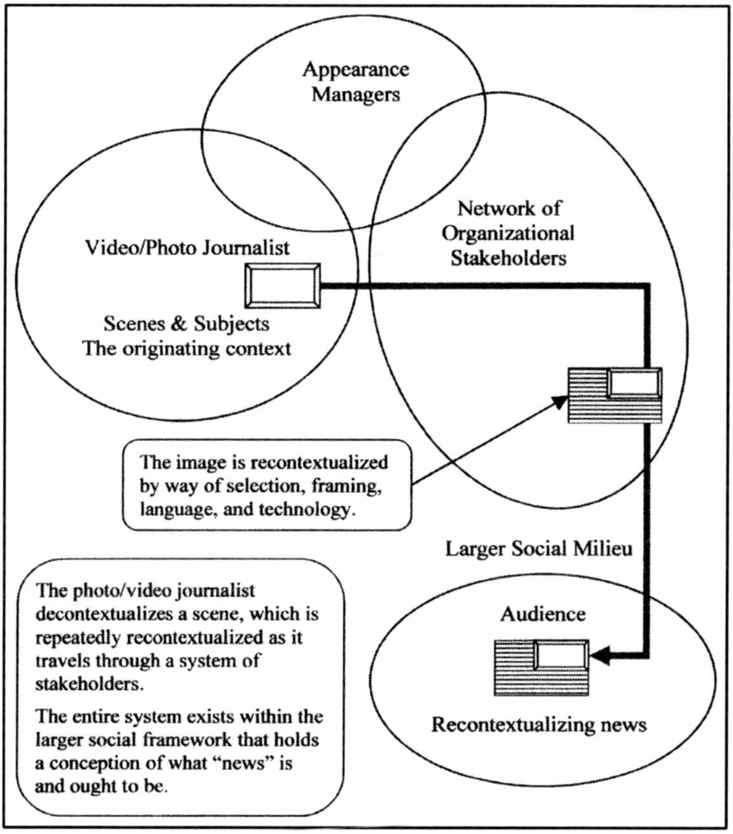

Figure 2.1: The photo/video journalist's environment

By looking at the process through the eyes of the system's stakeholders, it becomes possible to understand a VJ's decision-making process while constructing a news story. There may be times a photographer will risk losing a press pass if she perceives that larger moral concerns are at stake. Some choices are exercised out of pure fear or losing a job or status within a job. When someone's very livelihood is at stake in the process, their decision-making process will differ from those times when a relationship with a coworker might be temporarily unpleasant.

The meaning of those images and their contextualization is negotiated as they flow through news organizations, whether commercial and public news organizations or professional groups such as the National Press Photographers Association (NPPA). Editors, reporters, and other journalistic colleagues may select images a VJ might otherwise overlook, or write stories to accompany images that a photographer had not anticipated in the course of shooting. Photographers who work for large news organizations might be sent out on assignments without a clear understanding of the newsroom's plans for that image, being told simply to shoot a building's façade or signs at a street corner. Once the artifact is created, a photographer may have very limited control over how it is captioned, narrated, or used in the larger news product.

The meaning of images is further negotiated with and through the receiving audience, which brings its own perceptions, knowledge, understandings, and prejudices to their interpretations. An image that a photographer considers a statement against violence or an unjust war might be interpreted by an audience as sensationalism. Controversial images might spark dialogue between viewers and photographers about their meaning. Journalists are taught to keep the audience in mind as they produce their stories, and they may choose to create and publish certain images thought to be appealing. Other images are cut for fear they might offend. The audience, moreover, often overlaps with the subjects involved in news; the sources and subjects with whom journalists interact each day are perhaps a small percentage of their audience, but with disproportionate opportunities for feedback.

What's at Stake for the VJ

In the production of any news story, then, the VJ uses his or her body in concert with a camera to capture sounds and scenes in order to construct a coherent narrative that will pass through the network of stakeholders. He decontextualizes a moment in space and time to create a photographic artifact, one that will be recontextualized according to the norms and practices of his working environment. The video journalist's position as a stakeholder in the process is multilayered. At a news scene, the VJ might be most concerned about his or her immediate job assignment: What is the task for the newsroom? Have they been assigned to cover a ribbon-cutting? A speech? A fire? A VJ's most immediate stake, therefore, may be to answer to their manager and colleagues. This explains the single-mindedness so often displayed by photo journalists, who will risk their own safety above that of their immediate assignment. At a broader level, VJs also have a stake in their immediate relationship to the other human beings at the scene. What relationship do they have and want to have with the subjects, appearance managers (handlers, public relations representatives), and fellow photographers from other news outlets? The VJ might also consider whether there is an award-winning story at stake; competition is a significant source of status among photo journalists.

A VJ may be concerned not so much about her performance with an immediate assignment, but her job with a particular organization whether or not this particular assignment goes well. Is her job secure? Rewarding? Finally, the VJ's long-term career is always at stake on assignment. Certain mistakes can destroy a career, such as using digital manipulation to alter a photograph—even with benign intent—and certain iconic moments can make a career simply through the luck of being in the right place at the right time. For transitioning VJs, those who once performed a different role in the organization, their sense of self and ego may be at stake. Longtime still photographers who've become adept with one media form may not enjoy the frustration that comes with a new type of technology. Print reporters who consider themselves to be white collar, text-based professionals may find it threatening to be faced with the very physical, manual labor aspects of video journalism. And television reporters who've long been the de facto managers of their camera-carrying colleagues in the field might be unwilling to pick up that camera themselves.

Outside the organization, norms and expectations exist for video journalists working in the field. Union leaders may have concerns about changes in work practices as video journalism is introduced to a particular newsroom. In terms of day-to-day activities, there are written rules and state-enforced laws for photographic access to certain scenes; for instance, courtrooms, state legislatures, and other state sanctioned ceremonial events have specific codes of conduct. There are unwritten norms as well: usually, there is a moderately friendly spirit of cooperation with other photo journalists—even those with competing organizations.

What's at Stake for Human Subjects

Stakeholders, or the subjects at various events, generally have a strong interest in the way they are portrayed, and will use whatever means available to enhance their image, both literally and figuratively. When their image has been decontextualized by the camera, anything can be conceivably said about that image, which is why American[8] privacy and libel laws protect individuals in the recontextualization process. A subject's actions might be as simple as dressing up for a television interview, or avoiding cameras when one is arrested. Accounts of the paparazzi and their relationship with celebrities reveal the degree to which the relationship is a matter of co-construction, not, as popularly considered, entirely parasitic.[9] Beyond simply hoping for a flattering material image, subjects often wish to affect the recontextualization of their representation. Sometimes, what seems an innocent scene for a feature story can cause trouble for a subject, such as the man depicted at the baseball game when he'd called in sick to work that morning, or the woman walking in the park with a man not her husband. These individuals have stakes in the process beyond the aesthetics of their portraiture.

What's at Stake for Appearance Managers

The recontextualization process by which meaning is assigned and reassigned is a linguistic process, and therefore difficult to control. The United States, Great Britain, and other democracies have laws protecting freedom of language, making it possible to say nearly anything about an image in the recontextualization phase. The moment of decontextualization, that is, when the photographer interacts with the physical environment, can be, and often is, regulated. Private property owners, corporations, or governmental agents, such as the secret service or the US Congress, constitute another variable in the recontextualization process. Much of the power an appearance manager holds to is derived through their authority to control physical space in order to influence not only how stories are told, but often *what* stories are told.

Appearance managers, such as public relations representatives, event planners, and other handlers, are often under intense pressure to influence the way a news story is told by others. The difficulty, of course, is that while they might be able to control the way they themselves frame a message, write a news release, formulate their sound bite, or design their stage backdrop, they have only indirect control over the recontextualization of an image. If they are freelance public relations representatives whose only job is to handle one event for a client, their livelihood may be at stake should they fail to adequately protect that client's interests. Their professional reputation may be at stake. If they are in-house public relations executives, the overall image of their employer is in the balance. Also at stake is their long-term relationship with the journalists in their domain. While they may endeavor to have a positive and friendly relationship with journalists in the course of their work, they may be willing to sacrifice such niceties if they perceive that a story's angle is not going in their favor. Small wonder, then, that mediating agents will struggle to influence elements within their control: access to subjects and scenes, backdrops, props, and other "photo opportunities." Because the nature of available visuals influences the stories chosen and told by television journalists, such access becomes the means by which an image manager can exert influence on the larger story.

What's at Stake for Organizations

Video journalists work for a variety of organizations, whether commercial news operations, such as local television stations, newspapers, radio networks, or independent citizen-journalism groups like Indymedia, even groups that do not purport to produce news, such as *Witness.org*. The media logic of these various organizations is likely to vary, as will the norms and routines for the individual VJs. Each organization will have different norms and practices for the recontextualization of images gathered in the field. The expectations of a local television station are likely to contrast with a newspaper that is only starting to experiment with video. That newspaper's first video-photographer might have high status because of his special knowledge, or he might be shunned as someone breaking with newsroom norms. Union rules and trade organizations will add another dynamic to a VJ's "home base": the deployment of VJs to save money for media organizations might be seen as a means of career survival or suicide. The convergent newsroom has been touted as the wave of the future by media executives and critics alike, yet the details of developing such newsrooms remain devilish.

Members of a news organization have a stake in the work of a VJ at multiple levels—some practical, others intangible. Managers may be hoping to save money with a one-person crew, while enhancing local coverage. Photographers who've worked with still cameras for decades must contend with the fearsome possibility of layoffs or replacement. Forces within a VJ's organization might include everything from the speed with which news workers must operate to story choices, frequency of deadlines, publications, or the broadcasting of "news shows." Internal forces also include the financial pressures on newsrooms. The international recession that started in 2008 was especially difficult for traditional media organizations. Ad revenue plummeted and thousands of journalists were laid off (Associated Press, 2008; Edmunds, 2008; Rosenthal, 2008; Saba, 2008). Budget cuts might force newsroom employees to take on more responsibilities without additional pay (Singer, 2003). The consequences of economic and practical pressures may have critical consequences on the way journalistic reality is constructed.

What's at Stake for Organizational Leaders

Given the economic pressures that convergent technologies are placing on traditional media organizations, managers may perceive the very survival of their newsroom to be at stake. Managers who attempt to change the norms and values within their newsroom have a great deal at stake. Not only are they working to change the internal culture of their organization, but they must be sure that the product put forth by their organization is not harmed by changing work practices. Struggles with union rules and the labor relations are at stake, as are budgetary concerns. All the while, managers must maintain formal and informal relationships with their immediate employees; instituting change can alter those relationships permanently.

Other organizational colleagues may also fear the survival of their organization, their union, or their job. They may have friendly relationships with coworkers that become strained by the threat of changes in workplace organization. In some organizations, photo journalists are faced with the possibility of being phased out in order for younger, cheaper VJs to be hired; small wonder that they may not be willing to mentor their younger colleagues in the field.

Finally, there are larger questions of occupational and cultural identity, norms, and expectations for journalists generally. What does it mean to be a convergent journalist? Who is a convergent journalist and who is a text-based journalist? What of the norms regarding objectivity, fairness, public service, accuracy? Might the cheaper, faster, less collaborative ways of producing news stories threaten the ideals and norms that constitute the very identity of reporters?

What's at Stake for the Colleagues of Video Journalists

Because the norms and expectations are in a state of transition with the shift toward video journalism, VJs have an added stake in the process—they must "prove themselves" to their coworkers. VJs who are the younger, newer members of an organization, already attempting to make their way in a new organization, might feel this pressure acutely. More experienced journalists might feel the pressure to learn video-journalism skills a bit more intensely because they might be concerned for their very livelihood and job. These questions are in addition to the typical norms and expectations of a news organization: the imperative to bring back the story, the norms of objectivity and balance, the norm of appearing attractive when on camera. Deadline pressure is compounded as news organizations shift to a 24-hour cycle; in a sense, there are no deadlines because every minute is a deadline—there is no production schedule to break up the day. The constraints of time and space and the climate of political and economic upheaval cause the stakes to be felt keenly and often emotionally for most members of a news organization.

What's at Stake for the Audience

As news consumers, members of the audience have their own stake in the process. As I described in Chapter One, changes in camera technologies have historically changed the way information is presented, whether in the development of photo essays or live ENG reporting. The technologies of video journalism can be expected to similarly affect the construction of filmic news narratives. When one person uses a smaller camera, will their stories convey a stronger sense of intimacy with the subjects? Might they use a more personal approach and speak in the first person? How might that affect a viewer's comprehension, liking, and trust in a story? The audience is always present in the minds of intermediaries, organizational managers, and VJs, however, and their conceptions of what the audience wants and needs is presumed to be a guiding factor in their decisions and routines.

The social contract between journalists and a democratic polity have always placed the stakes for the news audience quite high. The news audience has its own interest in the way news is made, in ways it considers, and, perhaps more importantly, in ways the audience may be unaware. Viewers and readers often complain of bias. Some members of the audience, particularly blogging critics, have identified and expressed their opinions about the way news is delivered by demanding such transparency and accountability by their news organizations. In spite of some gestures, such as the provision of e-mail addresses for responses or information on anonymity policies, the larger processes of newsgathering, and especially video newsgathering, remain largely hidden from view, much like the man behind the curtain in *The Wizard of Oz*.

Might the audience be better served by VJs who are able to spend more emotional energy on a subject while working alone? Might a more transparent presentation of video stories, which include recontextualizing information about the circumstances under which a photograph was taken, be helpful to the audience? Or might the audience continue to see the same material more cheaply made? Will they turn away from news and toward more entertaining fare if the news product becomes watered down or poorly produced? Many of those who resist the changes posed by convergent media and the introduction of video journalism assert that one person working alone cannot deliver a product of adequate quality for the audience.

The utopian changes predicted by video journalism's proponents cannot be assumed. It may be that one person will create the same style of artifacts already produced within a particular newsroom, indicating that the media logic of an organization will trump the impact of singularity and/or expansion. It may also be that these two characteristics change the process and yield a new type of filmic story, as touted by video journalism's strongest advocates: one that is more intimate, transparent, or reflexive. It may be that the process changes, but the product is largely the same. With this research, I attempted to peel back the hope and the hype to see the reality of what video journalists do and what they create.

The Research

This book is based on more than a hundred observations and interviews with VJs and the people who work with them over the course of five years. I've met with VJs from a variety of organizations, such as commercial television stations, public radio, newspaper organizations, nonprofits, and freelancers, as long as they fit the definition of a VJ in that they shoot their stories themselves. The study includes visits to three professional photography workshops, a major national newspaper, a national radio network, a medium market newspaper, three BBC regional sites, a major market cable television operation, a small market television station, a major market newspaper, the US Capitol Building, and a nonprofit organization devoted to teaching video journalism to nonprofessionals. Some of the highlights include:

- A two-week stay with the BBC in June 2007 at the Nations & Regions (local television news) training site in Newcastle, England, a regional newsroom in Bristol, and a regional newsroom in Oxford
- A week-long field visit to a training session sponsored by an ownership group for newspaper reporters, writers, and editors to learn video journalism
- A workshop designed for print photographers interested in video at American University in Washington, D.C., October 2007
- A two-day workshop sponsored by the NPPA in Philadelphia in 2006, at which video journalism was discussed formally and informally
- A field visit to the *New York Times* video journalism unit
- A visit with a national radio network that has trained its reporters to use video
- A visit to Parliament in London
- Separate visits to Washington, D.C., in 2006 with the US Congress and with a national television network

- A field visit to a large market cable news operation that employs video journalists (all its reporters are expected to shoot their own stories)
- Four days with the Radio Television News Directors Association annual convention in 2008, where the merits of video journalism were studied and debated by news executives
- A field visit to a local television station that blends the work of VJs and traditional photographers for coverage
- A ride-along with a VJ who works for a major market newspaper
- Five days (over the course of three months) of field work with an independent citizen-journalist organization that trained citizen journalists to use video for union and community activism, a program known as *Our City, Our Voices*

I also looked carefully at the stories produced by the VJs to learn more about their storytelling styles. The next few chapters are organized according to the various categories of stakeholders in the process: the VJs themselves, their managers, and "appearance managers"—those outside of the news organizations whose job it is to protect the image of a particular institution, such as publicists, communication representatives, or public relations representatives. An additional chapter examines the structure and style of the stories produced by video journalists. Throughout this book, I look at how video journalism's two distinctive properties, namely singularity (the ability of one person to work alone) and expansion (its spread to new users), make a difference.

Significantly, for this is rare among journalistic ethnographies, my research includes observations of journalists actually covering stories in the field—not just working in a newsroom. These sites included a funeral for a young shooting victim, an apartment building fire, a feature story on a school building, an analytical story about physical therapists, a minor police event in an urban setting, and a feature story at an amusement park. To protect their privacy, everyone who participated in the study is represented by a set of random initials, e.g., "[LM]."

Of course, in the process of researching this book, I also relied on materials from institutional texts and trade literature. Such material includes rule books and guides for photographers covering various institutions, e.g., the Congressional administrative code that guides its photo galleries and news organization handbooks. Other helpful texts included trade publications for journalists, including *Broadcasting & Cable*, the *Communicator* (published by the Radio and Television News Directors Association), *News Photographer* (published by the National Press Photographers Association), and websites such as *The Photog's Lounge* or *Online Media Daily*, all of which include articles relevant to video journalism and its practices, as do a growing number of websites devoted specifically to video journalism. Some present VJ stories, such as those by Kevin Sites at *Yahoo* and Travis Fox, formerly with the *Washington Post*. Others comment on video journalism while presenting examples, such as those sites of Michael Rosenblum, David Dunkley Gyimah—*BagNewsNotes* (a blog devoted to photo-journalistic criticism)—or scholar Ken Kobre's online *KobreGuide*. Finally, a bulletin-board style forum called *The Watercooler*, where television journalists are able to post anonymous notes, complaints, and observations, has provided some helpful (not to mention vitriolic!) insights regarding their newsroom experiences.

Constructivist Analysis

The best way to understand a process or the structure of a system is to take it apart. The constructivist paradigm is itself a metaphor that implies a conception of a system that consists of interlocking parts, like a machine, and the best way to understand how a machine works is to take it apart and examine how the parts work together. That's what the rest of this book attempts to do, that is, *deconstruct* the process of video journalism to show the mechanics behind the scenes: those practices and daily decisions that contribute to the creation of video news stories by individual video journalists. Deconstructing the process makes it possible for us to see how the process both reflects and distorts reality, how time and space are compressed, and how forcing the chaos of our lives into narratives inflates the importance of some elements and bypasses others. The constructivist approach is as much about discovering the ways our shared understandings and meanings are created as how they are *not.* The analyst must not only observe the choices a subject makes, but must consider what other choices existed—the alternatives *not* chosen. My hope is that by considering the choices VJs make as they create a story I avoided producing a lengthy and detailed—but meaningless—description of professional practice, a common complaint of newsroom ethnographies (especially those written by former journalists) (J. Singer, 2009).

What of the stories themselves? Essentially, I centered my efforts on two basic dimensions: that of narrative structure and strategies of authorship/authority. To better understand the structure of VJ stories, I considered the *linkages* between word and image (borrowing heavily from a mapping technique conceived by Kracauer [1947]), as well as the nature and variety of visual scenes included in the final product. I looked at camera angle, composition, audio components (NATSOT, sound bites, etc.), and the use of graphic elements. I examined the way settings, characters, and actions are presented, and the editing technique used for transitions. In short, I looked for elements that might reflect differences in shooting technique indicative of a single producer working with a small camera.

Some Personal Notes

As Werner Heisenberg demonstrated, the act of measuring a phenomenon changes that phenomenon. This project is no exception to his uncertainty principle. Qualitative field research cannot be replicated in the way a laboratory experiment might. Life happens—and it's the ethnographer's job to take note of it. Her biases will cause her to emphasize what interests her and perhaps not even see other details another researcher might consider salient. If another researcher were to visit the same individuals in the same locations and ask the same questions, the moments recorded would still not be the same. This lack of replicability does not render such studies worthless though; indeed, the fact that this study has been undertaken during a unique and critical juncture in the development of digital journalism may *add* value to this project. The lack of laboratory control is the beautiful side of the qualitative coin. Life indeed does happen, and accompanied with explicit descriptions of field work, data, and analytical methods, another researcher might be able to follow my ontological path and judge my conclusions to be sound.

Therefore, I have attempted to work as transparently as possible, with my informants and my fellow scholars, sharing information about my research process so that others might assess through their own theoretical lens. I have shared my ongoing observations with informants, for instance, and have explained in advance what sorts of questions I will ask in an interview. I have attempted to explicitly outline my theoretical framework so that my colleagues might assess the value of the research. My observations, while not consistently detached, have the flavor of one who has empathy for her subjects, possibly reflecting greater intimacy with the phenomena being studied. I observed real video journalists working in real situations in a strategically considered variety of settings, all with the goal of presenting a detailed and informative account. So while I do not make predictive or causal claims, I do make a sincere attempt to provide a detailed portrait of the process and product of video journalism during a time of dramatic change.

My informants have the right to expect that they'll be represented here respectfully and accurately, and in ways that avoid unnecessarily embarrassing them. They gave time—sometimes days, sometimes hours—with an understanding that I would record their words and actions accurately. My stake in the project is different; it was part of my scholarly adventure. What for my subjects is their daily work, personal attitudes, their very career, became data for me to parse, examine, and critique. This is not inherently harmful or exploitative, but it is something which must be acknowledged.

The final complication for this project and my stake in it derives from my own background. I arrived at the academy with more than twenty years' experience as a journalist myself, nearly all of that time spent as a television journalist. In a sense, my credibility with my subjects as a journalist seemed more important than my status as a PhD researcher, and I found myself legitimizing myself with subjects more as an insider than an ethnographer would. I simply do not have an "outsider's eye." I identify with my subjects in ways only a person who has also spent time trying to obtain interviews, sitting on a sidewalk waiting for a visual opportunity, or struggling with a deadline can. I admit that I occasionally lapsed in my work as social scientist: holding doors for my subjects, sharing jokes with them about the boss, and at least twice pointing out photographic opportunities that I knew would help them in their story production. My instincts as a field producer took over when I would have preferred to have been detached. On the other hand, my knowledge as a field producer allowed me to create strong connections with my subjects. By occasionally helping them with a tripod or nodding in the direction of a key shot, I established credibility with those who allowed me into their daily work life. For worse and for better, therefore, I have injected myself into this research process. I endeavor to be as explicit about it as possible in the following chapters. Rather than pretend to separate myself from the observations, I will attempt to explain my own process in detail.

NOTES:

1. Webster's New Collegiate Dictionary (1977). In H. B. Woolf (Ed.), *Webster's New Collegiate Dictionary*. Springfield, MA: G&C Merriam Co.
2. Though this is really more a matter of degree, as any written text requires involvement of the body, whether typing, handwriting, or the copying of sheepskin manuscripts. The body can be easily forgotten when text is processed as "thought," but it is always there.
3. *The Daily Show*, a popular news satire program in the US, makes a frequent joke of this.
4. The first time I sat at a sewing machine at the age of nine, my mother explained to me that the sewing machine was "stupid" and would do whatever I told it to do, including sew through my finger.

5. I borrow this nomenclature from Carolyn Marvin and David Ingle's work on patriotism as civil religion and their theorizing of the "flag-body."
6. Interviews with [CL] and [RZ].
7. Or, to use Hall's (1973b) terminology, where meanings are encoded and decoded.
8. Such protections exist in other parts of the world, but I am only well-acquainted with US law.
9. For an excellent, though non-scholarly, account, see (Samuels, 2008).

Chapter 3:
The Video Journalism Process

> *"It is so characteristic, that just when the mechanics of reproduction are so vastly improved, there are fewer and fewer people who know how the music should be played."*
>
> *—Ludwig Wittgenstein*

Introduction

What makes the work of a video journalist special? How are the two characteristics of singularity and expansion manifest in the daily work of a video journalist? VJs work for a variety of organizations and many of them have taken on the role after working in another journalistic specialization. Is it possible that they have anything in common at all? After observing VJs at work, it was possible to pinpoint some commonalities. This chapter will describe the basic process and all the choices a VJ makes in producing a story. Then it will focus on how singularity and expansion affect that process and render it a distinct form of practice.

Deconstructing a process allows us to better understand it, but first, it's necessary to see the entire system. Here, then, is an illustrative example from my research. The VJ profiled here, [LT], works for a cable operation that relies entirely on solo VJs for its newsgathering. While the details of her process are unique to her own situation, job, and story, the basic steps she took on the day I shadowed her are common to the VJs I observed in a wide variety of settings.

One VJ's Day

During the newsroom's editorial meeting on this particular morning, [LT] was assigned to produce a story about the next day's presidential primary election. She was not present for the meeting of assignment editors[1] and producers, who based their decisions on information from news wires, local and national newspapers, and a file of news releases and other event notices. The news managers *preconceptualized* a story about the way the various local political activists were working behind the scenes on behalf of their candidates, and suggested that [LT] gain access to those offices.

Once assigned, [LT] immediately started making the phone calls necessary to arrange for interviews and access to campaign offices–to *locate and access the elements* she'll need to construct the story as it is preconceptualized. As another VJ puts it, it's crucial to answer the question: "What video can I use?" For this story, [LT] needed at least two things: access to the interiors of campaign offices for video of people working, and interviews with at least one person about the last minute push. She spent about a half hour making phone calls and requesting access before she reported to her managers that the story's preconceptualization needed to be changed—the offices would not grant her access. As an alternative, [LT] suggested visiting a local school to talk to young people about the campaign. She has a positive relationship with a private school in the area and was quickly granted access. The school serves a diverse population of teens, and because it is not part of a larger school district bureaucracy, its leaders can quickly make decisions about working with journalists. [LT] and the managers expected that the African American students would be enthused about the primary campaign between Hillary Clinton and Barack Obama.

Soon, [LT] was packing her gear and other supplies. VJs often carry multiple bags for their equipment: supplies such as pens and a notepad, and also extra shoes, makeup, and other cosmetic accessories. [LT] knows her clothes will take a beating from the physical work she does and says she's resigned to it. One way she gets through the day is to wear low-heeled boots with nice slacks so she has comfortable mobility. [LT] packs all her supplies into one of the cars that is shared by everyone in her newsroom, and heads to the school. She's been there before, knows the way, and is there by noon.

Once she arrives at the school and checks in, an administrator leads her up the stairs to the classroom of a social studies teacher. She carries a tote bag, her camera, and tripod up the stairs and refuses offers of help to carry her gear to the fourth floor. When introduced to the teacher, she explains what she needs to do and asks to videotape a class discussion about the primary. The teacher is able to oblige and [LT] sets up her camera and tripod inside the classroom to get started *shooting*. It is now more than three hours since she was assigned her story. She shoots a variety of shots from the front of the room before taking the camera around the classroom for additional angles. To shoot her own standup, [LT] puts a pen on a desk as a focusing target for the camera, then rolls tape and stands where the pencil was to make her presentation. As it turns out, the students are not nearly as interested in the democratic primary as expected; in fact, many are conservative Republicans. [LT] calls this sort of mismatch between newsroom preconceptualization and the reality of what she shoots "producer fantasy." She was confident she would still be able to work this material into a useable story.

By late afternoon, [LT] was on her way back to the station to narrativize her elements, recontextualizing them into a linear, real-time story structure that combines her voice, clips from the interviews she's collected, and illustrative images from the classroom. In the newsroom, she typed a script, had it approved by a manager, and then recorded her voice tracks in a small, soundproof room. She uploaded her video clips to one of several computer systems in a long bank of editing stations on one end of the newsroom, and spent about an hour crafting a story that lasted not much more than a minute. She met her deadline even after electricians working in the building caused the power to go out.

Figure 3.1. Access is always an issue for journalists, but for VJs, sometimes this is quite literal—simply opening doors when one is carrying equipment in both arms becomes a daily challenge.

In the early evening, her story was presented during the newscast. This is another form of recontextualization. In this organization [NBHD CABLE], most stories are introduced by a studio anchor, and VJs take turns as anchors in the small, automated studios for the frequent newscasts, operating their own teleprompter and adjusting their own unattended camera. Media organizations are often thought of in terms of their story recontextualization, whether on the web, in a newscast, or as part of a running loop of videos on a cable channel. Posting videos to the web sometimes requires a VJ to write out the wording for every sound bite (sometimes called a "verbatim") so that web users can read, not watch, the story.[2]

A Model for the VJ Process

The five basic steps [LT] took as she moved through her day were shared by the VJs observed in a variety of exhibiting organizations, whether newspapers, TV stations, or activist organizations. They are:

1. Preconception of the story and its elements
2. Locating and gaining access to elements
3. Decontextualizing elements: recording them for future use
4. Narrativizing the elements
5. Presenting the story

The process is similar to that of any other documentary filmmaker, and shares much in common with the process for writing a textual news story. It is also similar to the "News Factory" process identified by Bantz, McCorkle and Baade (1980). Very briefly, the first step involves identifying an event or set of circumstances as a news story, gaining access to the elements that must be recorded in order to create a story, shooting and recording those elements (or decontextualizing them), recontextualizing them into narrative, and then recontextualizing them again in a presentation (Linell, 1998). The process is circular: the fifth step informs the first. The demands of presentation influence the way a story is preconceptualized; for instance, the scheduled nature of a television newscast influences considerations for how long a story should run, which in turn informs the number of elements a VJ shoots in the field. Stories that are exhibited on the web do not have similar time constraints, so a story's length may not be so stringently preconceptualized. Recontextualization constitutes a media logic that shapes the entire process (Altheide & Snow, 1979).

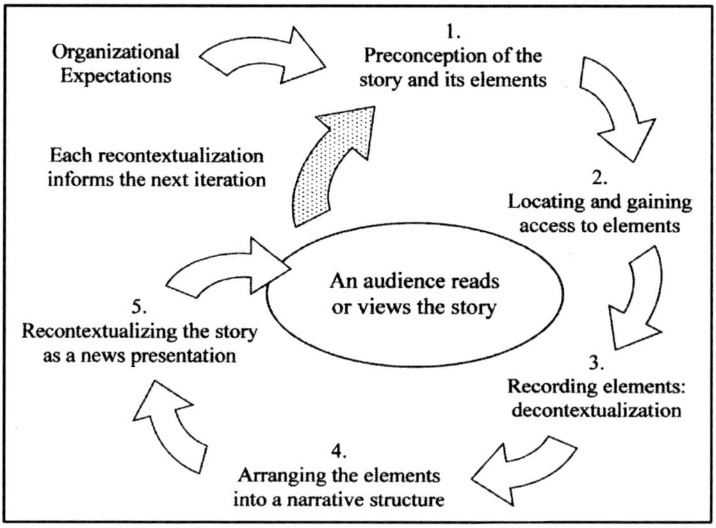

Figure 3.2: The video journalism process. Note that the process is self-renewing in that the presentational recontextualization informs the preconception phase.

The sorts of circumstances and facts that might be considered a *story* varies according to the form used by an exhibiting organization. Television, newspaper, radio, and activist organizations have different criteria for what is considered a story. As these forms converge, and as a video journalist cuts through these various forms, the connection between exhibition and preconception are likely to change. Nevertheless, each step has features unique to video journalism. While singularity and expansion both can be seen as affecting the process when it comes to the daily work of a VJ, singularity seems to make the biggest difference.

Step One: Preconception of the Story & Its Elements

To declare a particular set of circumstances, facts, or events to be a story, is to put in place what Searle has described as a "constitutive rule" (Searle, 1969; Smith, 2003). A constitutive rule allows for something to "count" for something in a particular context. The example Searle uses is paper money—certain pieces of paper count as money in our economic system. We use paper money by social agreement and a general understanding, or "collective intentionality" of its constitutive rule. Foremost among the attributes of Searle's notion of a constitutive rule is that it creates something new from an existing phenomenon:

> Collective intentionality assigns a new status to some phenomenon, where that status has an accompanying function that cannot be performed solely in virtue of the intrinsic physical features of the phenomenon in question. This assignment creates a new fact, an institutional fact, a new fact created by *human agreement*. (Searle, 1995, p. 46, italics added)

In a journalistic context, the declaration that a particular situation or event is a story sets off a series of practices, decisions, and rules that she, and possibly other journalists, will use to craft a narrative based on those circumstances. What constitutes news is a matter of human agreement; it is the way the group is instantiated as an interpretive community (Zelizer, 1993). A set of circumstances is declared a story by the identification of certain narrative elements. There may be an important character involved, i.e., Barack Obama, as in [LT]'s story. The setting might be the crucial element, i.e., the happenings at City Hall. The narrative nature of news requires a journalist to identify characters, setting, some kind of advancing action (e.g., conflict), and possibly a cultural lesson (Bird & Dardenne, 1988; Carey, 1989).

Journalists generally have understandings of what a story is, and as they gain experience with a particular newsroom, they learn what types of stories meet the expectations of their colleagues, managers, and (usually indirectly) the audience. Some stories begin as an idea, rather than a scheduled event. It may be related to a previous or ongoing set of circumstances—something called a *sidebar*—or it might be inspired by (or "ripped" from) a story from another news organization. Sometimes a story might arise from an investigation developed entirely from a journalist's curiosity, what's known as an enterprise story (Martin, 1998). Such stories involve active pursuit by a VJ. They might be side projects to be worked on a bit at a time in the course of covering daily news. Enterprise stories, "scoops," and investigative work are source of prestige in the journalistic community.

Tuchman's iconic *Making News* (1978) described how preconceptualizations help journalists make sense of the disorderly happenings of the world. Preconceptualizations are informed by the presentational needs of the organizational medium with which the VJ is affiliated. As Berkowitz, Kaniss, Altheide, and others have observed, the demands of a medium's form determine how journalists decide what stories to tell and how to narrativize a particular set of circumstances (Altheide, 1987; Altheide & Snow, 1979; Barnhurst & Nerone, 2001; Berkowitz, 1990; Kaniss, 1991). Thus, highly visual fires or automobile crashes are considered news for local television; stories involving abstract economic concepts are considered better for print.

Having a narrative preconceptualization is a form of bias, not necessarily a political bias, but a journalistic bias that favors narrativity: conflict, unusualness, interesting characters, and action. During newsroom editorial meetings, reporters and managers discuss the way individual happenings might be narrativized into stories of interest to their audience. At one station, a car junkyard without a privacy fence was considered as a "great story" because cars stained with blood from recent accidents could be seen by passersby. The visuals, coupled with the controversy generated by talking to horrified passersby, constituted a conflict-driven narrative. Changes in the situation can force a shift in the preconception. For example, a newspaper reporter might set out to write a feature story about a children's lemonade stand but finds out someone stole the children's money. His preconceptualization of the story shifts from a "sweet feature" to a "crime," and this requires a shift in the way he writes the story.

For day-to-day coverage, news institutions categorize certain patterns of events as story "types," such as elections (for the drama of their conflict), disasters (for their tragic impact on others), crime (again, for the drama and human conflict), and so on. Other sorts of events, such as council meetings, ribbon-cuttings, or charity fundraisers, may not present obvious dramatic narrative elements, but will be presented in narrative form nevertheless.[3] Journalists quickly develop formulas for writing various story types. Covering a fire, for instance, requires video of the flames, damaged property, and firefighters in action, plus an interview with a fire official, a witness, and, when available, a person who was affected by the fire. A narrative's demands for action and conflict further shape preconceptualization decisions. On the day I observed him, [NQ] made the choice of making an hour-long round trip for an interview that would add an opposing view to his story about the Love Canal anniversary, thereby adding conflict between "two sides" of his story. At [NBHD CABLE], [ES] was assigned to cover the funeral of a shooting that killed a promising high school student, a type of story that is sadly common enough in urban areas that he wrote out his entire script before shooting a frame. He joked that it's "cheating," but it is common practice for certain types of stories, and it can be done because of the way stories are so tightly preconceptualized. Another VJ with more than 30 years of experience, [EQ], also starts writing before the story is actually shot:

> As soon as I know what I've got to work with, I start writing. I'm usually writing in my head in the car, either to wherever I'm going to write it or on the way back to the station.

Unlike a text-based journalist, a video journalist must go a step beyond writing and conceptualizing. The characters, setting, and action must somehow be located in the world and recorded on video. The scenes and sounds VJs choose to decontextualize, and how these clips are recontextualized into a story and eventually a news presentation, vary according to the norms and expectations of the exhibiting organization, whether it's their employer or a nonprofessional affiliation. The choices are limited by the nature of the events, scenes, and people with whom the VJ camera-body interacts, but the choices are made based on a shared understanding of what the story is.

Newspaper editor [TI] believes the centrality of a narrative preconceptualization is the reason reporters can more easily learn video journalism than some photo journalists:

> Really, video journalism is more akin to…the work of a reporter than it is to the work of a print photographer. You really have to learn to tell a story visually, much the way print photographers do in a photo essay; they try to tell a story. But to just shoot one or two shots to illustrate a story is different and I would argue far easier than to actually do a video. It challenges the photographers to become true reporters and storytellers themselves, just like their reporting colleagues.

[HT], who works for a television station and must construct a story every day (three versions of it, in fact), plans out his stories in detail before leaving the station:

> You need to know how you're going to approach it and do it, partly because as a VJ you have so have so little time to do everything yourself you have to pre-decide how you're going to do it before you can leave the building or the meeting or you won't make your deadline. It's not like the old days when you'd go out and see what was actually happening and then decide how to cover it.

Video journalists for the *New York Times* often depend on the (text-based) correspondents to preconceptualize a story that the VJ will then produce in video form. Another common pattern for newspaper VJs allows them to pick and choose their own assignments from the events of the day. [KN], a self-assigned VJ for a major newspaper, does not start out his day with a preconception of a *particular* story; he only covers spot news. Because he was self-assigned, he could determine what he would cover, and his personal rule was that he covered nothing that was planned in advance for the benefit of news coverage—nothing that would require press credentials. To be sure, he'd never covered a specific murder or fire before, but as an experienced photo journalist, he knew what elements were necessary to narrativize stories categorized as "murder."

An exception to this form of preconceptualization of what a story is was observed with the *Our City, Our Voices* project, a citizen-journalism project wherein union organizers, immigrants, and other Philadelphians who often experience marginalization in media coverage attended an eight-week program to learn how to produce video stories. The workshop leaders spent hours, spread over four of the eight sessions, discussing storytelling and guiding participants into thinking about the types of stories they would like to tell about their lives. This appeared to be the most difficult aspect of the workshop, for while participants had a strong idea of something they wanted to say, this was often largely a negation of what they perceived as the typical news narrative ("Our neighborhood is NOT crime infested" and "People should be more sympathetic to unions.") It seemed difficult for these developing VJs to convert such propositions into a filmic narrative.

Singularity & a Tighter Preconception

The tendency of journalists to hold tightly to a story's original preconception recalls an old newsroom joke about the cub reporter who was sent to write a feature story about a flower show only to call back and say: "There's no story here—the convention center burned down." What is unique to video journalism, however, is the way certain exhibition forms *intensify* the need to preconceptualize. Generally speaking, *the more constraining the demands of the final presentation, the more intensely a VJ will work within the mental framework of a preconceptualization.* Because they work alone, VJs will be more apt to look for quick and easy access to story elements and they will be less likely to stray from their preconceptualization. Instead of the smaller cameras and simpler software making it easier to take chances, television VJs see themselves as having *less freedom* to take chances with their stories. That's not to say that video journalism is not opening possibilities for new sorts of narratives; newspaper VJs are trying to break new ground. VJs who do not produce a story a day can be flexible, but organizations that demand daily filings on tight deadlines are less likely to foster innovation, and more likely to rely on VJs to shoot feature stories instead of hard news.

Step Two: Locating & Gaining Access to Elements

Once the narrative is preconceptualized, its elements must be identified and located. Such elements include the audio and video recordings of tangible objects: the setting(s), happenings or relevant action, the objects or examples acted upon, and the human actors or "characters" who act, and provide interview sound to move the story. Note the way these tangible elements line up with the very basic components of narrative, namely actions, characters, and settings (Chatman, 1978, 1990; Herman & Vervaeck, 2005).[4] The art of narrative, of course, lies in arranging these elements effectively, for the components are not the story, they are merely necessary for its construction.

The added burden for VJs is that these components must be collected in a particular space and time, using their body and camera in concert with the physical and social environment. This imperative has a crucial impact on day-to-day story preconceptualization. In an editorial meeting, News director [MEL] asked whether it would be possible to go to an airport to shoot video of a family leaving for a funeral—the element necessary for a mourning story. During a morning meeting at [TV-MID], a reporter's idea for covering the way the local African American community was inspired by Barack Obama's campaign was rejected because there were no daytime gatherings where a VJ could record visual scenes of inspired people. In one BBC newsroom, a writer joked that they'd already shot the elements needed—"sunrises and weirdoes"—for typical coverage of the annual solstice celebration at Stonehenge.

Preconceptions make it possible to efficiently decontextualize the elements essential to a chosen narrative. [DT] says it took him a while to learn that he needed to shoot with the final narrative in mind:

> When I first started doing it, I was going out there and just shooting ridiculous amounts of video, you know shoot an hour of video for a three-minute piece. I just didn't understand the process. I'm getting a whole lot better at it now. I'm understanding a lot more than I did that capturing video is a lot different than just taking the pictures or even putting together a slide show.

[BEB] similarly says in the beginning "I was shooting way too much," and has since learned to trust himself to get the necessary elements without overdoing it.

Several instances noted during observational visits indicate that while a story's preconception drives the overall process, it is malleable and might be reconsidered in the face of changed circumstances. Recall, for instance, that when [LT] was assigned to cover the presidential primary as experienced by people in the Bronx, she first tried to reach Democratic Party leaders in the area. When they would not, or could not, be interviewed, [LT] and her managers decided to switch to a story about high school students. [EN] needed an extra day to shoot his story about high unemployment among physical therapists in England because he could not complete the story without video of a physical therapist working. Like [LT], he called and requested access to a nearby practice where he was able to shoot the scenes he needed.

Access in the Literal Sense

For a video journalist, access is both a matter of locomotion and social interaction. Traveling to and getting close enough to elements in order to photograph them often takes far more time each day than the shooting process itself. For the VJs who participated in this research, transportation was a daily challenge. A radio journalist at the Voice of America loaded up her equipment and used the Washington, D.C., subway rather than fight Capitol traffic, but her struggles with the equipment and subway escalators made for a long day. [NQ] spent more time driving to one of his interviews than actually conducting the interview, cutting his time for writing and editing the story very close to deadline. Traveling from location to location efficiently and on time was not only a source of stress for the VJs I observed, but a factor that influenced their choices of where to go and whom to interview. [LT] considers this part of her job to be the hardest: "I kill myself trying to get every single element," she says in the course of shooting a story. She went so far as to purchase her own personal GPS unit, an expense she called "well worth it" for the time and trouble it saved every day.

For some study participants, driving is an unwelcome task that signifies a change in professional roles. At crew-based stations, video-photographers are usually assigned to a news vehicle, so they do the driving, making it possible for a reporter to continue gathering information by cell phone or compose the story on a notepad or laptop. The VJs I observed did their own driving, however, which carves out a portion of their work day, not always insignificantly. This is nothing new for newspaper photographers or specialist video-photographers making the transition to video journalism, but has not always been such a significant part of the workday for some print reporters and most specialist television reporters. It's true, of course, that print-based reporters have long traveled to news locations, but the geographic imperative of video journalism *requires* it *every* time. Video stories cannot be constructed with a set of phone interviews. [DJ] says this adds a bit of pressure to his work because "you can't call up and get more video." [CC] has only produced a couple video stories for her newspaper, in part because she can't drive from her normal work location back to the main newsroom to edit. [KN] simply used his car as his office, and ensured that he could quickly respond to happenings he picked up by listening to a police scanner while driving around Philadelphia in a giant figure-eight route that maximized his access to major thoroughfares. VJs who allowed me to tag along were highly dependent on internet map services and navigational systems, and probably multitasked at the wheel more than they'd like me to report.

Access is one of the key areas where smaller cameras are making a difference, both in terms of geography and social interaction. They are less imposing than the conventional cameras, and VJs report that the average person seems less intimidated by them. Small cameras can be used to bypass official regulations against cameras, making it possible for [KB] to work in countries without press freedom:

> We've...gone places with smaller cameras on tourist visas and basically have been able to get our equipment into places that they don't want that equipment in, but we got it in, wearing shorts and funny shirts, walk around like tourists, even though we're doing journalism. We've done that a lot. And we, just recently were in China, where these cameras were valuable to us because they're high quality, [have] low power consumption...the smallness of the media storage. And when we began to have encounter problems with the...authorities, we shipped ourselves right out of the country.

> [CH]: The cameras that we have today, don't intimidate subjects. In fact, they seem to empower subjects, even subjects who are totally unfamiliar with the technology. They are empowered by the fact that the video journalist is using a smaller tool and despite that tool he or she, the VJ, can actually communicate with the subject and the subject can affect the end result.

[SG] credits his small Sony® with making it possible for him to approach a grieving father in the aftermath of China's 2008 earthquake. Because the camera was less intrusive, [SG] was able to gently approach the man and then follow him home for a longer interview and discussion with the man's wife. The result is an emotionally charged story about the couple's missing daughter, and their futile effort to find her body. It may simply be that the VJ working *alone* is also less intimidating, however. [PL] uses a conventional-sized camera, but believes an interview she conducted with a grieving family was more emotional and intimate because she was working alone. As video cameras become so small as to be nearly undetectable, it becomes easier to work around or bypass appearance managers who are hoping to regulate photography in a particular space.

Access & the Singular Body

Video journalism also presents physical constraints new to most writers, something that is occasionally a literal and metaphorical sore point. "I used to have three people to carry these things for me," remarked [WN], a radio reporter with the VOA who was training to be a VJ. The cameras might be smaller and lighter but, when added to a full kit with lights, tripod, tapes, batteries, and other accessories, can run between 60 to 70 pounds. Even something as simple as a door becomes an impediment; [NC] says she's developed a new appreciation for automatic ones. One convert says he lost 14 pounds after becoming a video journalist. A former television producer who once managed network crews of two or three people says, "Holy bananas, it's hard," even though he considers his work a vast improvement over his previous position. His colleague, [BF], is more profane: "It's a pain in the ass." But [DT] finds it exhilarating:

> That part I love. I have no issue with that. I'll be happy to get down in the mud to shoot something or climb on a building or I've climbed up antennas. I get on the ground on all fours to get a low angle. No issue there. I love it. I love it, that's why I got into this, you know, I love being out there.

[DT] does not have to use his body as ornamentation; in fact, he's never shot a standup of himself for the newspaper website. Unlike the typical TV VJ, he can get into that mud and not worry about looking "polished" for a TV studio.

Step Three: Recording Elements

Once a VJ has access to shoot the elements required for a narrative, a series of technical, mechanical, and aesthetic choices must be made in what is essentially a process of decontextualization. A VJ pulls pieces from the environment he hears and sees in order to construct a filmic story; he is the human bridge between scene and viewer. The VJ is a privileged witness who sees a 360-degree landscape and chooses portions of it to share. What is chosen depends on the story's preconception, of course, but is also guided by aesthetic and informational criteria. Certain portions of the scene might be relevant to the story at hand, such a school building for [NC]'s story about historic landmarks. She chose to shoot her wide shots of the building from the school's lawn, not across the street, in order to reveal only the building and not the parked cars in front of it.

Other choices may be based on symbolic understandings, wherein the VJ will replicate a visual trope with cultural relevance, such as a soldier cradling a child in the manner of the Pietà, or firefighters at the World Trade Center site hoisting a flag at Ground Zero in the same manner as the soldiers portrayed by Joe Rosenthal at Iwo Jima (Hill & Helmers, 2004; Huxford, 2001). One symbolic element of a scene might be chosen by a photographer as a generalizable representation. For example, Nick Ut's 1972 photograph of Kim Phuc, the little Vietnamese girl seen running from a napalm attack on her village, became culturally understood to represent all innocent victims of the war. It is possible that in the course of their daily work, photographers and VJs may not be able to fully articulate why they choose to shoot one element in a particular way, or the circumstances of the environment might force a particular angle or shot selection. Most important to this discussion, however, is that in making that choice, a scene is *decontextualized*, and only the person holding the camera is aware of the full context of a situation as the selection is made.

Just how should these elements be recorded? In training sessions, video journalism teachers worked to help participants break their stories down into easily recorded and identified elements, both narratively and visually. BBC training (based on Michael Rosenblum's method) focuses on the "five shots" that make it easy to edit a story together: wide shot, close-up, face, hands, and an alternative angle. This is known as a *sequence*, which allows the tape to be edited easily. Gannett's trainer simply suggested recording a variety of views. On the very first day of training, Gannett's trainees shot each other playing with a basketball, so that while editing they learned how to follow the action *and* shoot the ball's movements in such a way that the editing process did not create magical and nonsensical appearances of the ball.[5] At the *Washington Post*, [RJ] taught print reporters to use very simple formulas for a video story, such as shooting a very long establishing shot, then building their stories around only two sound bites.

The critical difference between a literary narrative and a VJ narrative is a matter of tangibility: objects, actions, and happenings in a filmic narrative must somehow be illustrated or described audibly using artifacts constructed by a human operating in concert with a camera. If the story is a profile of a local barista, at some point the VJ must shoot video of a cup of coffee being made; if the story is about an abstract concept, such as "unemployment," the VJ must find a way to illustrate the abstraction, usually by recording video of people in line at an unemployment office or filling out applications at a job fair. VJs cannot do any of this remotely; they must physically interact with the environment. VJ and trainer [NJ] goes so far as to call a VJ's body part of their gear pack:

> When you go into video journalism, the requirement for physical involvement and technical competence really jumps dramatically. You have to have, get a way to get that camera where it needs to be, whether you're holding it handheld or you're on a tripod, you've got to get that. That lens needs to *see* what you *need* to put the story together. So that means that you've got to be a bit pushy. You know, you've got to negotiate sometimes with other people.

Recording the elements requires a series of decisions regarding lighting, distance, angle, sound recording, framing, and steadying their shots. Often these decisions must be made very quickly—a challenge for those just learning VJ skills—and the reason, it seems, for the way more experienced VJs develop almost fetish-like relationships with their equipment. The more they practice, the more muscle memory they develop in manipulating their camera, lights, microphones, and tripods, and the more easily they're able to contend with the immediate pressures of shooting a story. Some aspects of shooting are affected more than others by the singularity. Lighting, focal length (and distance), lens filters, and focus, for example, are essential photographic decisions whether using a still camera, a conventional television camera, or a small VJ camera, but certain aspects of shooting are influenced by the affordances of lighter/smaller cameras, the incorporation of sound to the process, steadying, perspective, and composition.

Sound Recording

If narrative is the clothesline on which elements are hung to create a video story, sound is the rope that constitutes that clothesline. Interview sound can be woven into the spoken narrative and natural sound (NATSOT) can help establish the corporeal sense of "being there" for the viewer. [SG] used the sound of birds chirping in the background to add to the sense of pathos toward the end of his earthquake story. [BD] recorded sound of people playing African drums at the Jena Six rally, then used that music under most of the piece to foster the feeling of being at the rally. Knowing how to collect sound with the appropriate microphone is as important for a VJ as knowing how to focus a camera.

Adding sound to their repertoire is one of the biggest challenges for transitioning newspaper photographers. VJ trainers often encourage them to simply edit a few still images into a slide show with a simple soundtrack or a bit of music, to practice editing sound. During the workshops I attended, discussions often focused on sound considerations more than anything visual. Still photographers knew how to frame a shot and manage light but they are not trained to use microphones. [MN] counsels his trainees to put the microphone where the sound is, to get as close when collecting sound as a VJ ought to be close when recording an image. "If you want to stand out, get good audio," he told his students, "…there is a sound that goes with every story."

The consequence is that in addition to thinking visually, video journalists must also consider sound, how to gather it, how to use it to create a sense of place and time for the viewer, and how to produce a coherent narrative with it. "You're a slave to sound," says [HI]:

> If you want to do a package, you have to have sound, and sometimes that means waiting around for the fire chief longer than you would as a still photographer, you can go on to your next assignment, but as videographers you gotta wait and find people to talk, you gotta find people, witnesses, somebody to give you that sound to tie it all together, and that's probably the biggest problem.
>
> [TH]: Sound is the most important thing…I mean it's funny 'cause, I mean, to say I shoot video or I'll say yeah I'm a video shooter but it's really like, you're more of like a sound master because yes, the visuals are important, but you have to…take that care, time, and attention to set up your mikes…I have wireless mikes and all that, so I put more effort into that oftentimes…

[DT] has changed the way he asks questions:

> I have to find somebody to talk their way through a story, so what I do and what I ask for is somebody who knows a lot about something. And actually has the ability to tell a story…because it's about stories, ultimately. Another example I'll give you, I did a thing about the special Olympics Equestrians, which is posted over in Collegeville, and the woman what was in charge of it, and I interviewed her, and I basically said to her, I need you to describe this like I'm not here and you're telling me about it, it's not enough just to say oh it's a great event and the kids are so happy, you have to tell me like, "we're here today," and you know, so to get her to tell it in a different way. I had to learn that the hard way.

For [KN], his dependence on sound makes for some occasional discomfort. As a "snapper," he could take a shot of a person in crisis and go, but now "I have to engage them in conversation," and it's not something he relishes.

Knowing which type of microphone is appropriate to collect that sound is essential. *Lavalier* microphones, for instance, are the very small ones that can be fitted to a person's lapel. Larger, "stick" microphones are the ones a reporter normally holds while performing a standup. Microphones can intimidate subjects who have not assented to speaking on camera, so sometimes VJs are counseled to use the microphone that is attached to their camera, which allows them to start asking questions without invading a person's personal space. (The downside is that such microphones might not pick up the *right* sound as clearly.) Wireless microphones are extremely helpful in crowded situations (so no one's tripping over a wire), or for situations where the VJ wants freedom to move around a scene while recording uninterrupted audio. One print photographer who was teaching himself multimedia skills created a slideshow with still images and sound of children talking to Santa at a mall by placing a wireless microphone next to Santa's chair. The audio he recorded of spontaneous conversations between small children and Santa Claus simply could not have been created if he'd poked a large stick-like microphone into their faces.

Steadying

Smaller cameras are easier to manipulate, carry, or even hide, but they are harder to keep steady. Consequently, using a tripod is more than a matter of giving one's shoulder a rest, as it might be for a conventional camera. Shaky video is a mark of amateur or informal video; it can also sometimes convey a sort of immediacy that comes with amateur video from disasters (i.e., the Virginia Tech cell phone video taken by a student during the tragic shootings in April 2007). For everyday professional video, however, the norm is to record a steady shot. Tripods are therefore an indispensable part of a VJ's kit. They can be awkward to carry and set up, but there are methods for speeding up and easing the process; [MM] makes a point to show her trainees a proper method and extending the legs with a minimal aggravation.

Even when he's hurrying to a spot-news story, [KN] said he carries his tripod to the scene. He added his own strap to it for easier carrying.[6] With his tripod, he's able to overcome the fact that he's not allowed past crime-scene tape by using a longer (zoom) lens to shoot police activity. A zoom lens accentuates even the tiniest shake of a camera (think of using a telescope to view the stars—move an inch and you lose Venus), so using a tripod is essential. Tripods are also necessary for shooting a standup, or piece-to-camera, when a person is working alone. [KK] used a tripod to shoot video at the apartment fire aftermath, then turned the camera around so she could shoot video of herself making a short presentation with the burned-out building behind her.

When it's simply impossible to carry a tripod to a location, VJs at the VOA and Gannett are instructed to use a table, a fence—any immobile surface to steady the camera. There's even a product that looks like a bean bag with a screw on it that some VJs use as a cushioned tabletop stand. When he and his team forgot their tripod on a story, a newspaper VJ in training held the camera closely to his body and leaned on a post to hold his shot. All sorts of steadying gadgets are now marketed to VJs using smaller cameras, including very small table tripods and bean-bag-like contraptions that offer stability on uneven surfaces.

Tripods can also be a way for VJs to establish territory in group setting. By setting up a tripod on a riser, a photographer informally establishes a space within which to operate. [JB], a still newspaper photographer, actually refers to TV crews as "sticks" speaking with occasional resentment for the way their tripods command and dominate space. In a scrum, space is at a premium; the right space is essential to a good shot, and a tripod is therefore more than a steadying tool. At political events, where space is assigned by a communications representative, the assigned tripod spot can even be a mark of status within the press corps, with national network news getting a favorable position, and local or small outlets pushed to the back.[7]

Perspective

The corporeal metaphor of video is largely derived from the position of the camera in relation to a scene before it, and the way the resulting image is interpreted by a viewer. When a VJ shoots from above, a viewer is able to witness a scene from the bird's-eye view. Using the camera up close on a cricket player's hands and the viewer has a sense of being in the game. The angle of view is physically interpreted and created. Shoot someone from below, and they appear imposing; from above, and they look subservient; at eye level, we are in equal conversation. VJs use the angle of view to add a layer of meaning to the scenes they shoot, or to add a sense of aesthetic imbalance to scenes that would otherwise be visually dull. Using a variety of angles also makes the editing process a bit easier (think back to the basketball exercise) because when blended together, their juxtaposition can help the viewer follow action in a way that feels natural.[8]

During their training sessions, newspaper writers and editors, whose greatest physical demands on their day normally might be to pick up a telephone, were instead moving the camera in close to their subjects, walking the camera low to the ground, kneeling to interview children, or otherwise attempting to create compelling proxemic metaphors for their viewers. Changing the camera's perspective enhances the viewer's corporeal experience of video. [NJ] supposes it's one of the reasons people enjoy television, because a photographer's work can takes a viewer's eyes where they normally do not go. Video journalism has no monopoly on unusual camera perspectives; they've been part of filmic news and movie making from the very beginning. Smaller cameras, however, do make creative shots much easier to accomplish:

> [MM]: I'm a firm believer of putting the camera in some very odd places. And it was great in my training course...because when I went to open the fridge, one of [her students] said ooh, "What if you put the camera in the fridge?" and I went "Awesome, let's set the camera in the fridge! Set it up, flip the screen, put the camera in the fridge, make sure you check the exposure...while the fridge door is open, close the fridge door." Amazing shot!

Video limits some creative perspectives. Still photographers can raise their cameras very high or place them very low (using a vertical axis in relation to the body) to change the mundane to a scene that is more visually compelling. Photo journalists in Washington, D.C., for example, use extreme angles to add dynamism to public hearings and other somnambulant scenes. VJs can do the same thing as long as they are not in conversation with another person. When shooting an interview or a scene with people talking, it is necessary to remain at eye level with the speakers in order to maintain a proper conversational point of view for the audience. When covering the aftermath of the 2008 Chinese earthquake, [UG] put the camera on the ground to shoot a man's feet as he walks by, emphasizing the man's steps. But when shooting an argument between parents at the scene of the collapsed school, he shot the scene at eye level, maintaining his, and the viewer's sense, of normal place in human interaction.

Framing in the Visual Sense

A photographer visually contextualizes a subject by using appropriate *framing*. Here, framing is a literal concept in that the VJ must choose what to include in the viewfinder and what to exclude and how an object should be photographed in relation to other items in the scene. To complicate matters, this notion of framing and the rhetorical notion are related: the framing of scene *can indeed* impose a metaphorical and symbolic frame. For example, a photographer might compose an image of an athlete sitting on a bench so that the athlete appears very small in relation to a long, empty bench. The literal elements are composed, or arranged, in the shot in a way that imposes a symbolic frame that emphasizes the athlete's isolation. Therefore, the careful framing of a shot is more than a matter of making sure an object appears on the screen. Video journalists must consider *how* those objects appear on the screen. [MM] prefers to use her small camera to interview subjects very closely as they perform an activity. Another VJ might be more comfortable shooting an interview with a subject while activities are going on in the background—each choice presents a different witnessing experience for the viewer.

Photographic framing can make use of symbolic objects to cue the audience toward an associative interpretation intended by the photographer (as long as the audience and photographer share an understanding of what certain objects symbolize). A politician will be photographed next to a flag or a grieving parent might be photographed holding a child's teddy bear. One familiar trope identified in *National Geographic* photographs uses a composition that places a person living in primitive conditions next to a high-tech object or symbol of industry (Lutz & Collins, 1993). Video-photographer [RZ] likes to look for ways to frame at least one of shots in a way that summarizes the story that's being told. For instance, if the story is about a ribbon-cutting for a school for disabled children, he will try to compose one of his shots to include the school, the ribbon, and some of the children.

Framing does not simply include certain scenes and objects in the image; it cuts others out. Backgrounds and objects that do not serve the VJ's narrative purpose must be kept off the screen. Normally, for instance, still photographers avoid including microphone *flags* (the big plastic squares on microphones that identify a TV station) in their shots. But once, while covering a Pennsylvania Senator's campaign stop, [NZ] *purposely* composed the shot to include competing journalists and their equipment in order to show the degree to which the Senator's event was orchestrated for the media, as there were no members of the public in sight.

To shoot a scene that orients viewers to a scene, VJs often set up the camera on a far wall of a room or to the side of the action. To help the viewer identify a subject, the shot might include background objects or an easily categorized setting. A cook might be framed with a kitchen behind him or a teacher in front of a chalk board. A VJ might move around a room or scene several times looking for a shot that is both appealing and informative. Related to distance and angle, selecting an informative frame requires an aesthetic sense of balance (according to the artist's rule of thirds), and an understanding of the action. Again, to use the example of the Gannett trainees' basketball exercise, for the purposes of editing a coherent sequence, the future VJs learned to shoot the ball leaving the frame and entering a frame—not trying to follow it throughout.

There are special considerations for framing video as opposed to a still shot. The most critical arises when shooting interviews with human subjects. Convention calls for the top of their head to touch, or nearly touch, the top of the screen. Because photography works within a sensorimotor metaphor, the camera needs to be at a conversational angle and a subject's face needs to be pointed toward the center of the screen, not outside of it. (Imagine watching an interview with the person facing the edge of the TV screen!)

One technique that still photographers can use easily, but which is much harder when working with video, is called *cropping*. Cropping, which once literally and now digitally, cuts sections off of an image to remove objects and draw attention to what remains, can make an enormous difference in the aesthetics and symbolic nature of a still image. It is not, however, a normal part of video production. While it is technologically possible to freeze a frame, crop it, and put it back into a video story (this is often done for police surveillance video of wanted suspects, for example), it is time consuming and was not the norm for any of the VJs observed for this project.

Finally, video is always shot with a horizontal (or, to use a word-processing term *landscape*) frame. Still cameras can be turned to create a vertical (*portrait*) frame, but video cameras cannot; the image would appear sideways on the television screen. Former VJ [DZ] recalls that for her very first video story she tried shooting a helicopter moving logs vertically, an automatic choice for a still photographer, but one that would have appeared comical had she not remembered that a video viewer cannot be turned.

The sequence of shots in the BBC's physical therapist story exemplifies an effective use of frame choices. [EN] shot a massage therapy session with a variety of angles, distance, and frames. The opening sequence uses a shot of the patient's feet filling the frame, another shot displays the patient's face in full frame, yet another places the therapist's hands in the center, filling the entire screen, as [EN] starts his story with the words "healing hands." In order to shoot the sequence, he had to manipulate the lens on his camera, as well as move around the room several times, to record the scenes (with the patient's permission). He spent about a half-hour shooting the scenes needed for less than a minute's worth of edited material.

The story based on the aftermath of the Chinese earthquake also contained examples of meaningful framing in that the VJ shot the face of the Chinese official very close, creating a sense of intensity during an argument. [SG] shot the collapsed school juxtaposed with apartment buildings that remained intact in order to illustrate the parents' angry contention that the school must have been inadequately constructed as it was the only building destroyed in the earthquake. Video framing, therefore, is not merely a matter of making sure that a human subject is visible on the screen (in fact, VJs and their trainers note, placing a person face-forward in the middle of the screen is a mark of amateurism). The way subjects are framed can change the meaning of the image. Poor composition, which omits helpful background cues or includes extraneous objects, can confuse the viewer or get in the way of understanding the action. Framing has ethical considerations, and any photographer, still or video, makes choices about what to include in the image, what to cut out, and what angle should be used. These choices all have meaningful consequences.

The process of shooting video, or decontextualizing the world's physical essence into recorded artifacts of scenes and sound, is essentially the same for VJs across organizational categories. It is a technological artifact, in that a VJ uses the camera to shoot scenes according to her preconception of what elements might be needed. Her choices are limited to what she herself is able to view, and she uses variations in angle, distance, and so on to record scenes accordingly. The next two steps vary considerably according to the expectations of the organization and they are both forms of recontextualization. The primary recontextualization is the conversion of decontextualized recordings of sound and video into a narrative. Certain elements may be highlighted or others ignored depending on the expectations and requirements of the exhibiting organization. The second recontextualization places the story into an organization's presentational context, which might be a newscast, a website, or some form of exhibition.

Singularity & Recording Elements

Some of the skills that further differentiate VJs from other news workers are obvious, while others are somewhat unusual: opening doors while holding a tripod, steadying a camera when the tripod isn't available, shooting a standup[9] of oneself. Some of the VJs complain that it is difficult to concentrate on the content of an interview while shooting it. [ES] recalled missing a key scene needed for a story on a traffic problem because he was conducting an interview. For the television VJs, vocal and presentational skills are required as they shift from physical craft work to acting as ornamental presenters. Shooting their own standups becomes part of their daily work, even though, as [EN] notes, it can be awkward:

> When I first did it was just excruciatingly embarrassing, but you just get over it, you just kind of do it. People look at you and wonder who you're talking to. You look like you're talking to yourself. It's all just a bit odd....if I *do* [shoot standups] I try to do them away from big crowds of people.

Finally, the physicality of working alone constitutes a source of stress. *Every* VJ who allowed me to shadow them, *every* VJ who granted me an interview, considered the work to be physically taxing. [NC] says she goes home every day and lies on the bed for a few minutes before she can get on with her evening—and can't imagine trying to do this too far into the future or as a mother. [CH] and [KB], who have decades-long careers in solo-filmmaking, do not complain about the strength required but acknowledge that they have had to stay in shape. [KB] and his staff do calisthenics as part of their work routine.

> We're really serious about this; we do lots of push ups…I'm old now, so I'm not in as good physical shape as I use to be, but it's very, very important for you to be mentally alert and physically fit.

> [CH]: It's really physical. For me that's one of the challenges of the field. You're not going to see a lot of overweight VJs because you burn off too much energy doing it...We just took a class of 28 students to New Hampshire to cover the primaries—some of them are public communications students, some of them are journal-journalism students, and these are young people and they were shocked at the amount of technical skill and physical stamina necessary to form this craft...This is a craft that demands not only intellectual capacity but real physical stamina and a lot of people are not going to be able to do this simply because they haven't got the stamina.

Some younger VJs can't imagine doing daily stories past their 40s.[10] The chief complaint seems not to be the equipment itself, but of manipulating that equipment, traveling from location to location on deadline, climbing stairs and navigating doors, and the daily requirement of gaining access in the literal sense.

One way to overcome the difficulties inherent in working alone is to actively enlist the help of others. [MM] will go so far as to ask strangers for help when it's necessary, either to carry things or to literally watch her back when she's in an awkward position. While on assignment in the Bronx, [KK] was refused entry into an apartment building that had burned the night before. Only residents were allowed inside. One of the residents she'd interviewed was motivated to show the damage her apartment had suffered, and offered to go inside to use a cell phone to take pictures of the scene. [KK] could not allow the woman to use her news camera, so the cell phone[11] idea won, and the stills were incorporated into the day's story. The ubiquity of digital cameras and a stronger general understanding on the part of the audience regarding the way stories are constructed makes it easier for VJs to enlist help from laypersons. Many VJs report having very technical conversations with their subjects about camera technology. At the Bronx fire, the woman who took the cell phone camera into the building explained to a friend that the station won't be using her entire interview and all the shots, saying, "They're going to crop it up," indicating that while she may not know the vocabulary, she understands that news is an edited product.

Professional intermediaries, such as public relations representatives, are often accustomed to helping VJs who work alone:

> [BG]: I've done that quite a bit actually. I've even held the microphone. As long as I have something to look at so it looks like I'm being interviewed by a person and not having to look directly into the camera, it's OK. I really get a lot out of looking in the interviewer's eyes or looking at their face and reading their expression as they're asking the questions, it helps me to handle it. I prefer an interview where the questions aren't all loaded upfront, as in "Here are the questions, now speak." I prefer more of a dialogue with the person there. But we can make it work; it just may take one or two takes.

Figure 3.3: A VJ shoots his own standup. Since his camera does not have a flip screen, he'll return to the camera to check the standup, adjust the shot, then re-shoot until it is acceptable.

One of the keys to overcoming the difficulties of working in the field may simply be a matter of learning to ask for help. This is no small step for journalists accustomed to working independently, or for conventional, experienced photographers who prefer to use their camera as a social shield. Video journalism does not afford the luxury of working solely as a technician. The networking or "glad handing" sort of activities normally associated with reportage are part of a VJ's the routine.

Step Four: Narrativizing

Once a VJ has recorded the necessary elements to compose a narrative that can be understood by others, the physical work of narrativizing can begin. I use the word narrativize in order to distinguish this process from vocally narrating a story, which might or might not be part of a particular VJ's process. All VJs, however, must narrativize, or create a linear sequence of sound and images that is understood as a news story. There are two dimensions to the work of composing a video narrative. One is the physical and mechanical work that employs digital software to connect and layer the various elements. The other is textual, a matter of composing a coherent story that will be understood by others.

Chapter One briefly explained how the mechanics of digital editing are much like word processing, except that instead of one long line of thought, there are several layers: a primary audio track, a video track, and any extra audio or video tracks needed to add background sound, music, or special effects (see *Figure 1.3*). The product is chronologically linear, but digital edit systems allow the production to be manipulated anywhere along any line. Digital editing does not create a physical, taped story, but a set of software codes that command the editing system to pull a piece of video information from one place, a piece of audio information from another, and so on, to create a new computer file. This final creation of the new file is known as *rendering*, a computing process that can take a few minutes for a short news story to several hours for a complicated, multilayered production.[12]

Narrativizing a video story may or may not require a VJ to actually type up a script or plan. Gannett's trainers discouraged scripting for its newspaper writers making the transition. But VJs who work for television stations, such as [LT] and [NQ], write scripts that contain information for the broadcast, as well their own scripted narration, so that supervisors can check the work and show producers can understand how to appropriately place it into a program's chronological format.[13] If they do their own narration, they must track it, that is, read it aloud and record the bits of audio they'll use to craft their story. Most organizations, even the *New York Times*, have special audio booths for the job, but in a pinch a VJ can record adequate audio into their camera inside a closed car or even, as [SG] has, surrounded by a makeshift tent from a hotel comforter.[14]

Whether or not they type a script, they must have at least the mental plan of a narrative as they start reviewing their tape and downloading it into their edit system. This mental plan is informed by their original preconception, based on what they've experienced in the field and their understanding of what the organization expects. Video is transferred to digital editing systems according to the system afforded by their camera. Some cameras still use small digital tapes, some of which can be played back to transfer to a laptop system faster than real time; other systems are solid state, meaning that the original video is recorded to a hard drive. These files can usually be transferred to the edit system far more quickly. During this transfer process (also known as "ingesting") the VJ often starts making a formal or informal list of the shots that were recorded and the verbatim quotations of the sound bites, a process known as *logging* the tape. The process of logging is a matter of finding out just what sorts of material one actually has to work with. Sometimes a shot looks great in the field but lousy on the monitor at home. Sometimes, unfortunately, this is where inexperienced VJs learn that the great sound they thought they'd recorded in the field was missed because a microphone wasn't turned on, and so on. The contrast between the material a VJ *expected* and what he *actually has* informs this phase of recontextualization. The editing process informs the shooting process and vice versa. [KB] says it doesn't take long to learn how to avoid shooting yourself into a mess:

> You sure need to have spent a lot of time in an editing room and…if you've painted yourself into a lot of corners with the material you've shot and it was shot in a way that made it hard to edit…once…you're in an editing room without the proper cutaways boy, it's a pretty deep, fast learning curve. Because you don't want to let that happen again. I remember when we started…coming back with 50, 60 hours' worth of footage and the editor asked, "Well where are your cutaways?"[15] and I didn't know what he was talking about! We'd just lock...we'd just stay on the same shot for three or four minutes, "Ooh that's really interesting, well that's really interesting," and never have any way of getting between the shots.

The editing process can take as long, or longer, than the time spent in the field. Unless one has the luxury of an assistant to ingest video into the system and to log the tapes, the task can take hours, even days. [KN] rarely even bothered to stay at the newspaper to edit his pieces; he'd go home for dinner and edit for three to five hours in the evenings, which stretched his daily routine past anything resembling a conventional work day. Even with the long days, he said he was surprised by how much fun editing turned out to be when he made the transition from stills.

Of course, if all that's needed is a few shots of video to illustrate a breaking news story, the process is much quicker, and as VJs become more familiar with the process and what is needed, they shoot and log with great efficiency. Inexperienced shooters are more apt to fill hours of a tape with video and sound for a story that will only last two minutes. VJ trainer [RJ] required his transitioning writers to turn in a full video log for every story they shot in order to compel them to shoot more carefully, recording only what is needed and not much more. Early in their transition, VJs in training might spend more than a day working on a story; even experienced VJs say they may spend far more hours editing than shooting. [KN] said he never expected to enjoy editing as much as he does. [DT] says he has to avoid getting lost in the edit room.

To simplify matters and to construct a narrative that makes sense, the edit process starts with the main audio track. This is where a journalist's recorded narration might be blended with sound bites gathered in the field. If the VJ is constructing a story using only sound bites and natural sound, he'll choose the starting and stopping points for these various bits of sound and insert them into the edit system's timeline. This primary audio track will serve as the base of for the rest of the story. This is not to say that dramatic images might not set the stage for the story, or that the narrative might not be built around dramatic visual imagery, but the audio narrative is the frame upon which a filmic story is constructed.

Video editors often attempt to edit sound in a way that reflect the natural rhythms of speech, to create soundtracks that help transport viewers to a scene. Sound, after all, is part of a filmic story's corporeal metaphor. The editing process, as a result, has its own corporeal element beyond the physicality of button pushing. To edit according to the rhythms of speech requires kinesthetic awareness. The popular editing software, Final Cut Pro®, even includes a feature that allows for kinesthetic interaction with video. The software's "marking on the fly" feature allows an editor to mark a computer-editing timeline in rhythm with music or other sound as though drumming one's fingers to a song (Weynand, 2007). At Gannett, workshop participants were actually advised to shut their eyes after cutting and pasting their audio track together, and found it helpful to do so.

Figure 3.4. Two editing trainees shut their eyes to listen to the audio track of their story. The audio script provides the foundational narrative of a video story. These editors and others were also observed punching the air in rhythm to their audio track. The natural rhythm of speech and sound is sensed not through the eyes but the entire body.

When the story is finally edited and the final product rendered, the process still is not over. Editing a video story is only one phase of the recontextualization of its elements. Before it is seen by the larger, public audience, it is again recontextualized according to the practices of the VJ's employing organization.

Singularity & Narrativizing

One surprise of this project was the degree to which VJs report their love of editing, especially editing *alone*. [NQ] said, "I love the creative control it (the edit process) gives me." [HT] and [HI] felt similarly:

> [Traditionally when]...you worked as a photographer, you would shoot and then you'd hand over the story to the reporter who would write it, and the reporter would, if you were lucky hand it back to you to edit, and if not, they'd hand it off to a third person, an editor, and who you, maybe you don't even know his name...worked at the station. So it's like your work is completely lost through the chain. And so I would see pieces, I mean, we would shoot serious sweeps piece, they were like big topics...and the reporter and I would shoot it and we would hand it off to an editor who just completely botched the job because they obviously weren't on the scene, and didn't know where the good video was, or didn't know where the important shot was 'cause they weren't there. So it is ridiculous to have someone edit something who's not on the scene shooting. And that's what's still happening in the industry; that's weird. So creative control is like, well, I know where the best shot is, and I don't have to worry about someone else screwing up our work or making it look less powerful than it could be.
>
> [HI]: I tell [non-video] photographers...No one crops your video, no one leaves your cutline[16] off, no one puts a dumb headline on your video. It's all you and that's what's very good about it; in fact, it's what you saw, what you heard. You structure the thing. If it's good, it's all you, and if it's bad, no one, you got no one to blame but yourself, and that's cool. I like that about it.

And yet, while [HI] says he usually likes being in charge of his own pieces, on more complicated stories, he misses having a colleague to talk things through:

> I've done a lot of spot news, even as a photographer I did a lot of my own work so I'm not afraid to talk to people; I know what to ask in an interview, but sometimes...if something is complicated, you don't have that reporter to bounce the ideas, things off of, and you can kind of help each other distill down what the story is...Like with Obama the other day, you know I'm there reporting the whole thing. I was capturing it with a laptop...but you know, it's 35 minutes of speech, and it's a little, it makes me a little uncomfortable that I had to distill it down to two minutes, about actually three minutes, and I had no one to really bounce that off of; I had to work so fast, so sometimes you're wondering if your judgment is correct, and that's the biggest thing; am I going about this the right way?

One of the surprises to come out of observing training sessions was that, of the skills required for video journalism, editing confounded some transitioning journalists far more than using a camera. Recall the example timeline in *Figure 1.3* and the way it *layers* sounds, quotes, spoken narration, images, and so on; it is not a linear process, but one that requires multidimensional creativity. Add to that the complexities of ingesting video files from a camera to a computer, manipulating those files and preparing the whole production for a presentation, and the process becomes time consuming and occasionally overwhelming. Even experienced radio reporters, accustomed to digitally editing sound, were observed struggling with video editing. The difference may be that nearly everyone has used some type of camera at a point in their lives, and have some idea of what it means to use one, but digital editing is not an everyday skill.

Narrating & Narrativizing

One of the decisions a VJ must make in the course of editing a story is whether to record a vocal audio track. Television VJs generally have no choice—the broadcast program format nearly always requires a vocally recorded script—but VJs working for newspapers have greater freedom. Not surprising, since many VJs are former photographers accustomed to working in relative anonymity; the choice is to allow story subjects to tell the story and eschew a vocal track. [EQ] works for a television station and has appeared on camera throughout his career but prefers to remain unseen and unheard and so opts to let someone else from the station tell the story:

> I don't much like the sound of my voice...so lot of the times I'll write a story and have one of the reporters track it or one of the anchors track it, and put it in that way. I put my voice on just long enough to make sure my in-laws know I still have a job.

Another option is to let the story subjects tell the story, which often requires more effort on the part of the VJ in the field since she must collect enough sound to craft such an observational story. [SG], an award winning newspaper VJ, says he started out dead set against any scripted narration until it became too cumbersome to meet deadlines. [KN] similarly became more accustomed to using his own voice. [DT] also started using his voice in his pieces in the interest of time, but still keeps it to a minimum. "All you need is a couple of sentences," he says, "...sometimes it launches best if you just say it."

Exhibition: The Second Recontextualization

Video stories are recontextualized anew when they are put into a presentation by an exhibiting organization. Turow (2003) identifies exhibition as one of the primary activities of media organizations, which have historically been divided according to their presentational form: newspapers deliver news printed on paper, television news is presented as a scheduled program or show, and web news is presented as a series of screen pages, sometimes with links that allow users to choose how to follow the material. Though the situation is changing as quickly as this book is being typed, the procedural and intracultural differences between such organizations demand different forms of presentation for VJ stories. Web-based operations such as *Our City, Our Voices* or *My Urban Report*, upload their stories directly to a website. Newspaper VJs also send their work to a website, but in concert with the printed form of the newspaper. The *New York Times* VJs often work in concert with the organization's writers, so their videos are presented alongside a text version of the story on nytimes.com. VJs at [MID-TV] post their stories to the web after those stories are broadcast within a news program. The timing for posting or broadcasting stories ranges from a system without hard deadlines, granting the VJ freedom to decide when a story is ready for view, to very stringent and demanding daily deadlines, which force a VJ to adjust his work practices to fit those demands. The exhibiting form, whether a tightly timed and produced television program broadcast in real time, or a newspaper website that is available according to a user's schedule, dominates the process.

Deadlines

One significant shift, as observed by other scholars of convergent news operations, has occurred within newspaper organizations whose journalists historically worked with only one, or possibly two, deadlines in a 24-hour cycle (P. J. Boczkowski, 2009; Dupagne & Garrison, 2006; J. B. Singer, 2003). A web presence allows a newspaper to post news as it happens, something radio and television journalists have done for decades. Still, the deadlines for such operations seem more story-driven than program-driven. In other words, if there's a breaking story that compels immediate coverage, it can be posted instantaneously. Less urgent stories can be posted when they're ready. Newspaper photo editor [IE] has struggled with his staff to get them thinking in terms of 24-hour news. [DT] starts his day around 6 a.m., and constantly adjusts his shifts to work at night or on weekends in order to make sure his pieces are posted before they get stale. [UJ], a longtime live blogger for his newspaper, is already accustomed to the clock's constant tug, and it almost seems to energize his work.

A radio or television broadcast, however, happens at a particular time, and the clock is not forgiving. VJs working for television program organizations may have multiple top-down deadlines, for a noon and five o'clock broadcast, for instance, which require *something* to be presented no matter whether the VJ would like to pursue more details, add an extra shot, or change a line of narrative.

Formats

Sending a piece ("posting it") straight to the web is a matter of understanding the organization's interface with the web. This part of the presentation is also more demanding for television VJs. For example, program format at [MID-TV] requires VJs to present their story live in the studio, standing in front of a screen from which their video will expand to fill the screen once their introduction is finished. A studio anchor first introduces the VJ (though this title is not used; they are merely introduced by name), so this format establishes their connection with the story. [NBHD CABLE] doesn't use this live in-studio format, but instead requires taped standups to be inserted into the story—an alternative way to establish the VJ's ownership of the story. For television station VJs, these presentational formats require a dramatic shift in active to passive body work, from carrying, lifting, and moving a camera to create a story, to presenting their own body as an attractive object for the viewing audience.

Until very recently, the two types of body work were generally divided between different occupational categories. Skillfully navigating this shift requires male VJs to check their hair, possibly put on some face powder, adjust their tie, and wear a suit jacket. [EN] wore a suit during his work day, but took off the jacket to shoot, for instance, as did [NP]. For female VJs based in television organizations, the transition might be a bit more elaborate, as their hair styles require a bit more care, and the requisite skirt suits must be paired with shoes that limit mobility. [NC] solves this by bringing a change of shoes to work; this way, she can shoot in flats, and wear high heels for her live studio appearances so as to meet the height requirements for the automated studio cameras.

The exhibition format's temporal demands will also dictate the length of stories a VJ produces. The *New York Times* may have a story that lasts as long as 10 or 12 minutes; there are no hard and fast rules on the web. On the other hand, other newspaper organizations may impose guidelines to keep the workflow under control, or to ensure that a VJ produces a certain quantity of stories per week, for example. Those guidelines are easily stretched when necessary—again, because the audience of a newspaper website chooses when and how to click on a posted video. The rules are very different for a television story. A television news broadcast has very strict requirements for timing. It starts at one time and ends at another, and a certain number of stories have to fit within that finite, unforgiving schedule. Consequently, the typical television VJ will produce stories no longer than two minutes; longer pieces are reserved only for special situations. [EJ], a former television documentary producer, is thrilled that the work he does now for the web has been freed from such constraints:

> Unless you're shooting for a magazine show, a typical TV news story will never exceed 2 minutes and 45 seconds. More often, they'll be anywhere between a minute and a minute-thirty and that's because you're dealing with an appointment-based medium, which has only so many minutes in which to tell its story. Everything is dictated in television by hit times. So if you are a producer and you are scheduling a news show, you have your schedule in front of you and if you have a piece that's a minute-thirty, you're going to schedule that piece for 6:19 and it's going to run to 6:20:30. And that's it. Period. It doesn't matter how good or bad the story, you're going to fill that block of time. We don't come to the table with those constraints.

The skills required for VJs in this presentational phase vary widely. The issues of appearance are irrelevant for print reporters unless they choose to start shooting their own standups. But for television station VJs, the dramatic contrast between physical demands for both muscle work and ornamentation require skills that may actually conflict with one another. Male VJs did not complain about this, but some of the female VJs interviewed for the project did comment on the difficulty of looking TV-ready at the end of a day's physical exertion.

Presentational Differences

The way an exhibiting genre influences a VJ's preconceptualizations and daily routines seems to influence job satisfaction. As one might expect, greater freedom in terms of story choice and style led to greater job satisfaction. A former TV producer, now with the *New York Times*, is thrilled with his new situation that allows him to choose story topics that he finds professionally meaningful, and to take enough time to craft pieces that give him a sense of pride. Other self-assigned newspaper VJs enjoyed their days even with the added physical stress of working alone. In contrast, TV VJs often used the phrase "daily grind." [HT] called the demands of his job "really really really really really really [yes, he said this six times] hard." Television station VJs had the least amount of freedom, as their work fit into a rigid temporal and production framework. Missing a deadline for television, that is to not *make air*, may not be a firing offense if it only happens once, but repeated misses are a quick road to the unemployment office. Of course, while those working for newspaper organizations had a bit more flexibility, they still contend with deadlines and a need to post their pieces while they're still relevant in the news cycle. Only the VJs allied with independent organizations, such as *Our City, Our Voices*, had *total* control over subject choice and the pace of their work. Their stake in video journalism is one of voluntary community participation, a hobby of sorts, not a livelihood.

Summary: A Distinct Process

As I conducted these observations and interviews, I expected that the new technologies of video journalism would affect the process of filmic newsgathering. It has. What I did not expect, however, was the degree to which the fifth step affects the first in this circular process, and how much pressure an organization's media logic would have on preconceptualization. Television station VJs who are assigned a story a day reported that they shoot elements to fit a mental, or, in some cases, prewritten draft of their stories instead of attending to a situation, shooting its various elements, then crafting a narrative. This is not to say that they did not shift their attention or process should the situation not conform to their expectations, but the intense deadline and scheduling demands of daily television production do seem to constrain a VJ's choices. In contrast, VJs whose work appears on the web are free from such constraints, and were better able to let a story "breathe"—to use a video photography colloquialism.

While the practices for preconception and presentational reconception varied according to an organization's presentational demands, the other steps—that is, locating and gaining access to elements, recording those elements and narrativizing them—were remarkably similar interorganizationally. Here, singularity, one of the two primary characteristics of video journalism, significantly influenced the process. The essentiality of working with one's body on location means that a significant portion of a VJ's day is spent negotiating with sources for access to locations. Working alone caused them to favor single-location shoots and simpler stories. The attention and skill a VJ employs in the recording of scenes and audio varies according to their experience, but all those who participated in the project had a sense of what is necessary in the recording process, such as framing and steadying their shots to gathering compelling sound. VJs have their own unique set of strategies for accomplishing certain tasks alone, such as shooting their own standups or steadying their camera. While many of my informants report that they enjoy the creative work of narrativizing a story with digital editing software, working alone forces them to make a critical decision about whether and when to record their own voice to their stories.

The way presentational form affects a VJ's daily process is not the only manifestation of the divisions that still exist between television, newspaper, and web-based organizations. Such divisions are also affecting the way video journalism is being adopted and incorporated into organizational structures. The next chapter is devoted to the ways these exhibitors are using video journalists and their stories to fulfill organizational goals.

NOTES:

Portions of this chapter have been previously published in *Journalism and Mass Communication Quarterly*, and are used here with permission: Bock, M. A. (2011). You really, truly, have to "be there": Video journalism as a social and material construction. *Journalism and Mass Communication Quarterly*. *88*(4) 705–718.

1. Assignment editors are the logistical managers of coverage for a television newsroom.
2. Converting the video story to a textual story is a new task for television workers who, until recently, did not even have to type with punctuation or proper spelling.
3. This is the source of many complaints, of course, by individuals involved in news stories who say a reporter blew the tiniest bit of conflict in a public meeting out of proportion; the events were converted to narrative form.
4. From Chatman, 1978, p. 26.
5. Imagine that you are watching a video in which a ball is in one person's hands and gets tossed to the left, but in the next shot, the ball is suddenly and inexplicably moving to the right. The best way to shoot this sort of action is to allow the ball to *leave the frame* so that the edited result makes physical sense to the viewer.
6. It is not uncommon for news photographers to adapt their equipment to fit their personal preferences by adding straps or inventing carriers. One of my former colleagues converted a golf bag to tote his tripod.
7. During the Iowa caucuses of 1988, I was once assigned to spend an evening doing nothing but sit on a platform prior to a rally in order to save a tripod location for a photographer.
8. Of course, it isn't at all natural! Still, it matches what we've come to expect in filmic news, which is reflective of the way we experience the world spatially. When we watch a basketball game in person, we certainly do not lie on the floor to see the players' shoes close up, we don't float above the court to view the whole scene, and we don't get into the face of a fouled player. Nevertheless, these things "feel" right to us because of movie and television conventions familiar to us in contemporary culture. See (Messaris & Moriarty, 2005).

9. A short presentation that depicts a reporter or VJ on the scene. In Britain, this is known as a "piece to camera."
10. Though this may be the ageism common among people in their 20s.
11. It was my phone, in fact, since [KK]'s phone was not compatible.
12. Rendering for mere sections of Hollywood feature films can take many hours.
13. Called a "rundown" in the US or a "running order" in the UK.
14. The implications of the differences between recorded journalist narration, known authors, and other forms of narrative voice are addressed in detail in Chapter Seven.
15. A cutaway is a shot of something static, usually away from or reacting to the main action in a scene that allows editors to cut between sections of action in a way that feels natural to a viewer. Without cutaways, coffee cups appear on tables out of nowhere, people run on the same street in two places, and someone's head can move awkwardly from place to place with no apparent reason.
16. The photographer's name, and possibly employing organization, which credits their work.

Chapter Four:
Organizations & Video Journalism

> *"Going in there every day was such a joy—the wit, the cleverness, the feeling of being together and making something happen every day. A newsroom is a completely magical place."*
>
> *—Carol Ann Campbell,*
> *formerly of the* Newark Star Ledger *(in Carr, D., 2009)*

Introduction

The foundations of journalism are shaking as this book is being written. The impact of the internet, coupled with the recession of the early 21st century, is accelerating a shift that started in the 1990s when broadband internet was in its infancy. Newspapers and television news operations are shrinking—if not shutting down completely. Experimental web news organizations are struggling to find ways to finance their operations. The situation is much like days of the American frontier, only this time www stands for the "wild wild web." Most journalists and their managers see a need to use the web effectively as a presentational platform, yet the ideas for harnessing the web continue to move faster than advertising dollars arrive. In the midst of this wild frontier, video journalists are a new sort of gunslinger, considered a hero by some, a villain by others, often struggling not only with outsiders in the field but within their own newsrooms to establish their place.

This chapter examines the way video journalism is developing in three organizational categories, focusing on how its two distinctive features, singularity (working solo) and expansion (the spread to new users) are affecting that development. The organizations are distinguished according to their historic presentational form, even though all three are converging to the web: television, newspaper, and community-web group. Members of these various organizations have different backgrounds with regard to filmic news: television journalists currently produce video stories, so video journalism presents a new way of doing it. For newspaper and radio news workers, video journalism presents an entirely new way of creating a story, and for web-based citizen organizations, both the *video* and *journalism* tasks are new activities. Video journalism's singularity and expansion pose significant challenges for news work in these three domains: television journalists are being asked to take on *more* tasks, newspaper journalists are being asked to take on *new* tasks, and nonprofessionals are assuming roles once reserved for members of journalism's interpretive community.

Whether among themselves in online discussion boards or during interviews with me, journalists usually frame their arguments about video journalism as a conflict between utopian and dystopian possibilities: Is it a means by which to improve filmic journalism in terms of quality and quantity? Or is it a cheap way to do things the way they've always been done? I would argue that framing the argument this way is simplistic. It's more useful to ask: "What does a VJ employee afford this organization?" "How might a VJ be useful?" For newspapers, a VJ might present the possibility of live news coverage on the web, or enhancing a text-based story with video. For television, it affords the possibility of expanded coverage areas or creative approaches. For community organizations, it affords a new way for participating in the public sphere. As with any change, the situation is better understood as a matter of complex change, with both troubling and liberating possibilities.

Television

For television operations, video journalism presents an economic advantage: one person does the work of two, three, or more. Even so, one person cannot necessarily do the same work as quickly as a team of two or three, nor can one person be in more than one place at a time—an obvious observation, but one that is critical for understanding video journalism. Most relevant to television organizations is the enhanced flexibility that video journalists afford when it comes to assigning journalists to stories and locations, allocating resources to generate more unique and local, or "hyper-local" news, or in some cases simply extending coverage into areas heretofore ignored.

The BBC

In 2001, the BBC's Nations & Regions division[1] embarked on an ambitious video journalism program, hiring consultant Michael Rosenblum to start training VJs at a specially-equipped facility in Newcastle Upon Tyne. In seven months, about 500 BBC Nations & Regions employees took the three-week course. Many of the trainees were already BBC journalists, but about 20% had never been involved with newsgathering. A special agreement with the technical union of the BBC ensured that the VJ training would be encouraged for everyone, and not used as a tool for displacing jobs. The training dealt with more than the technical aspects of video journalism and challenged its participants to engage in new ways of telling stories in order to better serve the BBC's diverse audience and attract new viewers. Rosenblum is a longtime critic of conventional television, who's said that "news is produced on a conveyor belt in which every story is cut to the same template" (Broadcast, 2001). At the BBC, his workshops instead promoted original news stories driven by "characters" or "real people," avoiding officials and news releases. His BBC trainees were encouraged to let stories unfold naturally in an intimate, observational documentary style. One BBC newsroom executive sees this as an advantageous alternative to conventional TV coverage:

> [MZ]: Imagine then if you are dealing with very sensitive issues, very sensitive situations and difficult situations with individuals, and on top of yourself as a journalist carrying the camera, you also have a cameraman, in certain cases you may have the light person, and you have the sound person and so on, and any sense of intimacy is gone because pretty much what you have is a posse.

Rosenblum's ideas received a mixed reception at the BBC. Some executives embraced the approach, seeing it as a way of bringing greater relevance to the news programs. Yet, for other executives and journalists the approach didn't match up with the media logic of their organization; it was difficult to produce such stories at the rate typically expected. "He wasn't working within the practicalities that we do," concluded one VJ from Oxford. Some journalists, like [EN], were insulted by the institution's insistence that video journalism was a matter of "better storytelling" and not a way to save money.

In time, the less conventional approaches to content and narrative style were subsumed by the everyday demands of broadcast news, exemplifying the way recontextualization informs preconceptualization. Years after the initial training sessions, a conventional BBC video-photographer, [FD], remarked to me, "You have to cover all stories, even ones that are picture challenged." Today, the BBC training program continues to hold up the subject-driven, observational model as an ideal, while at the same time accepting that the temporal demands of a daily broadcast impede the development of compelling, intimate observational stories. "They want it both ways," says a leader in the multimedia training division of the managers;

they want a VJ to be able to shoot something quickly for the daily show, but also with the pathos and depth of an observational documentary.

Video journalism's most powerful influence in the BBC's Nations & Regions division has been in its contribution to hyper-local coverage in two of the country's smaller communities, Oxford and the Channel Islands. Oxford, England, was one of the first to establish a hyper-local newscast using VJs. Prior to 2000, Oxford news was covered by London's operation, about 50 miles away. Producer [JM] says that meant that either a story had to be a deadly disaster or that the London office had such a slow news day it could send a crew to do a feature story about cows. Now, using a digital system that switches from a national feed to a regional feed, and then a local line, the BBC produces a news program with a section devoted especially to news from Oxford and its environs. For the viewers in greater Oxford, the newscast appears seamless. Those outside the area see a slightly different version of the newscast without the Oxford news, but it too appears as one program. Staffed almost entirely with video journalists (there is one specialized video-photographer on staff), and with everyone pitching in (for instance, news editor's administrator frequently moves cameras and runs the teleprompter when other employees are out on assignment), the newsroom provides residents of Oxford local video coverage they would not otherwise have.

Video journalism gives the BBC network a less expensive way to cover local news, allowing it to expand its coverage. Managers who favor the creative observational style believe it will remain an option for coverage, much the way some textual stories might receive day-of front page coverage and others get the "glossy magazine" treatment:

> [MZ]: I think there's a variation. The idea is that the VJs will be able to treat their stories differently. I think the mixture we have is, in some cases it will be what we would call perhaps the more classic sort of VJ, the one that goes with a camera to develop a more intimate relationship with his or her subjects or stories and probably taking a longer lead time in terms of bringing that story. That's one type.
>
> Now increasingly what we're having as well is the day story, the story of the day, that basically can be put together by one person without necessarily relying on crews, so that, technically speaking, would be VJs but perhaps not with the same treatment we refer to when we're talking about VJ work.

Video journalism was introduced to the BBC system less than ten years ago, and has already undergone shifts in the way it serves the historic institution. One VJ trainer, a fan of the intimate observational style, remarked that Rosenblum's heavy-handed approach may have backfired because of organizational culture:

> [MM]: He walked into the BBC, which is a mammoth organization, real massive, and said "Right, everything that you're doing is shit, absolute rubbish. You want to stop everything and do it this way." And it's just like "Yeah, well, we're like some ten-ton train. You can't stop us, you can kind of slowly change our direction, but by trying to say 'Stop! Move!'—not going to happen."

What is certain for the BBC is that video journalism is part of the organization's long-range multimedia strategy. The local news division's training corps no longer teaches video journalism as a single subject, folding it instead into a multimedia web curriculum that also includes writing for the web and website production.

Hyper-local Cable

In the United States, where one-man-band video has long been a mainstay in small rural communities, similar models are now in play in the top markets. New York City, for example, is home to one of the first all-VJ, major market news operations, known as NY1. Rosenblum trained the first team at the 24-hour cable startup in the early 1990s. Founding executive Steve Paulus says the VJ model was cost effective. Speaking to a trade magazine upon the station's 15-year anniversary, Paulus explained that the VJ model increased the station's productivity and coverage capabilities:

> Our philosophy was to have no boundaries between technology and journalism.…One of the first things we did was to teach everybody how to shoot with a camera.…When you have a journalist who can shoot the camera, you're relying on the number of cameras you have, not the number of camera crews. And we have a lot of cameras. I like to say that when you have a camera crew and you need to climb a tree to get the shot, it's hard to get the cameraman to climb the tree, but if you're the cameraman, you'll climb the tree. (Caranicas, 2007, p. 20)

NY1's organizational structure, in which nearly all employees of the newsroom work as generalist VJs instead of specialists who work as part of teams, has been adopted by a competitor, [NBHD CABLE], which has applied the VJ model to urban hyper-local coverage. Advertising and subscriber supported [NBHD CABLE] operations cover portions of the greater New York metropolitan area: the Bronx, Brooklyn, Long Island, and so on. As with NY1, the VJs there are young and paid intentionally low salaries right out of school, and they are expected to leave within one to three years because the job is treated as an entrée to the more lucrative larger markets.

Even with these ascetic conditions, competition is strong; the news director is able to hire graduates from Ivy League universities, class valedictorians, and other academically high achievers. The manager saw herself as a teacher as much as a news director, helping to groom her VJs to move on to bigger markets and more prestigious jobs. The workload is rigorous. An experienced New York VJ and longtime documentary producer, [KB], used the word "insane" in his assessment. [ML] says the system has made it possible for [NBHD CABLE] to provide neighborhood-level coverage for the community:

> If you take a look when the decision was made to launch these…operations and you know you have X amount of dollars to get the job done, at some point if you're sitting behind a desk, you're saying well, I can get eight crews with a photographer and a reporter to cover the news in the Bronx, or if I went the one-man-band route I've got 16 crews, and can I penetrate a larger area, can I hit more stories?

This strategy of using generalists instead of specialists to increase productivity is apparently financially viable. [NBHD CABLE]'s parent company reported a 10% revenue increase from 2008 to 2009 (Cablevision, 2009). Is the product truly hyper-local? It does, after all, focus on one borough in ways the larger network affiliates do not. On the other hand, the population for this section of New York City is about the same as Orlando, Florida, so a hyper-local story here is not necessarily at the level of a small community or neighborhood. Moreover, by building high turnover into its business model, [NBHD CABLE] ensures that none of its VJs ever develops close ties to the area, and never has a stake in the community they cover, so their journalism never reflects the sort of understanding that develops from experience.

Local Broadcasters

[TV-MID] is a more traditional operation than [NBHD CABLE], with newscasts scheduled between other network-affiliated[2] programming. Its newsroom employs both traditional reporters, who work with full-time video-photographers and a handful of VJs, or "backpack journalists" as they are called here. The VJs for [TV-MID] usually use the smaller cameras, but might pick up a conventional camera when it's necessary. Decisions about who covers which story are made during the editorial meeting and by the assignment editor. The product has not changed because of the station's use of VJs; the newscasts are essentially the same. The difference is primarily a matter of saving money and stretching station resources.

But [GE], a news director who manages a newsroom of similar size in another state, says the cost savings are illusory. So far, he has resisted converting his staff to the VJ model because he finds the specialists easier to deploy and move as needed:

> We're producing here two, three, four—five hours of news a day so, and most of what I've seen from the VJs across the street, they're OK, they're all feature-y, it's all like a day in a tattoo parlor...When the fires happen, we destroy them. I mean, they couldn't do anything. A reporter with a laptop and a handheld gets nothing, because at that point it's all about immediacy and that person can't deliver that and a two-man crew and a live truck can.

In [GE]'s experience, a VJ takes twice as long to produce the same number of stories as a two-person crew, and he'd rather have two people do more, and do it quickly. "I'm not saying it's completely worthless, I'm just saying for day in day out, where the rubber meets the road—not happening." An illustration from [TV-MID] supports his premise: [NC] has occasionally come into conflict with the assignment editor over VJ deployments. The assignment editor started sending the VJs out to the more distant stories in order to keep her more specialized double crews in the city; this would give her more flexibility. For [NC], this only meant adding more driving to her workday. Since a VJ can't drive and write or edit at the same time, the distant assignments were difficult to complete on time, a point she believes the assignment editor now understands.

A news director from another large market station agrees—in part. [QE] says her entire staff is now trained to shoot video; she herself shot dramatic weather footage the night before speaking with me. Yet, while she agrees that breaking news requires more than a solo VJ, assignments in her newsroom are made on a story-by-story basis, with some going to VJs, other stories to teams:

> The distribution of skills has helped us be very nimble. We are getting more stories covered and more enterprise journalism because of it. So it's an expanded news-gathering culture that has really been very effective—very effective.

[QE] argues that with continual training sessions, her organization (which has won numerous awards for video photography) has been able maintain high standards for photographic quality. She concedes, however, that it's essential to maintain checks and balances on solo VJs to ensure that fact-finding and story integrity are not lost in the pressure of constant deadlines.

The Impact on TV Organizations

Broadcast programming, especially all-day coverage, is such that quantity matters a great deal. The proverbial newscast "beast" needs to be fed often and without fail. For these operations, the recontextualization of news stories into a real-time broadcast program is a determining influence. The VJs I observed created stories in much the same style as their conventional crew counterparts: short packages shot according to formula using the familiar expository spoken narrative. More so than VJs with newspaper organizations, television VJs were more likely to use phrases like "endless grind" or "burnout." One columnist for the NPPA detected a similar trend: "I hear from a lot of frustrated storytellers who are getting tired of being handed a stack of press releases and told to get it back as soon as possible not just for air, but for the Web too" (Wertheimer, 2007, p. 16). The National Union of Journalists in England is starting to hear health complaints, such as exhaustion or back problems, from VJs who've been on the job a few years. Television VJs are being used to do the jobs two or more people once did and, in some situations, at the same pace two people once did (Personal Communication, NUJ). BBC managers are aware of the demands on those working solo, and generally have adjusted their productivity expectations. VJs with the BBC are not expected to produce a full story a day; three or, at most, four a week is reasonable, and this allows the VJs to spend some time in the newsroom setting up stories, doing research, or otherwise collaborating with colleagues. But at [TV-MID], [NBHD CABLE] and other local TV operations in the US, VJs are expected not only to turn a story a day, but sometimes more than one version of the story.

It should be made clear that the all-VJ organizations I visited continue to hire some specialist camera operators or photographers to assist with live shots or extended coverage. Live-shot stories from the field can be (and have been) sent by way of VOIP[3] wireless connections engineered by one person, but the organizations observed still utilize specialists, either news photographers or engineers (or both), to quickly set up a live signal from a portable microwave or satellite truck. With video journalism, organizations have greater flexibility in terms of allocation, and are able to enlarge their coverage area or increase overall productivity in terms of unique content. VJs do not necessarily increase productivity in terms of speed, as there's no opportunity to write while another person drives, or to work the phone to collect facts while another person shoots. BBC executives say they believe there will always be a need for specialist camera-operators or specialist editors, only that there may be fewer of them, and that they will be assigned to stories requiring specialist treatment. Similarly, stateside television reporter

[CA] works both with specialist video-photographers and by himself, but he is not expected to produce a story every day on his own. Instead, he has a small camera he carries all the time, giving him (and his station) more flexibility in terms of time and geography:

> I've done actually quite a bit of shooting and it's come in handy most for me, with breaking news type situations...I am on my daily turn with a photographer every day still, but when there is some kind of breaking situations when that photographer is editing my package, that is already in the show for 11 or after the show and I'm...still around, it's really come in handy being able to capture the breaking news.
>
> The other thing it's really important on, if there's an element I want for my story outside my normal hours or outside of my photographer's normal hours, it's something I can real easily zip and dish up without having to worry about scheduling a photographer, or coming in on a day off, I can really just make it happen fairly quickly.

[CH], a former Video News International VJ turned academic, believes the singular model with smaller cameras is especially valuable for international news coverage:

> The old model, the traditional model of elite foreign correspondents, particularly for television is just not viable, at least not viable in the realm of the accountants who were more concerned about cost than they are about the quality of journalism. So we're thinking that overseas this model is becoming more and more in use and my forte at the university is foreign correspondence...I encourage students to embrace this new technology and this new model because it is the technology and it is the model of the future.

An extraordinary example of the way conventional cameras combined with VJ cameras can afford television news organizations greater allocation flexibility presented itself in London on the day Prime Minister Tony Blair stepped down and power was transferred to Gordon Brown in July 2007.[4] The scene outside the official residence of the British Prime Minister, 10 Downing Street, was replete with journalists and cameras of every possible style. Behind a set of gates guarded by soldiers carrying automatic weapons, traditional media were set up on steps, tethered to live hook-ups, across the narrow street from the Prime Minister's door. Outside the gates, the situation was more fluid, with an assortment of cameras—conventional, still, small-format video, and consumer-grade cameras—wielded by the general public. The conventional live cameras inside the gates had the best, most privileged view of Blair's exit, but they could not move. Outside, photographers were mobile and had views of the street, the protesters, and members of the public who were there to look on—or quite disinterestedly walk by. Among those outside was a pair of VJs using two motorcycles, a small-format camera, and a small microwave transmitter that fit into a suitcase carried by one of the motorcycles, offering extreme flexibility in terms of mobility and live coverage. No matter how large the crowd or how intense the traffic became as the Blair motorcade traveled to the Palace, these two ultra-mobile journalists could move quickly into position, record the scene, and transmit it back to their newsroom in real time.

Organizational Struggles for Television

The introduction of video journalism to the local television organizations in this study was often greeted with skepticism, if not outright hostility. Certain stakeholders in the existing process have much to lose in terms of their status and identity. They can and have, in some situations, lost their jobs. It should not be surprising that there's as much passion to the debate between those who embrace video journalism and their colleagues who resist it. Part of the emotion likely comes from the fierce relationship photographers of all stripes form with their equipment. Some of the arguments about small video cameras echo the battle between glass plate cameras and the Leica® in the first half of the 20th century. Conventional television photographers and reporters, for whom video journalism adds responsibilities, tend to be the most vocal about their objections, but they are not alone. Objections to video journalism tend to cluster around five themes:

1. Diminished quality
2. Conversion of high-paying jobs to low-paying jobs taken by young journalists willing to do more for less
3. Loss of journalistic collaboration
4. Burnout
5. Loss of status as a specialist or performer

Understandably, even with promises of anonymity, my subjects tended to be diplomatic in their assessments of video journalism. The discourse in another anonymous forum, an online bulletin board for the television news community, called *The Watercooler*, was far more vitriolic.[5] I followed conversations there in the course of my research to enrich my ethnographic material because I found that journalists would say things to each other behind the cloak of internet anonymity that they would not say to me.

Diminished Quality. Conventional television photographers who dislike the VJ system say that no one can both write and shoot well. As specialists who've built their careers by focusing on using their cameras well, understanding the aesthetics of lighting and composition, they have a great deal at stake in protecting their occupational territory. Even in the years before the VJ movement took hold, Lindekugel (1994) noticed that videophotographers resented a reporter trying to tell them how to approach a shot. The idea that video is easily learned by someone accustomed to working with words offends some longtime specialists like [FD], who told me,

> I don't like it.... Stories get told better by two people, one to concentrate on the words and listen, the other to concentrate on the visuals. We used to call viewer video "home" video—we can't call it that anymore. Our stuff looks like it even more? We can't call it professional video anymore.

[NC] hears criticism from specialist photographers that she doesn't properly frame her interview subjects. One of her specialist colleagues believes the visual quality of stories from [TV-MID] has declined, but he is sympathetic:

> [DH]: You'll hear complaints from some of the managers recently about some of the reporters' videography...and the reporters under their breath, look back and are like "What do you want? I'm doing all this stuff, I've gotta set up the story, I've gotta set things up down the road, you want me to do series,[6] you want me to do this and that, and on top of that, you want me to have good videography and editing skills? You're lucky the story gets on." That's what I hear quite a lot from the reporters, but you know what? I give them a lot of credit because to keep your head above water with all the responsibilities...and just showing them that they can do it, is commendable.
>
> They didn't give up. They didn't give up and they're still storytellers. It's just they're not 100% *visual* storytellers, they may get good overtime, they may not. It may just be a means to an end and I think that I am worried about quality, 'cause I think it really comes from corporate people on down that basically videography, quality is not as important as it used to be. It really is—"video is just video"—it's just like a means to an end, the way of telling people information. The cinematography end of things...beautiful pictures and eye candy? That was really nice, but in the final analysis for me, I don't know if it's as important as just telling a story, getting the information out there.

The only response to a general query I posted to an NPPA bulletin board was more critical:

> I had to train 2 of the shooters that were hired as OMB's.[7] THEY STILL HAVE PROBLEMS white balancing and shoot shaky video, audio is over modulated and sometimes missing. One of them didn't even know what end of a camera to look

> into. He came from radio. The other was a WX[8] forecaster that wanted to report. He told the ND (news director, the manager) that he had experience shooting. He may have, but it was minimal at best. I don't think corporations are worried at ALL about quality.... This is all about cost cutting."[9]

But [MN] argues that the complaints about quality are coming from within, not from viewers.

> The real pushback that I see is the quality argument: "Well, this is going to change the quality of my work." And that quality is generally based on how their work is perceived inside a television station. Or inside a newspaper newsroom. It's not based on the people that actually use the products, the people who are sitting in their living rooms, or the people sitting in their kitchens watching a newscast. Or, picking up the paper from their driveway...I was a photographer for a long, long time. I still consider myself a photographer. I've worked in this industry for more than 25 years and I think if we use that quality argument, I would have had somebody setting up my lights, and somebody setting up running my audio. That was the definition of quality 25 years ago.

For news video, there may be a greater appreciation on the part of viewers for an image's witnessing authority than its aesthetic quality. Video from a cell phone of the Virginia Tech massacre, or from the killing of an Iraqi woman during the 2009 protests, were shaky and partly out of focus, and, yet, they became cultural reference points for those events. For the average viewer, quality is not always defined according to cinematic standards.

Arguments about quality also center on the skills of photographic, editing, or reportorial specialists (and occasionally overlap with the "youth" complaint discussed shortly). Because video journalism is generally seen as a more economical model for television production than the crew-based system, it is targeted by critics as an inferior model, frustrating VJs like [MM] who sincerely believe that singular video production has the potential to improve the product.

> That makes me really angry! It's not just about saving money. It's about doing the things that we went and did yesterday, which involved going out with a small camera and talking to people and coming back with a piece that people actually really liked watching.

[QE], the news director of an organization that requires all journalists to be able to shoot video, says that photographic quality is a concern, but it's one that can be met with continual training, and, she notes, it's an area where she still hears some criticism.

The issue strikes squarely at long-simmering resentments and rivalries within the television organizations. On the day WUSA announced it would convert its entire newsroom to the VJ model, *The Watercooler* overflowed with incendiary argument. Posters like "Citijock," and "NYCStreet" sparred with an anonymous news manager with the nickname "NoBSNews": eCityjock:

> The only future for VJ newsrooms are low ratings and smiley warm features *(feature stories)*. They will LOSE when covering NEWS.
>
> *NYCStreet RE:* Being a Moron, Rosenblum style
>
> Gannett is one of the companies in financial distress. They're trying anything to cut costs. They're fourth in the market and fading fast. This will save their GMs fat salary for another 90 days. It won't save their newscasts. Even the Young stations have backed off after VJ failed there. No one has made it work…
>
> *NoBSNews:* RE: Stupidity and Denial:
>
> The level of ignorance by the anti-VJ posters is astounding.
>
> 1) The current VJ stations do not require that everyone shoot alone every day. If safety, content warrants they sent two people (including live shots) yet you morons continue to try to make that point as if it's reality.
>
> 2) You say Young and Gannett are doing it because they are in financial trouble. Guess what dudes? In the current environment, the old model of doing business puts EVERYONE in financial trouble. Everyone has to change!
>
> 3) The quality argument is an absolute joke and insult. I've watching ht KRON and WKRN product. It's good, certainly no worse than competitors. As long as you grade quality as "The same old tired tripod-ed long standup in the middle, some nat-sound and a bite from two politicians as quality…viewers will continue to drop like flies. At least three stations are trying some new approaches to storytelling.
>
> 4) Don't give me the…veterans who know city hall bullshit either. I've been in TV management a long time. The veteran who knows the city, knows city hall blah blah shows up to the morning meeting with NOTHING. Same tired, boring crap that means nothing to viewers. You veteran reporters are gigantic pain in the ass. You don't work hard, turn in the same crap everyday and your stories frankly SUCK.
>
> Give me some people who are willing to dig, open to new ideas and care about what they do. YOU DON'T CARE. You stopped caring until you found out you might have to go VJ!
>
> *(Obscene sign-off omitted)*

The WUSA argument continued through dozens of posts, representing in microcosm much of the fear and anger that surrounds the debate over video journalism. Much of the rift was not merely between VJs and non-VJs, but seemed to be generational.

Younger, Cheaper Workers. Some of the resentment surely stems also from the youth of video journalists. [NBHD CABLE] hires VJs straight out of college. As newcomers, they are often willing to work for less in order to get a foothold in a very competitive business. In the field, my informants rarely spoke very negatively about VJs or the imposition of video journalism into their organizations, even with promises of anonymity. But where they are certain of anonymity, as on *The Watercooler*, the resentment is loud and clear. This message was posted July 12, 2009, by an (apparent) television photographer who goes by the online nickname, "about2retire":

> Do you young squirts have ANY idea how much change us "lazy old-timers" have seen, and had to adapt to, in just the last 20 years?? I've been at this for 33 years, more than likely since before you were born, so don't tell me we are lazy and don't accept change. Believe me, NOBODY sat on their ass in "the olden days." And those still in the business, that I know, bust a hump every day! The VJ concept is nothing new! It's SO small market and yes, in my early career we did it but had no idea it had such a fancy name. We just called it a one-man band. This is far from hi-tech progress. The cameras may be more expensive, but the shooters are far cheaper and it shows. I still work in a top 25 market but it sure doesn't look like it. While other stations in the market have gone this route, Thank God my station hasn't…yet.

Here's another, posted February 9, 2009, by "thisisnewstoday":

> Here's my problem with VJ's…I agree technology is making doing this easier. And that's great. But the big issue for many of us pro's…is not so much shooting you're [*sic*] own stuff. It's the PAY. And the quality of people. Stations that are going VJ are not doing it because "the technology is there." It's because those who agree to do it…do it for much less money. And those of us who have been in the business a few years…don't want to make 40K in a large market. Problem is, the people who are being brought in to VJ…are making 40K…which means…they probably suck. Which hurts the product. Because the only people who would agree to make 40K after a few years in this biz suck.

Many of the VJs in local TV news indeed are younger journalists who graduated from multimedia programs like [NC]. Some are willing to put in the longer hours and harder physical work as a means to move up to a larger market, like [ES] and [LT] at [NBHD CABLE]. The salaries are incredibly low. [NC] was paid $26,000[10] her first year, and was able to negotiate a raise when she re-signed a contract to work part-time as an anchor (an indication of the way television news values performative skills more than journalistic ones). [ES] and his colleagues at [NBHDCABLE] similarly earned barely half the median income for television journalists on the east coast.[11] [LT] did in fact get hired in a top-ten television market between the time I shadowed her and finished writing this book. But VJs like [NJ], [KB], and [CH] have decades of experience behind them and continue to shoot. The fact that the younger VJs are working for less money, and threatening the conventional pay structure, seems more relevant than age itself.

Loss of Collaboration in the Field. Some VJs also miss a certain amount of collaboration while on a story. Whether in a newsroom or on a campaign bus, group discussion often serves to give reporters a sense of security about story treatment, with, of course, the concomitant problem of "herd" journalism. [MM] says there's a need for organizations to find a new way to provide VJs with a collaborative environment:

> I don't know if it's just news or the world in general but people are quite insecure, and if you work on your own you have be bleeding confident or have a very thick skin because there's no one else to turn around and say "What do you think about that?" And it is quite a lonely job.

[MN], a former television photographer turned corporate trainer and manager, says he hopes that VJs in his organization will still find ways to collaborate with colleagues in the newsroom about stories:

> One of my biggest fears is that the single-person crew is the…single-person focus. Say we're going to do a story on water rates and we send Tom to go do it, well, Tom's not bouncing ideas off of anybody. Tom takes the assignment, goes in the car, goes and finds somebody in favor, somebody against, and he comes back. We get Tom's perspective on that versus, you know, one of the things that we have with a two-person crew is, hopefully they are talking to each other…I'd like to think smart journalists realize that and before they walk out the door, they start bouncing things off each other.

[QE], who appreciates the nimbleness VJs have brought to her newsroom, similarly notes that it's more important than ever for the rest of the team to help with checks and balances.

Collaboration and quality may not necessarily be positively correlated. While discourse among journalists is what leads to decisions about what constitutes news, it can also lead to homogenization. As Zelizer, Crouse, Boczkowski, and others have noted, conversations between the boys and girls on the bus or in the van can homogenize news content and lead to practices that please one another, without regard for what the audience needs and prefers.

Burnout. Concomitant with the loss of collaboration is exhaustion. Its routines are physically demanding whether or not a VJ is expected to produce a daily story. [NC] hopes to move up to a market where she could stop shooting her own stories because she hopes to marry and have children someday and "can't imagine" being pregnant and doing this. [MM] had to explain to one of her trainees' managers that a VJ needs some days to recover:

> There's an awful lot of video journalism burnout because they're doing three jobs and they're doing four ten-hour days…I had a word with our television editor and said look, "He cannot produce a package a day for those four days 'cause it'll kill him." 'Cause he is doing the job of three people you can't ever forget that. So she was very receptive, really receptive. So he'll occasionally get a crew or he'll occasionally get an edit suite and he does a really good mix.

In this case and others at the BBC, managers have taken note of the physical toll daily work has on VJs (as has England's National Union of Journalists), and tries to set realistic expectations for productivity; rather than a story a day. Regional VJs for the BBC are expected to produce three or four stories a week, using at least one day a week to arrange interviews, write, edit, and simply recuperate. The demands of commercial television, though, often do not allow the luxury of a VJ "down day." [ES] reports that in the summer of 2009, some of his colleagues at [NPHD CABLE] have worked ten days straight on daily-turnaround stories. [HT] and [KQ] not only are expected to produce a story a day, they're required to do three versions of that story.

Loss of Status. Carrying a small camera oneself is also seen as a mark of lower status, both within a newsroom and outside of it. When her newsroom started requiring all journalists to learn to shoot, [QE] says reporters literally cried in her office: "It seemed counterintuitive to career growth. It seemed like, 'Well I'm going backward.'" [EN] says he and his colleagues are regarded as "scum of the earth," by specialist photographers and correspondents. BBC executive [MZ] hopes this will change with time:

> There is a sense of status that may be an issue for some that is, "If I'm in a certain position, that basically I should have people working for me. I should have someone driving my car, and I step out as the reporter, the journalist, and I don't have to worry about whether the camera is on or off, or the light is on or off, or the sound is right

> because that's how it used to be." Again, it touches on something...that is a generational aspect, and where people see themselves...in a certain place in the pecking order. My hope is that over time that won't be the main reason, the main barrier, why some people may decide not to go and not embrace...video journalism.

In the field, size seems to matter as well. [DT] likes the fact that he can blend in with his small camera and says he's been treated collegially by TV photographers using larger equipment. But [KN] says that while carrying his little video camera he's been ignored by public officials who don't consider him to be part of the mainstream press corps. He doesn't think the local Chief of Police would have walked by him like that if he'd had "a big camera and some middle-aged white guy standing next to me." [NC] jokes with the specialist photographers at her station about her "baby camera." At [NBHD CABLE], [ML] believes her VJs have a competitive edge because they carry the larger cameras.[12] While covering the 2004 presidential election, [NJ] noticed that poll numbers and camera size seemed to be positively correlated:

> Every time I went out from one state to another there seemed to be more small cameras. And of course, the less important your candidate was, like if you were watching Al Sharpton, there were ten small cameras pointed at him...

The power of a video from one of those small cameras, though, destroyed the campaign of another 2004 candidate, Howard Dean, whose so-called "scream" derailed his presidential attempt after it was posted online. By the 2008 campaign, small cameras were part of the landscape at all campaign stops, including those with the frontrunners, such as John McCain, Barack Obama, and Hillary Clinton.[13] As far as news strength, small cameras seem to be losing their stigma.

Adapting & Converging

Video journalism, therefore, allows conventional television organizations to create more unique content for real-time shows at lower cost. A few VJs reported using their small cameras to contribute to spot news coverage as part of a team, but most were observed spending a full day producing feature or general news stories.

Elements of sound and image are adapted to fit the program, not vice versa. Consequently, video journalism's greatest impact on television news stems from its accessibility and ease. More people with more cameras can expand coverage areas and allows for easier, faster, more easily maneuverable deployments.

In San Francisco, one station's experiment is instructive. The utopian trade-off presented to employees of KRON who made the VJ transition and started shooting their own stories was that they would have greater control over their story selection and construction. They could focus on a story they considered important, and devote the amount of energy to it they considered necessary. In other words, they would be better able to perform according to their beliefs about what constitutes professionalism: autonomy and ideology. For a while, this was the case. The station assigned VJs to "beats" (areas of specialization) and granted them two or three days to work on deeper, more analytical pieces (Russell, 2006). But when the format failed to attract more viewers (and therefore more advertising revenue), KRON shifted the emphasis back to spot-news and daily-turnaround stories, leaving the remaining VJs with a more intense workload but less of a chance to serve their journalistic ideals. A former manager[14] posted his mea culpa to *The Watercooler*:

> I Was One of the "Guys": My name is (   ) I was…@ KRON tasked with the job of helping to create the V-J concept. I supported…and continue to support…video journalism. My initial plan…endorsed initially by Young management…was to allow participating staffers to work from home, develop sources and spend whatever time was necessary to report stories with perspective and relevance. The original plan was to have V-Js propose pieces, submit ideas which…after green-lighting…we would post on the KRON website FIRST. Line producers would then cherry-pick stories for broadcast. With 40+ staffers generating content, our story-count would exceed anything the competition could produce. Most importantly, our V-Js created pieces that actually made a difference to our community. It all fell apart and those of us who were committed to the idea were forced out. In our place reside individuals with a limited & archaic vision driven by economic imperatives. When I was finally forced out, I spent my final day apologizing to my staff for my naiveté. These pros were right…this V-J idea was always a cost-cutting project. I was wrong to believe otherwise. That said, I still believe the idea is the future. I believe that because I was once a one-man-band and, as such, I believe I contributed much more to my community than the standard crap we see on the air today.

Television news organizations have processes in place for creating filmic news, and video journalism affords it the opportunity to change those processes without necessarily changing the product. What about news organizations without a system already in place, or ideas about how it should be done? Filmic news is entirely new for print organizations working to establish a web presence. For these organizations, video journalism offers the opportunity to invent something entirely new.

Newspapers

A decade ago, the thought of a newspaper employee with a video camera seemed downright bizarre. Today it's commonplace. Even though the overall business prognosis for newspapers in 2009 was grim, one bright spot existed for online news, which continued to expand (Saba, 2008; Sass, 2009). Online news videos, in particular, became a revenue center for newspapers, as publishers found they could sell what are known as "pre-roll" ads, commercials a viewer must see before the news item starts (Nason, 2008). Small wonder that newspapers are working to incorporate video into their product. Just how best to incorporate it, however, is up for negotiation. All manner of interactive and visual elements are being posted to newspaper websites in addition to video: still-photo slide shows, interactive graphics, and user-comment pages.

In the previous century, video was the territory of local television news, seen by print journalists as a callow, shallow version of journalism (Singer, 2003). What was once the competition is now part of the internet survival kit. Gannett video trainer [MN] joked about the rivalry when he was training employees from both types of newsrooms, "How scary can this be, putting newspaper and TV people here at the same time?" Managers faced with incorporating video into their newspaper's internet product must choose which parts of the TV model work, and which ones can be abandoned. The internet affords freedoms that broadcasting does not. Because a website is not broadcast in real time according to a schedule, video stories on the web can be of any length. Second, websites are part of a larger network: a video story can be linked to print information, statistical graphics, still photographs, or any other sort of resource for the end user. This is why, at the conclusion of a video technique workshop in which he covered camera, microphone, and editing skills (everything that a television journalist does in the course of a day), he could declare without irony that "This is not TV." Newspaper organizations are actively working to distinguish their product from TV news by seeking ways to incorporate video in ways that allow them to reinvent filmic news and to provide an alternative to an appointment-style, time-constrained TV news model.

Local Newspapers

For [IE], a photo editor at a major local daily newspaper, motivating his department to acquire new skills has been a challenge. He delegated the task of worrying about the front page photo on the printed paper so he could, at least temporarily, focus on the organization's online product. When he arrived at the paper several years ago, everyone in the photo department started at 10 a.m. In order to foster a real-time mentality, he changed the staff schedules to cover a greater part of the clock, to change the focus on the constant deadline of "now." He scheduled one staff photographer/VJ to start at 6 a.m. The department is unionized, so no one can be forced to learn to shoot video. Instead, [IE] says he's doing his best to be a supportive cheerleader for convergence, with the overall message, "Hey guys, we've got to change!" To that end, [IE] purchased equipment for each of the 25 members of his photo department (some of it via *eBay* to save money) and invited each person to come in for training. He does the training himself, having acquired video skills on his own. Not everyone has taken up his invitation.

[IE]'s emphasis is on learning video, but he has no strong opinions about format, narrative structure, the use of graphic titles, and so on: "That will all shake out." When I ask him whether the photographers who learn video take on the title of multimedia journalist, backpack journalist, VJ, or something else, he dismisses the question. "Who cares? At the end of the day, it comes down to storytelling." [IE]'s approach to convergence strategy is not surprising, as his former employer has adopted an across-the-board multimedia strategy that anticipates a day when labels like *newspaper* and *television* are no longer relevant for news organizations.

As part of that long-range strategy, the Gannett Corporation has trained more than 600 of its employees, many of them based at newspapers, in video journalism skills. Gannett is the largest media company in the United States, with 84 daily newspapers including its flagship national publication, *USA Today*, more than 800 nondaily publications, and 23 TV stations. It also has newspaper holdings in the United Kingdom. Gannett executives allowed me to observe a four-day training session for employees in Florida. The session was hosted by the newspaper *Florida Today*, and most of its participants were employees of the newspaper, though a few representatives from Gannett television properties were also present. Gannett calls its VJs backpack journalists, or BPJs. The company's stated goal is for nearly every journalist to be proficient with a wide range of multimedia skills, with video as part of an overall toolkit. The manager who coordinates the training says the trainees are eager to acquire video journalism skills:

> [BT]: Out of the 640 people, I could count, probably on one hand or even less, the people who really didn't want to be there. By and large they love the opportunity, they're clamoring to do it. I have editors asking me when are you going to do another session? And I have, you know, reporters and editors asking their bosses when can I start doing this?

Like the BBC, Gannett's long-range strategy also is geared toward the concept of hyper-local news; it's the one thing that local journalists can deliver that other media outlets and websites cannot. For the Gannett group, the average traffic for a video in 2007 was 3,700 a month. By February of 2008, traffic rose to 1.9 million streams a month. As of July 2009, the *Florida Today* website has an automatic video player—go to the site and an anchored presentation starts with a short newscast. It's not exactly a news program, but it uses a traditional desk. To that end, a newspaper like the *Allentown Morning Call* has distributed 45 video cameras to its staff, 30 of which are to be used by reporters, not the photographic staff.

[RJ] explains that "The long-term goal is to have a news organization that can talk in any medium." [MN] tells his trainees, who might work for television stations or newspapers, that now "We're all in the same business." He notes that a TV station on average has about 12 reporters, while the typical newspaper in the same market has 36 reporters. When everyone is trained in multimedia and video journalism, the playing field is even. He summed it up this way:

> I think we are going down a great road because we are going to create newsrooms full of journalists...Will it be less people than there are today? Sure, but my hope is that it will be a newsroom full of multiskilled journalists who are interested in digging up unique local content. So much of what gets in a paper or gets on a television newscast is produced outside that of that television station, it's from CNN or AP or whoever it is, but all of that information is available to me somewhere else. I think our future is in local content produced locally.

A National Newspaper

The *New York Times* video unit was not imposed on the organization, but instead evolved independently. The *Times* purchased a controlling interest in a company called Video News International, the independent company led by Michael Rosenblum in 1995 (*New York Times*, 1995). The company evolved into New York Times Television, and the unit continued to operate as an independent production arm of the corporation. Eventually, the newspaper sold the documentary unit, but hired some of its leaders as in-house video producers. The current division now operates out of the new building in Manhattan, along with the rest of the *Times* journalists, with 15 full-time VJs. Two more full-time VJs work out of Washington, D.C., and about 20 more cameras are in use by *Times* journalists around the world.

The editorial director of video and television for the *Times*, Ann Derry, is an award-winning documentary filmmaker. Her assistant is a former Emmy-winning television network executive. Because the unit developed independently, its members are not converted photographers from the newspaper's stills department (though one has trained and joined voluntarily), so no one in the organization was forced to learn multimedia skills. *Times* VJs are not expected to turn a story a day, nor necessarily even pursue and research their own stories on a regular basis. They do not respond to spot news. ([BF] quipped, "We're not New York One.") They are expected to work as visual partners to the print reporters on the *Times* staff, some of the best writers in the world and often highly specialized beat reporters.

The unit does include some employees who are not VJs but editors who work with raw material sent from the field for the website. Interns are available to help, especially with the tedious process of logging tapes.[15] Stories are preconceptualized in one of a few ways: they might be conceived independently by an individual VJ, or a story is suggested by a print reporter for "translation" to video. VJs are not expected to produce a piece a day; in fact, one of their best, ([BF]), has been allowed up to a month to produce a story. Derry says her driving principle is to consider the best way to use the *Times*' resources, especially its beat reporters. As of 2007, the video unit officially became a "desk," which in newsroom parlance means it is an independent department. Derry says she no longer works to convince journalists on the print side to try out video—they have started coming to her. *Times* reporters usually track their own spoken narration (Derry estimates about 80% of the time) using a format she calls "reporters' notebook." Other pieces are narrated by the VJs themselves, and still others are observational pieces with no scripted narration. Occasionally, a *Times* reporter will appear in a video, as with a regular feature the department produces with the golf writer.

VJs in this department seem genuinely enthusiastic about having the autonomy to adapt their storytelling style to the needs of the subject, instead of the other way around. "Video storytelling has been liberated!" declared [SU]. "If it's compelling and we want to make it 12 minutes, we make it 12 minutes…The story is what we think it should be, and not what some line producer[16] thinks it should be."

Organizational Struggles for Newspapers

Unlike television organizations, which are struggling to incorporate video journalism into a system of filmic news production already in place, newspaper organizations are starting *de novo*. While they already have routines in place for newsgathering and for photo journalism, incorporating filmic news into a web product constitutes a different set of struggles over identity and practice. Two themes emerged in the course of this project: One is rooted in the tension in their cultural identity as text-workers in relation to TV news. The other stems from the more basic struggle to simply learn how best to use a new form of media.

Cultural Clashes. Television news dominated and defined filmic news during the second half of the 20th century. Local TV news and its reliance on dramatic visuals, fast-moving graphics, and attractive anchors were often perceived as a less serious form of journalism, a perception with roots in the larger text-picture hierarchy (Becker, 2003; Singer 2003; Zelizer, 1995a). Consequently, managers who introduce video journalism to print (and to some extent, radio) newsrooms have encountered resistance rooted in this belief. [NN] reports that some of his writers thought shooting video would hurt their reputation with their sources as "serious" journalists. [MN]'s training sessions are peppered with jokes about the rivalry: the reputation of television reporters being "pushy" and "jerks," and the danger of having print and television journalists working together, "to have dogs and cats in the same room?" [NJ]'s background is in print and in radio, and explains the way her colleagues often see the clash:

> When I was in journalism school and I think a lot of people have this feeling—that in order to…get into video, with television, you had to be pretty. Because everyone thought of the anchor and you gotta look right…So people didn't think of video journalism—in that sense of you're the talent and you stand up and tell stories—as serious. You just had to be pretty and well spoken. And radio people think, "We're the ones that tell the real stories, because we don't have to put on hair spray to get in front of the mike."[17] I think radio people are put off by video in that way. They don't care about whether my tie's on straight; I'm just going to give you the straight story.

One way newspaper journalists respond to the desire to avoid the perceived shallowness of television is to use a simple observational approach and never appear on camera. [HI] only produces observational NATPAKs for his newspaper's website, and [DT] will record his voice but never a standup. Interestingly, though, some newspaper websites are starting to incorporate presentations from reporters. Some newspapers now use small studios for reporters to work as anchors for short online newscasts. The blending of visual and textual cultures is likely to create new normative standards for what constitutes serious journalism.

Another source of discord arises in the differences between still and video photographic practice in the field. One of the tenets of the NPPA's Code of Ethics instructs visual journalists as follows: "While photographing subjects do not intentionally contribute to, alter, or seek to alter or influence events" (NPPA, n.d.). For still photographers, this has been interpreted to mean that unless they are shooting a person's portrait, they must not ask a person to move a certain way, repeat an action, or otherwise pose for the camera. This dictum is related to norms of both anonymity and objectivity; the photographer is expected to observe and not participate. For TV photographers and video journalists, however—particularly those working on a daily deadline—such a demand is difficult to follow. If a VJ is to record a particular element with enough time to edit a piece and recontextualize it according to its original preconceptualization, waiting for events to unfold might mean missing deadlines repeatedly (which, as explained previously, can lead to unemployment for a journalist). Therefore, in order to get the work done on time, many VJs merge the norms of portrait and news photography, occasionally asking subjects to wait just a moment before entering a room, or to flip a few more pancakes so the scene can be shot from another angle. The subjects of news video are often complicit in the stories created about them. [MN] says he's heard the complaints from still photographers who believe asking someone to flip another set of pancakes is unethical, but says that such a request is acceptable for news portrait photography, and that such a move is not a reflection of lower standards. On the other hand, [DT] continues to avoid making such requests, and chooses instead to live with the consequences in the edit room:

> I have not really had an issue with it; I'll tell you why, because I just use what I get—like, having somebody re-do something. I actually still don't do that. If I were doing television—yeah, and I've seen the videographers work, the TV guys, and they'll say "oh yeah, could you walk this way again? Could you do that again? Can you…?" I haven't had to do that.
>
> My videos are obviously going to suffer because of that. You know, the shots, the angles may not be quite right, the lighting may be a little funny, that's I guess, my choice…

Newspaper editor [NN] says it's occasionally difficult to convince his colleagues that there are alternatives:

> Their only point of reference…is TV, so they try to mimic TV; they come up with ideas that are very TV-esque instead of trying to create their own way. "So there's a little bit of a push-back on that occasionally from me," he says.

While it sounds inviting, "creating their own way" is not an easy proposition. What should video journalism look like on newspaper websites? How should it be presented? The nearly unlimited possibilities proffered by multimedia journalism can seem overwhelming, and the organizations that participated in this study are experimenting with a variety of approaches.

Building Something New. Newspaper leaders respond by not trying to compete with television at all, but to look for ways web-based video journalism might be an improvement upon television news. Viewers use the web on their schedule, so presentation is not tied to the clock. The web also offers as much space for material as an exhibitor's servers will allow, so there is essentially no limit on the amount of time a story can run. Finally, with the choice of using stills, text, or video, stories can be treated with a form that best suits them. Highly visual stories can be covered with a VJ. Stories about complex, abstract ideas can be covered with text.

The print reporters in transition who were most enthusiastic about video journalism saw it not as an imposition but as a chance to add a new dimension to their stories. A *Times* reporter who pursued VJ training did so because he found that with certain stories, he "couldn't do it justice with writing; at least not my writing." He wanted to occasionally have the means to show a scene rather than describe it in language. A Gannett trainee who worked out of a remote bureau wanted to be able to shoot her own video stories for those times when she was on the scene (because she was based in a remote bureau) before anyone else, and knew she could effectively compete with the local TV stations. An urban crime reporter used video to show exactly what she meant by an open-air drug market, when a textual description didn't seem nearly as dramatic as video of drugs being sold in broad daylight from a truck. As newspaper photo editor [IE] explains, "We do not have the restrictions…we have the ability to let the subjects speak for themselves. These guys could not do what they do for a TV station."

Derry is gratified by both the freedom the web format offers her unit in terms of time, subject, and form for their videos, and by the current acceptance of her unit by the rest of the newspaper's staff. She notes that previously, the *Times* held a meeting every day to decide what the next day's front page would contain. Now, the editors in that meeting decide what goes on the paper's front page and the web page—and how video will be used. Derry says that for years she had to drag her nonvideo colleagues at the *Times* into a video journalism mindset; her unit was treated like a nuisance, as "those people." Now, she says her colleagues are enthusiastic about video, and she believes the organization is headed for the day when all stories will be treated with the appropriate medium, with written articles, graphics, slide shows, or video, according to the nature of the subject.

The Challenge for Newspaper Organizations. Newspaper organizations have an advantage in their competition with local TV newsrooms in that they generally employ more reporters. For Gannett's holdings, the newspaper organizations generally have at least twice as many reporters as its station properties. Their disadvantage, though, comes in their lack of experience with video and the need to invent routines and practices for incorporating into the overall product. [IE]'s struggles to change his staff's working hours to better reflect a 24-hour news cycle is just one example of the kinds of adjustments print organizations must make. Add to this the pressure from citizen journalists who desire greater participation in news discourse, and it is easy to see why organizations have yet to settle on a singular set of practices, and why the struggles can be expected to continue.

Such economic realities seem to also be at play for the newspaper journalists making the transition to video journalism. While many of the subjects for this book were early adopters who might be expected to have positively embraced the new form, there seems to be a sense of resignation among others. Resistance on the part of textual journalists, who have little interest in the blue-collar nature of physical, sometimes dirty photographic work, seems almost futile in the face of yet another year of double-digit losses in the print industry. Some of my informants reported feeling as though they are being squeezed to do more with less time and less training, a sentiment echoed in a quantitative survey by a former photo journalist (Yaschur, 2011).

The hierarchy that once existed between text and image journalists is crumbling, and not without the pain and discord that naturally accompanies such a shift. As one VJ put it, "the scribblers" are finally going to have to give some ground. At the same time, some of those scribblers are happily embracing the new multimedia model as a chance to tell stories in new ways. Of course, some of that enthusiasm is likely a symptom of self-preservation, but some of the writers interviewed for this project do seem genuinely happy to have a new tool at their disposal. Their complaints are not necessarily directed at multimedia practices as much as at the way organizations are imposing the model on them.

The challenge of the current economic environment, coupled with the inexorable shift in the media environment toward internet-based presentation, will only intensify the pressure on media organizations to exploit the values of video journalism. The individuals charged with doing the work, whether a television professional who's asked to "go it alone," a still photographer who's expected to learn how to edit, or a citizen journalist challenged to participate more fully in the public sphere, will undoubtedly feel the negative aspects of this pressure. In the organizational domain, therefore, video journalism presents a double-edged sword—one that allows for a greater number of people to participate and to do so alone, but one that could impose hardship, job losses, and threats to the professional identities of those faced with its adoption.

Citizen Journalism Organizations

Community journalism, also called citizen journalism or "indy-journalism," takes advantage of the expanding, democratizing nature of video journalism, with its lower cost and more user-friendly equipment. Current TV, a project started by Al Gore, is perhaps the best known project of its type, inviting contributions from nonprofessionals and paying more experienced community VJs for their work. In 2009, *YouTube* added journalism tutorials to its news contribution section. The IMC (Independent Media Centers, also known as Indymedia) is another pioneer in the genre, though it's not entirely video-driven as its network of activists use a variety of media forms to convey a more populist agenda. IMC has its roots in the historic "Battle of Seattle" riots when the organization loaned video cameras to a team of activists to record their own video of events so they could provide a counter narrative to that given by traditional television networks.

At the core of these efforts is the notion that everyday people finally have the opportunity to make multimedia contributions to the public sphere—to add their voice to the debate using video. While the internet's role in the process of public deliberation is yet to be adequately understood, there are indications that it may well be a "useful tool" (Delli Carpini, Cook, & Jacobs, 2004, p. 336). Taking a cue from musician-activist Jello Biafra who said, "Don't hate the media, BE the media," community journalism encourages nonprofessionals to produce multimedia projects that contest mainstream media discourse. Unlike typical news websites, community video websites do not use balanced language or make claims to factual objectivity. Their purpose is to give a (metaphorical) voice to new and discernible points of view (Coffman, 2009). In this way, they operate from a documentary film tradition. Community video can also be used as a way of building group cohesion; the very work of creating a video story requires discussion and debate, and helps individuals acquire the sorts of language skills necessary to articulate their views (Ananny & Stohecker, 2002).

Our City, Our Voices (OCOV), an organization in Philadelphia funded by a Knight Foundation grant, was one such effort. In 2008, the organization provided free instruction to a class made up of union organizers, taxi drivers, and immigration activists on how to shoot, write, and edit video stories. One of the workshop leaders, [MK], says video has long functioned as an evidentiary tool for activists, but is fast becoming a part of community organization strategy in the US:

> Depending on what the outcome, it does get used a lot and increasingly more and more. I think people are using kind of social documentary or different types of video work for kind of policy, advocacy, for educators, for all sorts of ways that I think that previously it was more constricted to kind of activists talking to activists and now it's sort of more about how people are using video to talk more broadly to different audiences.

[MK] and her colleagues spent the bulk of their time helping students with preconceptualization, eliciting ideas from the group about what stories they'd like to tell. Many of the answers were deeply personal, such as the woman from Asia who struggled to establish herself as a registered nurse in the United States because her home country's credentials were deemed worthless here. Other group members wanted to talk more broadly about the importance of a union for worker protection or for the need for people with diverse backgrounds to live harmoniously. [BD] enjoys being able to offer an alternative to a typical broadcast newscast with reports centered on the African American experience:

> If I was reporting on air, I'd look like the same dime-a-dozen reporter in any market in America, you know, it's like blah blah blah: Police say "what it is," track, sound bite, track sound bite end of package, standup, whatever. Having the freedom to do my own media…it sits outside the box; [I] tell the story how I want to tell it. So in that, I'm trying to stay fresh and do something different each time. That's where my focus is: Issues that are my experiences, my life stories, it's reality-slash-news-slash journalism…a hybrid of all those genres out there…It's kind of obvious that minority voice, whether African American community or Asian or Hispanic or whatever, [are] kind of marginalized in the media.

One of the reasons [TC] joined the OCOV class was that she perceives mainstream news organizations' coverage of issues dear to her, such as union activities and the situation in her own neighborhood, is incomplete:

> Video lets you show what you feel is more important. 'Cause you watch some things, you read things, and it don't have all the necessary information sometimes. Sometimes it's just a little bit of this and not enough of that.

OCOV's teachers worked from within the documentary tradition, with a clear point of view, and one that ideally lets subjects speak for themselves. The students, however, didn't necessarily embrace the verité style, and some of the films were more imitative of TV news, with a spoken narrator (though one who made opinionated statements). While each person in the class was exposed to the work of the entire process depicted in *Figure 3.2*, no one was expected to work alone. This was in part a matter of resources—there were too few cameras and laptops, so the students had to work in teams. The result achieved a result not related to skill-building but to community organizing:

> [MK]: I think also it does form a cohesive group…This class was an interesting example because all sorts of issues are being raised that aren't being directly addressed by the film, but the opportunity to sort of be in the same room and think about these issues is allowing—for example, last class we had an issue that [a colleague] had spoken about previously about feeling sort of like there's this extra attention to immigrants in an unfair way; where it's like her position sort of as a working person, why should someone who's an immigrant who just got here get more attention or more privileges and those sorts of things. So those kinds of conversations are happening as a result of the class and maybe will work their way into a video which will work their way into a more public dialogue.

Organizational Struggles for Citizen Journalists

Shooting stories for the web on a regular basis poses a challenge for members of OCOV and similar organizations. Resources in terms of equipment and time are scarce. Activist groups can make cameras available on a loan basis, but time, for people who work and have families, is a luxury, and creating video stories can take hours, even days. A citizen journalist who runs a local news website in San Mateo was enthusiastic about providing an alternative to the mainstream, but quickly discovered that, "I wish I'd known how hard it is to do journalism well. I've now learned by doing it how time-consuming it is to report, write, edit, and fact-check news stories with integrity" (Parr, 2005). Another self-described (occasional) independent journalist, [DE], enjoys the work but has largely abandoned it in order to make a living:

> Citizen journalism is a little rough…you can't put so much time into it…I like it but I had to make sure I had some other projects.

Students with OCOV were not always able to fit the Sunday afternoon class into their schedules, and opted to take the cameras home to shoot. Taxi drivers from the class shot part of their video stories from their cabs between fares. Current TV, considered a leading project of this kind, made a decision in 2009 to lay off 80 people and shift to a more traditional form of production in order to attract advertising (Flint & James, 2009).

In spite of these challenges, Philadelphia's Indymedia site is continually updated with contributions from students of OCOV and its partner organizations. Video journalism affords such groups a way to call attention to issues that interest them while pressuring mainstream media to be more open to public participation. Resources limit the nature of the work in terms of technical quality, but the fact that video is no longer the exclusive province of conventional news organizations is changing the journalistic landscape. Newspaper websites often invite comment and participation, and traditional TV organizations, such as BBC, CNN, and other news organizations, invite video contributions. Such contributions made a dramatic difference in the way the American public learned about election protests in Iran in the summer of 2009, from web bloggers and video posts to social media sites like *Twitter* and *Facebook* (Associated Press, 2009; Cohen, 2009). In a study in which he interviewed Indymedia, journalist Mark Deuze concluded that this "may yet prove to be the crucible for new ways of reconnecting journalism, news, and media professionals with ideals of sharing access and participatory storytelling in journalism" (Deuze & Platon, 2003). As more and more nonprofessional individuals learn to use video as a storytelling device, this crucible is likely to get hotter.

VJs & Competing Colleagues

So far, this discussion has addressed the way video journalism affects individual organizations within their newsrooms. Another dimension of the organizational impact stems video journalism's expansion, which can be seen in the way journalists from different organizations interact while covering stories. As the lines between text and visual news degrade, inter-organizational relationships are adjusting to the new norms and routines of video journalism.

Some subjects have reported negative responses from colleagues in the field. [NC] says specialist video-photographers from other stations seem to respond to her coldly when they encounter one another in the field. She attributes the attitude as much to her solo work as to the fact that she is not a union member.[18] An early account of the transition at KRON reported that a new VJ was told by a competitor "I hope you fail." One of the justifications [NBHD CABLE]'s news director makes for requiring her VJs to use conventionally sized cameras is that they appear more competitive in the field when working alongside photographers from other stations in the New York market. [KN] has experienced situations that support such a justification. With years of experience in his market, he's been ignored by longtime sources when he carries his small video camera, noting that "I'm sure if I had a bigger camera and a middle-aged guy at my side" it wouldn't happen. "They don't understand, let alone respect" his role as a video journalist. Such complaints were the minority among the subjects for this project, however. [TH]'s experience was far more common:

> People were very helpful...I hadn't found or really ran into anyone from the video community that was not willing to share something they know or just chat you up...
>
> I would say like a year ago when still photographers started carrying video cameras some of them would just kind of look at you a little crazy...This was probably near 18 months ago, like why are you carrying a video camera, because I think at that point that's when the wave started to turn and then I just think they don't, they didn't know what was going on with the print media. And now, obviously, the fact that we're shooting basically video for the web which is different, you know we're not, we're not trying to come in and take over what they do, they, they're the work that they do...

Similarly, [DT] says his small camera is more of a conversation starter than an impediment to working with competitors in the scrum. Veteran photographers point to having a basic bond from working in the field—no matter whether they're shooting video or stills. As [NZ] puts it:

> Everybody knows each other, and somebody's got to be a real jerk, I mean a real, real jerk to step on somebody or push somebody out of the way. We usually work pretty well together.

In contrast to the fierce competition that exists on an organizational level, the norm in the scrum is a sort of friendly, even helpful competition. [HI] will hold a microphone for a TV station colleague who can't get close enough to a news podium; he's even looking into the viewfinder of solo colleagues who need help shooting their own standups. During an observation, even I experienced the spirit of cooperative competition when my camera batteries died, and a stranger from the scrum loaned me a pair of AA batteries.

> [KL]: They have that competition but the way they also cooperate with each other and ok, there's a set space, there's four of us, we're going to cooperate so we can all get the picture. We'll all go back in and hey, my computer's broken, can I borrow yours...They're constantly tutoring each other in Photoshop, "Oh, I learned a new way to do something, learn this way, um, how's this camera work versus that camera. Is this one better? How do you know? I see you've got the new D5. How does that compare to its old one." So it's always—they're constantly working with each other and helping each other out. You know, in the old days, they say they used to cover each other. Someone would be sick on a, like a campaign trail somewhere. A guy would shoot two cameras: one roll of film for him, one roll for the other guy, and throw him a roll when he came back.

Why might this be so, in spite of rivalries between employing organizations, and the desire to compete on a personal level? Such behavior may stem from a photographer's identity as a professional with a certain amount of autonomy, shared discourse, and shared physical experiences while on assignment. They are employed by a particular organization, but they may consider themselves autonomous practitioners in the field. It would seem that a photographer's identity, whether shooting video or stills or both, is as a photographer first, and an employee second. Even within their organization, their identity as a photographer who works with their body, in the field as opposed to the newsroom, seems to predominate. [ES], [NC], and [KN] are just a few of the participants in this project who complained about their colleagues back in the newsroom whom they perceive as being ignorant of conditions in the field. If one spends more time in the field with other photographers than in the newsroom with organizational colleagues, it seems logical that one's reference group, and loyalty, would shift to the people with whom a photographer faces mutual challenges on a daily basis.

Summary: A Network of Stakeholders

Just as a small video camera is an object that presents its human user with a set of affordances, the skills and body of a VJ affords organizations a means to accomplish certain goals. Each category of the organizations observed for this section is using video journalism for different ends. Those ends might be financially or journalistically inspired or—realistically—both. Television stations are using the single-person VJs for increased assignment flexibility and as a cost-effective way to provide hyper-local coverage to communities that were heretofore without their own television news. Newspapers are looking to video as a new revenue stream. Might the newspaper model, which enhances story treatment on the web, be the form that prevails in the long term? Can community journalism get off the ground without commercial support?

As video journalism develops in different organizations, it is possible to see the results of oppositional objectives for the various stakeholders. Commercial news organizations require profits to exist, and for commercial media, profits are connected to the size of an audience it can attract to see advertisements. Local television and newspapers are using VJs in different ways, but with the same end goal of financial solvency, if not prosperity. The BBC is not commercially driven, but instead answers to a trust that oversees its spending practices. So while ratings don't matter in an advertising sense, the BBC must still use its resources and attract enough of an audience to justify its public support. Video journalists who work for such organizations have financial stakes in them as well; they are, after all, working for a living. Yet as a professional community, they have other stakes in the way they, as working bodies, are used by their organization. Their resistance represents the inflammation of those other stakes, notably autonomy and the norms of public service as described by Singer, Deuze, Zelizer, Schudson, and others.

The degree of latitude and individual VJ experiences for the preconceptualization phase varies according to their membership in an organization, as well as their status within it. [KN] was granted the power to be "self-assigned" with his newspaper after having won a Pulitzer Prize and then teaching himself video skills. The VJs at [NBHD CABLE], however, are younger; indeed, the organization's business model relies on the employment of younger journalists willing to work for lower salaries in return for an opportunity to build a resume tape for more prestigious jobs in larger markets. With minimal experience, high turnover, and limited tenure, they have less power to argue over story choice and development. VJs at the *New York Times* have wide latitude regarding story choices because they are not in the daily mix, but instead are part of an enhancement for the product.

The ultimate new form of collaboration may not be inside a newsroom—it may be between journalists and would-be journalists, or simply between citizens. Video journalism's expansion to new users means many more nonprofessional journalists can participate. A longtime videophotographer with the BBC observed that the so-called amateur contributions are occasionally so good they're comparable to professional work. Community VJs have a different stake in the process, one that might be more personal—a need for self-expression or a desire to contribute to the public conversation—and their volunteer status can interfere with their ability to make regular and visible contributions to what's increasingly being called the "conversation" of the public sphere (King, 2008). Perhaps it's not necessary for a citizen to take up video journalism as a hobby in order to participate actively. Lower costs and easy access to the internet allow individuals to make occasional but valuable contributions in the form of one of the primary journalistic verbs: witnessing. In such cases, viewers are not worried about shadow ratios or perfect shooting technique; the authority of witnessing, especially when combined with the vetting of a institutional recontextualization, made the images from Iraq extraordinarily powerful (Associated Press, 2009; Cohen, 2009).

The current business environment for conventional media organizations is dire. Video on the web is a bright spot on this dark landscape (Nason, 2008; Sass, 2009), so there is little wonder that exhibiting organizations are encouraging, if not forcing, employees to learn VJ skills. For many of my informants, video journalism represents a significant career shift, something they never expected to be required to do. Some embrace it enthusiastically as a way of enhancing their own work, while others approach their new duties with "adapt or die" fatalism. Some have dropped out entirely. At WUSA in Washington, Gannett's decision to convert the entire staff to a VJ model prompted some reporters to simply resign (Farhi, 2008). The rhetoric surrounding the shift, whether online discussions like those on *The Watercooler* or in conversation, could be classified as cruel. During a NPPA workshop devoted to multimedia skills, the word "dinosaur" was directed more than once at those who would resist the transition to video. At the BBC, a former radio reporter confesses he "hates" video journalism, but was given no choice but to take on additional responsibilities if he wanted to remain employed. The employees observed at Gannett's workshop were not forced to attend, but were encouraged, and many seemed sincerely enthused about learning a skill that might preserve their career. Still photographers have sought out workshops on their own in response to the dramatic economic shifts affecting newsrooms.

These may be difficult days, but with crisis comes the opportunity of reinvention. So while news organizations continue to experiment with ways to best harness video journalism for their purposes, all signs are that this emerging form will remain part of the landscape.

News is not made in the newsroom, however, but in the world. How are video journalism's distinctive features of singularity and expansion manifest in the reporter-source environment? How does it affect the relationships VJs have with external intermediaries, sources, public relations officers, and other so-called handlers? This domain is also undergoing a shift, and this is the subject of the next chapter.

NOTES:

1. The BBC's Nations & Regions division is essentially the local news arm of the BBC. It operates separately from BBC International and the BBC's national networks. It has 12 English regions, and includes the term "Nations" for its local operations in the nations of Northern Ireland, Scotland, and Wales.
2. US network affiliates share the programming day with the national organization. Usually, the national programming includes national news, soap operas, and primetime entertainment. Local access hours allow the affiliate to run syndicated programs, such as game shows or talk shows, and local TV news. Ad revenues are shared between the local company and the affiliated network.

3. Voice over the internet protocol, that is, phone service on the web.
4. On June 27, 2007, then-Prime Minister Tony Blair stepped down and leadership was handed to Gordon Brown.
5. And profane, too—far more in line with what I experienced as common newsroom conversation when I was a journalist.
6. Local TV news series are multipart stories, usually covering a topic in greater depth than a typical daily story.
7. One-man bands.
8. Weather.
9. In an ironic sense, his posting underscored his point about specialists and quality in that it contained three misspellings that appeared not to be typographic errors.
10. Roughly two thirds of the average college graduate in 2007, according to the Federal Bureau of Labor Statistics.
11. Based on salary data from (Weaver & Wilhoit, 1986).
12. It would also be extremely expensive to re-equip her entire staff.
13. Chapter Seven discusses the role of small cameras at one of her campaign stops in greater detail.
14. He confirmed by phone that this was indeed his posting.
15. Transcribing audio and listing shots.
16. The person at a TV station who plans and times a broadcast program.
17. Microphone, pronounced like "mike," but broadcast journalists spell it as an abbreviation, mike.
18. Her youth and gender may also play a role; as an attractive on-camera reporter, she does not look or act like "one of the guys."

Chapter Five:
Appearance Managers & Video Journalism

> *"It is not essential, therefore, that a Prince should have all the good qualities which I have enumerated above, but it is most essential that he should seem to have them."*
>
> —*Machiavelli*

Introduction

Not long after photography was invented, politicians, military leaders, and social activists began to learn how the craft could be harnessed to suit their interests. The usefulness of images not only to elucidate but to convince, inspire, or persuade was immediately clear. In the United States, the Civil War served to foment techniques for cultivating an "image" in the abstract with an image in the material. Abraham Lincoln credited his eventual electoral success to a portrait by Matthew Brady. General Ulysses S. Grant is understood to have very purposefully posed with his jacket unbuttoned and without customary military pomp in order to advance the impression that he was all business—too involved with the battlefield to be bothered about his epaulets. Theodore Roosevelt welcomed photographers as he fought the Spanish-American War as a way to promote himself as a man of strength, courage, and vigor. Military officers during the First World War imposed some of the most stringent censorship ever in an effort to maintain morale back home. Only years after that war ended were its true and extensive horrors witnessed by way of photography.

Eventually, critics will argue, the tail started to wag the dog. Instead of photographers and filmmakers capturing an event as it happened, events would come to be designed and held entirely for the benefit of photographic recording. Critical researchers have chronicled the way political conventions turned into TV shows, mutating from self-standing spectacles to what Boorstin (1961) labeled "pseudo-events." These events are planned with cameras in mind and, as the numerous cognitive researchers have found, the message of the resulting images can trump facts in the minds of viewers. To control the image is to control the story.

Key to this discussion, however, is that images, as tangible artifacts derived by camera-bodies operating in relation with the physical world, can be controlled not only discursively but through physical means. Those who control a space can control how that space is depicted. The authority to control the bodily freedoms of others can control how and when an image is decontextualized by a VJ, and adds an additional source of power to those who would control their literal image.

Over time, public relations professionals have learned how to be coproducers of news stories, and governmental institutions (which have control over human bodies) are able to use that power to control their own images, literally and metaphorically. Whether by releasing images that they themselves have produced (as with video news releases), controlling journalists' geographical access to locations, or by carefully orchestrating camera placement at events, image managers endeavor to enhance and protect the message they want to convey on the part of their employer, business, or personal interest (Bock, 2008; 2009). Sometimes, their efforts may seem banal, as with the sports team PR representative who says his rules simply keep photographers safe from speeding football players. Other efforts are more blatantly manipulative, as when the Pentagon was found to have vetted the work of journalists applying to be "embeds" in the war in Iraq and Afghanistan, favoring those reporters whose work was categorized as sympathetic to the military (Reed, 2009).

This chapter describes the practices within the domain of appearance managers: campaign handlers, public relations representatives, and other actors who work as literal "gatekeepers" to the locations, subjects, and interviews that journalists seek in order to construct their narratives. Much of what is covered here applies to all forms of visual journalism, but again, the video journalism's two distinctive characteristics of singularity and expansion can be expected to have an impact. What happens when appearance managers, as stakeholders, are suddenly faced with far more reporters carrying cameras than ever before? What is the consequence of the use of cameras so small that it's impossible to sort professional journalists from everyday citizens committing journalistic acts? Does the singular nature of the work render a video journalist even more dependent on the information subsidies[1] provided by an appearance manager? How does the physicality of video journalism affect the source-VJ relationship and the stories that result from their interaction?

Much of this discussion is relevant not only to video journalism but to camera coverage generally—a domain often bypassed by news scholars who tend to focus on the newsroom and not the field. Whether or not a photographer is working alone, matters of access and control significantly influence the choices made in the construction of news stories, and these choices are left largely opaque by journalism. This chapter is based on interviews with VJs and other photographic journalists, enriched with a set of interviews with intermediaries, including a press aide to a mayor of a large US city, coordinators from presidential campaigns, a former district attorney, and several veteran public relations freelancers. Their contributions indicate that the practice of video journalism is indeed changing the source-journalist relationship.

Access & Autonomy

Geographic access is a matter of both the laws of physics and social control. Just where a camera-body may operate is regulated by trespassing statutes, privacy and libel law, administrative regulations, as well as moral and social norms. Even on public property, photographers might be restricted from recording certain views, such as court proceedings, certain governmental meetings, or locations that might be considered terror targets, such as bridges or power plants. Restrictions on the latter tightened considerably after September 11th. Libel law further regulates the recontextualization of images, even those shot on public property. I cannot take a picture of a crowd of people in Philadelphia, focusing on one person in particular, then add the caption "Statistics show that one in ten people is a sociopath," because to do so would imply that the person highlighted in my picture is a sociopath. A complete review of photographic law is not possible here, but a general understanding that video journalists must often navigate formal and informal regulations on their daily work is essential.

Assisting them—or impeding them—in navigating access to narrative elements are public relations liaisons, campaign handlers, press aides, and other social actors who control the gates to information and geography. News scholars have already documented the way journalists' dependence on sources shape the news in favor of the status quo (Gitlin, 1980; Molotch & Lester, 1974; Sigal, 1973; Tuchman, 1978). Official sources serve as nodes in the "newsnet," and provide a means of claiming the authority of facts. Appearance managers provide information subsidies that save journalists time and money while furthering the interests of their client or employer (Gandy Jr., 1982). This phenomenon is intensified for video journalists, who not only need "facts," but physical access, and for whom specific visual elements are often tightly tied to a story's preconception. The additional provision of what might be considered a "visual" subsidy in the form of a spatial accommodation can be similarly expected to further the interests of those who control a physical space.

Working with appearance managers to negotiate physical (and therefore photographic) access to locations was a primary activity common to all of the VJs observed for this project. As soon as they'd precontextualized their stories, [UJ], [LT], [ES], [CP], and [NC] set about gaining access to the locations that would provide the views and interviews necessary to construct their narratives. [LT], [CP], and [NC] each called upon communication representatives for private schools. [UJ] reached out to a contact at a local tourist attraction, and [ES] made a personal visit to the funeral home where a viewing was to take place for a shooting victim. [ES] thought a face-to-face conversation would be a more appropriate and effective way to obtain permission to record part of the victim's viewing, and he did succeed. In all of these cases, permission was granted, but with restrictions. [ES] was allowed to stand in one part of the room with his camera. The others were allowed access to certain areas and were continually escorted on the property. None objected—this was accepted as normal protocol, and in each case they were able to shoot the elements required for their stories. Spot news, of course, does not require this kind of planned access. VJs like [HI] and [KN] use police scanners to listen for events and generally shoot them from the public street. In such situations, a photo journalist might be granted access to a crime scene, or inside a firefighting perimeter, if the rules of local press credentials allow. [KN], however, had the goal of putting himself in the place of the general public and avoided any stories that required a credential.

Gaining physical access is only part of the challenge for journalists who use cameras in the course of their newsgathering. Autonomy within a space—the freedom to move and position oneself in relation to a scene—is an additional concern. Because the photographer's position has an impact on the nature of the resulting image, the rules regarding position are a matter of contestation between photographers and appearance managers. Position rules are one of the ways appearance managers set a sort of "price" on access. As with many of the other sorts of exchanges for access, the price is rarely, if ever, mentioned in journalistic accounts.

Rules of Engagement

Many news scholars have observed that the source-journalist relationship is a matter of interdependence (Cook, 2005; Gans, 1979, 2004; Sigal, 1973; Strentz, 1977; Tuchman, 1978). There are moments of antagonism, but journalists require the assistance of their sources, or appearance managers, in order to make sense of the daily barrage of events—and appearance managers need journalists to convey a message to the public. Therefore, controlling access is not a simple matter of yes or no, but of when and how, and with mutually beneficial goals. Experienced appearance managers know that video journalists, and any other journalists who work with cameras, need certain elements for a story's preconception. They understand that by granting access to those elements that a story's preconception can be met, and often speak of helping a journalist "get what they need" in order to fulfill a shared understanding of a story's preconception. Interactions regarding access can be considered a sort of game, or an exchange-based system: access is exchanged for a position requirement, limits on the nature of the photographic access, or simply an implicit agreement that the images constructed will be narrativized according to a shared preconception. These sometimes agreements, which may or may not be overtly discussed, constitute the rules of engagement between appearance managers and journalists.

The Shared Preconception

Appearance managers will often work to determine a journalist's preconception before granting access to locations or subjects. The tourist attraction in Florida where [UJ] visited normally requires journalists who wish to bring a camera to fill out a form in advance explaining *in writing* what the story is about and what elements are sought. Most requests are granted, but [BG], the liaison, says occasionally,

> We do say no if it's a...project that doesn't have an actual airing date, if it's a spec [speculative] project, we usually say no to that. We have limited resources and we have to look at how we allocate our resources. We also may [say no] if it's a program that's not documenting history or travel or tourism—if it looks like an implied endorsement we're not able to...so we have some guidelines.

A mayoral press aide, [EP], will ask an inquiring journalist a bit about the story they're pursuing:

> I'd like to know the types of questions...What's your story about? Just in general and by asking that question you can typically find out what their disposition towards the story is. You know, saying "I'd like to know why all of the homeless people at the airport are still there." Well, geez, I get a sense of where that story's going, so, OK, all right, I know how to start...versus um, "What effort is the city taking to assist the homeless?" It's the same issue, homelessness, but two different slants...You can learn a lot just with that simple question, so we'll ask what the story's about.

[LM] considers one of the main parts of his job to be that of building a shared preconception with journalists:

> My responsibility is to manage, and to the extent that I'm able, control the message on the campaign and therefore I want to make sure reporters understand what we're trying to do in the context of the campaign—so that they don't walk into an event with little or no understanding of what's going on and try to draw their own conclusions. *I want them draw our conclusions.* (italics added)

[EP] says that if he's unacquainted with a particular journalist, he does his best to get to know their work before granting access to the mayor.

> If I've never worked with you before, uh, as we're talking I'm probably Googling ...the people on my team will probably be doing the same, in the sense of stories you've written in the past. You don't have to read everything about a person, but just sort of the tone they take on stories.

He'll also ask about the questions the journalist intends to pose in general terms because "it helps [the mayor] and it helps the person who's doing the interview because you won't have all day." In other words, [EP] says that with preparation he can ensure that the journalist "gets what he needs." Similarly, [UC] likes to know what to expect ahead of time so he can prepare his answers in accordance with a TV news program's production schedule:

> I think, most importantly, it's to come with a message, to know what the major points that you want to make and to do it somewhat coherently...to do that very crisply, and concisely...That goes for like the day before when I do the...live interviews. You know, they're longer, two and a half minutes, or whatever, but I know what I have to do, what's really important to be able to communicate in that short time.

Longtime local politician [CD] learned from the journalists who covered his work as a prosecutor how to make his news conferences more inviting for the photographic press: "That's why we always tried to have pictures and dope out on the table and money and guns and you know, time lines and maps or whatever it is so it would make good TV." But [CD] not only knew how to provide visual elements for a narrative, he understood television work routines well enough to assist with a journalist's geographic challenges:

> Well I knew...that [a station does not] want to have to use more than one crew to cover a story, so I always made certain that when we were arresting somebody...that it was done at a time when [a station] could send a crew to me, leave there, and have time to go to [the] next location to get the shot. So I never set those things up so they

> would be at the same time, because I knew better than to make [a station] have to have two crews.
>
> I scheduled press conferences so that [TV stations] would have time in the mornings to get [their] assignments and get out to...where they needed to get. I knew that I couldn't have a press conference at 9 o'clock in the morning because [TV stations] couldn't get [their] act together and be out there unless it was an emergency.

By sharing a preconception of what a story is, and how it might be shot, an appearance manager can control the way that story is told. A shared preconception is at the root of the source-VJ relationship. The school where [LT] interviewed students about the primary understood that she would be doing a story about student perceptions and granted her entrance to a classroom because they trusted she would follow through on that understanding. Sometimes, the shared preconception is presumed based on daily interaction. This appears to be the case in Washington, D.C., where the nature of the story being covered seemed to be presumed and never discussed, as press aides shouted instructions to photographers and reporters in the hallways of the Dirksen Senate Office Building as a Supreme Court Justice nominee (Samuel Alito) made the rounds to meet senators. In exchange for following Senate rules for photo opportunities (still photographers first, video-photographers second—each visit lasting only a few minutes), everyone could "get what they need." One experienced handler says that balancing the stakes for members of Congress with those of the journalists is like walking a tightrope.

> [KL]: In general, the biggest problem's always access. I mean, you're trying to, photographers want access to an event or a meeting, and trying to accommodate their access with, accommodating the Senate rules or the House rules or their wishes too...We say we control chaos, managed chaos. We try and limit the chaos...Part of our job is to sometimes educate people [in Congress] that aren't around these photo ops like Kennedy[2] every day, saying "Yes, this is the way it goes. It's a little messy but it's controlled and it's going to end in thirty seconds. Just relax."

The definition of what they need depends on a story's preconception. In this case, the Senate press aides could presume that what each journalist required was a still shot of the nominee shaking hands with a senator, or a short video clip of the same scene. The preconception was that the narrative for the story was, at its simplest, that "Alito met with senators in Washington, D.C." If either the press aides or the journalists held a different preconception, the cooperative dance in the hallways of Dirksen would not work. The result, however, is a system of highly staged ceremonial photo ops, which allows for stories to be constructed according to the preconceptions shared by journalists and the Washington intermediaries.

For journalists and sources, shared preconceptions of a story allow for mutually beneficial relationships. Sometimes, however, the preconception is misunderstood or misrepresented by a journalist in order to gain access. [BG] says it's only happened to her a couple of times, but she has had journalists request access on the basis of one proposed narrative—only to change their angle once inside the park. In those instances, she has asked them to leave. The teacher in [LT]'s story was not so offended that he refused to cooperate with her, but after the fact said he thought her questions indicated a stereotypical preconception about the political leanings of his mostly minority students:

> [KX]: I felt that [she] was fishing for information that she assumed she would get from minority students in a minority neighborhood. I do not think that she got what she thought she would get.

While shooting the historic building story, [NC]'s interview with a press liaison had an awkward moment when the liaison could not answer questions about the process of obtaining a historic designation. Even though [NC] had advised her that she was pursuing this angle, the liaison appeared to have a slightly different preconception, one that focused more on the building's historic features, and repeatedly referred [NC] to a press release to that effect and to interviews with longtime employees of the school who could address the building's architecture.

Disagreements about a story's preconception, and about how and in what context information and images might be recontextualized, harm the relationship between journalists and intermediaries, sometimes with finality. [CD] used advance tips to assist television journalists because he knew they would be more likely to cover his events if he eased their transportation logistics (and such coverage reflected well on him as a crime fighter). [CD] only tipped those who would not betray such confidences by publishing or broadcasting the links: "I had very simple rules. Anybody in the media, whether it be print or electronic, whoever f----ed me never got any consideration again."

Another clash of preconceptualization, one that occurred outside a journalist's immediate control, involved a still photograph taken by [SK]. As [SK] described it, his photo of President George W. Bush bicycling was printed in a national newspaper adjacent to a photo of then-campaign-rival John Kerry hard at work on the campaign trail. In this instance, the White House originally preconceived the bike trail story as a portrayal of the president's strength and fitness, but the photo was recontextualized as a president at play. For a short time thereafter, access for photographers to view the president at play was denied.

Illusory Access: Pools & Feeds

Studies of news practices (Bennett, 1996; McManus, 1994; Schram, 1987) have observed that television news is skewed to what can be photographed. To understand how video journalists are able to record narrative elements, it is essential to understand the social and physical processes that cause certain things to be pictured and others not. One way to control images in the news is to produce them without the involvement of a news photographer. Much of the work of government press aides and public relations professionals revolves around providing what Oscar Gandy has called information subsidies in visual form (Gandy Jr., 1982). Video news releases (VNRs), for example, allow news stations to obtain video from inside factories, hospitals, military tanks, and other locations without the expense or trouble of sending a photographer (Harmon & White, 2001). Another form of subsidy is known as a "pool feed." The organization of such feeds constitutes a cooperative between news organizations and intermediaries, and can range from an informal agreement between news organizations in taking turns in covering a trial and sharing the video amongst the group, or a more formal, mediated system as is found in the US Capitol and Britain's Parliament. A pool system uses minimal staff—often one photographer—to shoot a story, and the material is then shared, usually by way of a video "feed" by cable or satellite. It might not employ a news photographer at all, but would instead be staffed by a government or corporate employee. The system constitutes a financial savings for the news organizations, and minimizes the number of photographers in a single event at a time—and is used far more by television and video news than by still photographers.[3]

Video coverage of the US Congress, many White House events, Britain's Parliament, and many US statehouses[4] is almost always pooled (Bock, 2009). The Capitol in Washington is wired with fiber lines from building to building, and any member of the pooling cooperative can plug into the fiber line in the Dirksen "hub room." Fiber lines from throughout the Capitol complex wind into this room, where each network has machinery that sends signals to its bureaus around Washington. Other members of the pool can come to the hub room and plug in a tape deck to record an event.[5] Registered members of the pool, who ostensibly take turns providing a photographer and the necessary equipment to cover an event on behalf of all the other members, contact a liaison with the Gallery who works with committee leadership to assign turns for camera coverage and regulate camera placement. A handler who works for Congress administers the pool and understands the various elements required to construct a video story, and works closely with producers, photographers, and technicians to ensure that each is able to obtain feed video. [WK] knows where all the connections and light switches are in the various committee rooms—and even where windows in the building can be opened—so that a technician can use a portable microwave unit to establish a live shot. She will also accompany a photographer into a room so that news organizations may obtain something known as "cutaways," or shots of the audience, which might be necessary to show that a particular correspondent was in the room (Bock, 2009).

C-SPAN, a cable organization that works in cooperation with the government, is tapped for pool coverage a disproportionate number of times. C-SPAN's coverage of hearings is unique in that it assigns three cameras to each event: one is placed in the back, another is behind and to the side of the hearing panel table (on the minority party's side), and a third camera—often a small, remotely controlled robotic camera—is placed at eye level in front of the witness table. C-SPAN managers consider this third camera part of their organization's visual "signature," something all of its photographers are trained to use. By photographing witnesses at eye level, they appear neither childlike nor regal,[6] with the goal of refraining from using the camera to make political judgments (Ourand, 2004). C-SPAN video-photographers say their goal is to shoot events so that the viewers feel as though they are there. In fact, the television coverage is actually better than being there. The public sits many feet behind the witness whose back is to the audience. Much the way cameras at a sporting event capture the touchdown on replay better than the crowd's eyes in real time, watching a hearing on C-SPAN grants a TV audience a clearer visual view of the official event.

Some government agencies now have their own robotic camera feeds from the rooms where press conferences are held, without any of the involvement of a news photographer. The Federal Emergency Management Agency found itself in a public relations bind in 2007 when it was discovered to have planted agency employees in the room to ask self-serving questions during a robotically covered briefing. Many state legislatures provide gavel-to-gavel video feeds staffed by state-employed production staff operating robotic cameras. For example, Pennsylvania has a cable-funded gavel-to-gavel channel that relays the signal from statehouse cameras and also covers hearings and meetings with its own cameras (staffed by legislature employees), much the way C-SPAN covers Washington but without the mediation of a journalist. Still other governmental bodies simply send streaming audio of deliberations to the internet, again, without any involvement of an independent reporter or photographer.

England's Houses of Parliament have tighter restrictions for cameras within Westminster. Unlike the US Capitol, which professes to be the "People's House," the palace in which the House of Lords and the House of Commons convenes belongs to the Members of Parliament—there is no presumption of any public "right" to visual access.

> [SG]: The similarity I always quote about rules, because people ask me about rules all the time, is if we go cover cricket or soccer or any other, any other live event, if someone decides that it has stopped raining and it would be a good day to take their clothes off and run all the way across the front of the cameras, we don't transmit that.
>
> So it's, I don't really see the big thing about rules. It's good for theses and for articles but really, you know, it's one of those things.

When [SG] uses the phrase "proceedings of Parliament," he is talking about the legally defined proceedings. The view is blocked for the opening prayers by members of the House of Lords and when proceedings are interrupted by protest. When a protester in the House of Commons threw purple powder at Prime Minister Tony Blair in 2004, the BBC was able to record a few seconds of the incident before the feed was interrupted. The network's airing of that video drew a warning from Parliamentary officials to broadcasters, and [SG], who is a production manager, not a journalist, shrugged off the controversy:

> In fact, disorder takes place—can take place—instantaneously. Things were thrown at the Prime Minister last year. That was an instantaneous event. And we transmit live all the time. I don't think anyone was hanged or sent to the tower or, you know, put out and shot.
>
> It isn't a big issue for us...We're here to transmit the proceedings of Parliament. We know the proceedings don't include things being thrown at the Prime Minister, invasions of the Chamber floor, and a dozen other things that you could write down.

Much like [KL] in Washington, [SG] is pressured by both sides—journalists and leaders of Parliament. Parliament's interests are served by the "Yeoman Usher of the Black Rod," who dictates where, how, and under what circumstances a video camera might be used within the Palace. For example, a correspondent cannot be photographed for television doing a piece to camera (or a standup, in American journalistic terminology) except under special circumstances, and *absolutely not* unless the topic of their report involves a matter of Parliamentary business. "The members…it is their house—and they don't want some or any old body, appearing on television talking about their house." [LZ] is explicit about his desire to assist members of the House of Lords control their image their way, and avoid imparting any image indicating that the institution is old-fashioned, or in his words, "fuddy duddy." To that end, despite numerous requests, he has never allowed camera coverage for the annual search of Parliament's cellars by the Yeomen of the Guard, who wear traditional Beefeater-style uniforms, in a ceremonial search of the building's lower level for Guy Fawkes[7] and his gang. Parliament's website describes the traditional ceremony as "picturesque,"[8] and yet pictures do not exist for Parliament's fear of appearing out of touch.

Corporeal Controls

An additional tension that exists between camera-bodies and intermediaries concerns the degree of corporeal autonomy *within* a space. Video journalists must contend daily with formal and informal attempts to control their freedom of movement. Controls on physical autonomy might be overt, by making permission to enter contingent upon remaining in one assigned space, or it might be more subtle as when a public relations representative escorts a photographer throughout a visit. The demands of light and sound might also constitute unintentional or passive controls—video-photographers at Philadelphia's City Council Committee meetings, for instance, cluster in one location, not by administrative fiat but because of the placement of an audio mult-box.[9] Interestingly, though not necessarily surprisingly, the research suggests that controlling photographer-bodies is positively correlated with a subject's political and economic power. Those who live in poor or lower middle-class neighborhoods live out their lives largely in view from the public street. Upper middle-class Americans may choose to live in gated communities, which prevents the public from witnessing their comings and goings. Those with secret service protection are able to use the force of law to retain their privacy. As these examples from campaigns, Congress, Parliament, and other governmental bodies indicate, elected officials impose stronger corporeal controls than average citizens, and the more elite the organization the more elaborate those controls become—and the more strictly they are enforced.

Jurisdictions that allow cameras for court proceedings provide another example. Every jurisdiction is different in its details, but generally judges have strict control over camera placement, the use of lights (usually prohibited), even photographer attire. [RZ] has experience in the New Jersey court system:

> You have to get the OK from the presiding judge, tell him what equipment you're bringing in, whatever you're recording, who you're recording for, and when will it be used, and you fill out papers every time you do that...Most of the time, you cannot move; they tell you to stand in one position and that's pretty much it, and you have to get everything from where you are, and you shouldn't move and disturb the court.

State agents and private property owners similarly regulate where camera-bodies may stand. The Philadelphia City Council, for example, has a fenced-in location for photographers, except for the staff photographers working for the city who take ceremonial pictures at the start of meetings.[10] In the US Senate, photographers are bound by an intricate set of regulations about what they can shoot and where. News photographers are not allowed to shoot the Senate chamber itself, nor any other room or entrance to a room, deemed as part of the Senate. Even the doors to a formal lunchroom where Senate briefings occur are considered part of the Senate and are off limits. Senators can grant or deny access to their offices or meetings in order to control how and when they are photographed. Major entertainment events, such as concerts, regulate where and when news photographers—whether still or video—may operate in order to protect their financial interests. So will professional sports organizations, such as the National Football League or Major League Baseball. The NFL also places tight restrictions on video's recontextualization in news, as explained by a team press representative:

> [EC]: That content is very valuable content, and...it's lucrative that content, during the week. So they limit it so we can, you know, we want to promote ours at NFL.com and the team's website first and foremost.

Political campaigns and events often control camera location informally by placing risers in a key location, as was the case in Blue Bell, Pennsylvania, for a rally with then-primary-candidate Hillary Clinton. In the early stages of campaigns, for instance in Iowa and New Hampshire at the start of presidential campaigns, photographers experienced in campaign coverage report that regulations are loose—so much so that one network photographer says he's been asked where he thinks his best shot might be. But those same video-photographers also say that as campaigns progress, as security tightens, and the subjects' stakes go higher, camera placement regulation becomes highly regimented. Photographers learn where they will be placed hours before an event when they report for a security sweep, the process by which police officers inspect their equipment by hand and with trained dogs.

> [VF]: For the president, you can't move...you have to stay in your spot...pretty much for the press, it's risers. You're stuck with the tripod on a riser.

> [WB]: Usually they want you to stay in one position; it's not like you can move around a lot...and that can be a pain. If you want to kind of have a little bit of movement, usually they confine you to one space, one area. You go and come as they tell you so you know they pretty much dictate everything to you.

> [NZ]: They put you in a space and you're just stuck there. It's like this picture of [a federal official]. They allowed us when he came and spoke at Penn for graduation. They originally were going to put us like 500 feet away, and then they allowed us for a few minutes to walk up and shoot from an angle for three minutes and then they brought us back...They were worried about security. So I had to make an interesting photo but it's very boring, so I had to figure out what I could do, so I had to use the screen behind him. You have to be creative. A lot of my job is making chicken salad out of chicken poop.

Restrictions on sound mean coverage is generally limited to the scripted event, as with pool coverage of the US Senate. Photographers might get ambient sound on the microphone attached to their cameras, and reporters might try to talk to the president, but that's usually forbidden:

> [WB]: I usually broke the rules because a reporter told me, "Push the envelope, then break the rules a little bit until you're reprimanded." (*What happened?)* They'll say, "You can't talk to the candidate," but a reporter will stick a mike up there anyway and shout a couple questions, and even though they told you you're not supposed to do it, and sometimes you get sound and sometimes you don't.

All the photographers report they've experienced quick corrections from secret service agents when they cross a literal or figurative line. Usually, force isn't involved, but [WB] says the agents will touch and move a photographer to keep him or her in the designated spot.

It doesn't always take the force of law, though, to keep camera-bodies confined to what one VJ calls a "no petting" area. Sometimes just by cordoning off a section where cameras and tripods can be set up apart from the rest of the crowd, with a head-on view of the anticipated action, is enough. Clustering together also ensures that photographers do not get into each other's shots, something that is generally avoided unless press presence itself is part of the narrative. [NZ], for instance, generally avoids including mike flags in his shots—those plastic markers on microphones that advertise for a particular TV station—but in one case, he purposely incorporated them into his shot of a woman on trial for corruption in order to illustrate the mayhem that surrounded her "perp walk."

Appearance managers might not always use fences to group the visual press in one area. Sometimes it's as simple as providing electrical outlets or microphone-quality sound in a way that induces VJs and photographers to work from one vantage point. [UC], a former political campaign staffer who now runs a popular annual charity event in Philadelphia, blocks out his events as though he was a staging director, working

> very strategically. The weekend before, [I] went in there…I think of it as a studio. I think of it as…what is the shot I want? The shot I wanted was sort of two-fold; it was when we sort of started off with a little program…I decided who should be in that shot, and what should be behind that shot that's going to get picked up, and of course I had the banner with all the sponsor logos and the name of the project, and I literally am deciding who is going to be sort of standing where. I put the tape down and the names on the tape and I kind of step back and I kind of pretend my eye is the camera and I sort of strategically put things at certain heights and position tables so that…there's a certain distance between the subject and the cameras.

Political intermediaries are well aware of the importance of camera placement:

> [LM]: In the bigger picture context of media, earned media,[11] specifically, press relations news coverage and also managing a message, cameras play a significant role because people tend to get more information from what they see rather than what they read.
>
> You can deliver a more thorough message, perhaps, through print media, but more people get their information from electronic media, and especially in this day and age when you're talking about not only nighttime news, local and national, but also blogs and websites and *YouTube* and any other sort of electronic medium that's out there. So, cameras play a significant role and you want to make sure that…not only they do get a compelling message delivered by your candidate, but a compelling picture that sort of evokes an emotional response from the viewer.

The role of the so-called stagers has become so large that [PD], a Washington TV photographer, says that while on the campaign trail in 2004, he'd often have handlers actually request to look through his viewfinder to check the way he was shooting it. Members of the White House pool note that the handler who managed the image of George W. Bush on the road knew what television "needs" because he was a former network video-photographer. "The guy has talent," says one photographer. Another explained:

> [WG]: He is the guy that positions the flag behind the president. He is the guy that makes sure the backdrop is well-lit. He is the guy that comes over and asks you if the feed is clean. He is the guy that makes sure that the riser is the right height so that it looks the President in the eye.

Staging efforts for political leaders is not a matter of partisanship; Democrats and Republicans alike are careful to control the context in which they are photographed. When Hillary Clinton appeared in Blue Bell, for example, more than one image manager was involved in the event's staging for camera coverage:

> [LM]: There's a whole team dedicated to press advance, which are the people that figure out "OK, we're going to put the press riser here and this is going to be the shot of the stage that most people get, and we'll put, you know, a cutaway riser here so that cameras can get a different angle, perhaps over the shoulder of the candidate." ...And they'll also sort of work with the site people to figure out, you know, "Let's get a big sign, you know, on a particular part of the...in this case the gymnasium" so that the camera shot and the cutaway riser shows the sign with the message on it, "Women for Hillary."

After clinching the democratic nomination in 2008, the Obama campaign tightened its controls so extensively that two women wearing Islamic head scarves were not allowed to sit behind the nominee during an event, ostensibly to ensure that Obama was not photographed with Muslims literally (and more important, symbolically) behind him (Rutenberg & Zeleny, 2008).[12] Confined, literally and metaphorically, to one location in the room, VJs and the rest of the visual press would be unable to record anything but the image presented to them by the campaign.

Conflicts in the Field

What happens when photographers are denied permission to enter a location? In the cases presented here, [UJ] would not have had a story. His feature was based on a ride at the park and, without access, he would have had to pursue a different topic. Similarly, [LT] and [NC] would have had to adjust their story preconceptualizations; after all, [LT] had already done so once. She was originally assigned to interview members of the local Democratic Party about the primary; none were available for interviews and therefore none could be videotaped in their environment. [LT] adapted her assignment to cover "how *students* were talking about the primary," in part, because she was able to gain access to a school. Without permission to enter the historic building, [NC] could have shot exteriors of the architecture from a public space on the sidewalk, but without interviews from the people inside, she would not have had the sound bites considered essential for a scripted package. At most, the station might have run some images with narration from an anchor person (known as a voice-over) and [NC] would have been assigned a different story. [ES] had access to scene where the shooting occurred and a makeshift shrine on the sidewalk, both on public streets, so he could have proceeded without access inside the funeral home. Yet, because he was allowed inside the funeral home, he was able to refer to the scene in his script (and, some might believe, add an emotionally powerful element to a story about urban violence). In each of these cases, access—or lack thereof—played a role in the way a story is constructed.

There are times when a video story can be constructed in spite of efforts by intermediaries to block access. Photographic journalists choose from strategies that might include shooting scenes from a distance, shooting the blocked scene (i.e., "negotiations are taking place behind these closed doors"), deception, or obtaining video with help from another source. The VJs who allowed me to observe them followed one of the first two choices. When he arrived at a shooting scene, for example, [KN] was not able to get his camera close to the scene because it was cordoned off with police tape. He had to stay across the street, so he put the camera on the tripod and used his longer lens. To cross the line would have risked his relationship with the police department at best or, at worst, could have resulted in his arrest or the cancellation of his press badge. Even from this distance, he was able to shoot video of the police on the scene and of a woman who was apparently taken to a squad car for questioning. One of [KN]'s strategies for contending with officers who may try to overplay their power at a scene is to turn on the camera the moment he leaves the car, that way anything police say will be recorded. (He also believes officers are more sensitive to the possibility of being recorded on video, and since starting his work as a VJ, he says he hears the word "sir" a lot more often.)

[ES] had permission from the family to be inside the funeral home for a young shooting victim's service, but opted to gather more shots outside the funeral home—especially at a street shrine constructed for the victim, a familiar trope for urban violence. When he was interviewing students outside the victim's high school, however, [ES] hit a barrier. School security asked him to leave the sidewalk outside of the building. [ES] could have stood his ground and argued with the officer, since a sidewalk is a public thoroughfare, and one of the places photographers typically can count on being able to work freely. Instead, he explained later, he chose to not waste time in debate. He had already shot the sound bites he needed; it was past three o'clock in the afternoon, and the only element he still needed to shoot, his own standup, could be done from across the street.

In England, [EU] stood his ground on public property. Upon arriving near a construction site that was causing concern among its neighbors, a leader of the worksite approached [EU] and asked him to leave. [EU] explained that he was standing on public property and continued to work while the work site leader stood and watched.[13]

For appearance managers, conflicts in the field can often be handled at the very start, during discussions of the preconception. [BG] says it's rare but she has turned down requests to shoot video at the amusement park she represents:

> Every once in a while it happens and it may happen…maybe it's more of a [government agency] story, [and they're] trying to find anyone who will comment on that story. It's not appropriate to happen [here] and I would say you could go to get those man-on-the-street interviews somewhere else.

One strategy for getting around intermediaries when a long-term relationship is desirable is that of feigned and friendly ignorance. Sometimes, it's a matter of jovially talking one's way in. [MM] and her trainee attempted this technique on the day I observed them when their appointment at a fitness clinic was too late in the day to work within their deadlines. They arrived at the fitness clinic early—on their terms—and cordially asked to be allowed in. The public relations representative attempted to hold them to the schedule, but eventually compromised and allowed them in a bit earlier than they'd originally agreed upon.

Not all such conflicts are so easily diffused. Sometimes, they are physical, particularly in riot or demonstration situations when photographers and VJs clash with police. [KN] has had enough negative conversations with police at crime scenes that he now starts his camera as he walks up to a location. The most dangerous source of conflict for photographers and video journalists is not with professional intermediaries, however, but with angry or distraught subjects. Photo and video journalists have been punched, knocked over, even attacked with garden tools, by individuals in a rage. In fact, one of the BBC's health and safety rules discourages VJs from working alone outside of courthouses because of the frequency (and virulence) of such altercations.

Implications

The shared preconception of how a particular event ought to be narrativized serves the purposes of journalists and mediating sources. If each of these stakeholders is able to agree on a preconception, then it is possible to arrange for photo and video journalists to gain access to the elements required for story construction. Such arrangements, though, come at a price of image control, whether in the form of bodily access to some scenes and not others, technological controls such as pools and feeds, or corporeal controls within a space. The largely unspoken assumption of such arrangements is that video images are fungible, factual recordings of the world—that "video is video" and "sound is sound." The constructed nature of the video and sound is largely ignored.

Controlling photographic access makes it possible for appearance managers to influence the resulting images. They are able to decide which parts of a scene can be viewed by the public and which cannot, protecting their own self-interests in the name of privacy, order, and formality. The impact of such controls is not lost on video journalists who work under these conditions, but the requirement to obtain story elements trumps their desire for autonomy:

> [WB]: I'm in the news business so I'm going to put the camera wherever I can; it's kind of meat and potatoes. But you're talking about "Hollywood" in some ways there. I'm sure if you shoot someone low they're going to look more powerful; if you shoot someone high they're going to look weaker. So there are these things but to be honest I'm thinking of the story so much that I'm not even going on that path on a day-to-day thing.

When journalists are dependent upon such intermediaries for access to visual information, that dependence can cede control of the story to appearance managers whose stakes compete with those of journalists or the audience. The relationship grows over time because of a mutual dependence and the benefit each derives from one another. [BG] does her best to foster positive, friendly relationships with journalists, even as she carefully monitors what they do when on the property:

> We really try and balance it and we talk to the crews ahead of time and just explain that we're there to make sure they get what they need and that our visitors enjoy the experience and that is our job…I'm not expecting the film crew to really care that much about the visitors, that is my job. We balance that and usually works quite well and I think most of the crews walk away feeling like they've got special treatment.

Close working relationships and "special treatment" may be pleasant and not all that consequential in the short run for stories at a theme park. But over time, the relationship between journalists and appearance managers can make it easy to forget and neglect the stakeholder who is not physically present—the audience. Journalistic convention does not require that journalists explain the source of their video or the circumstances under which it was shot; video is treated as "fact," not as a constructed artifact. Scripts rarely include information about pooling arrangements or positional requirements, for to do so would undermine the indexical authority of news images. This lack of transparency with regard to the ontology of the video shores up the claims to authority by journalists or, as Krippendorff writes, locates power at the source of transmission:

> To conceive as a transmission from another place or time a violent news episode on television, for example, or a political speech heard on the radio, surely entails the ontological claim of representational accuracy or at least the absence of intentional biases and locates the evidence that could validate this claim in a reality outside the receivers' reach. This puts the receivers of such supposedly neutral messages at the mercy of the authority of the information suppliers who successfully claim privileged access to the very reality that the notion of transmission denies its receivers. Thus power metaphors objectify power by locating it at the source of transmission. (1989: p. 184)

The opacity of the source-journalist interaction is rooted in their shared preconception of the story. When an event is preconceived as part of a television show, the show and its format prevail through the rest of the process. Journalists work to obtain the components needed for a show, rather than let events unfold. By granting journalists those components in a sort of information subsidy, appearance managers are able to influence the nature of those components: deciding which parts of a scene can be viewed by the public and which cannot.

Members of Parliament, their staff, and those physically present for the session may witness the pre-session prayers, but the general public watching on television cannot. Members of Congress, aware of the rules for when a microphone can be on or off, are free to have one kind of social interaction for the benefit of the news audience, and an entirely different interaction in front of those present in the room. If a reporter's preconceptualization required that then-Supreme Court Justice Nominee Samuel Alito answer questions about abortion or civil rights, for example, not only would they have been unable to collect that sound bite (such ceremonial photo ops discourage, if not outright forbid, questioning), but they might have been disinvited from the press tour that day. In Washington, [WB] says he has seen how the pooled photo opportunity system discourages difficult questions:

> You know, people do get one-on-ones [direct interviews] with the candidates but it's always—they pick the journalist that's going to be the nicest and not the ones that ask the hard questions, and as a result the whole White House, this is a good point, all the White House press reporters, they're so scared of covering the president because if they ask any tough questions, they lose their privileges. I mean they lose access. And it's all about access.

The result of the system is something one handler calls "scripted spontaneity." Participants know most of what will occur in front of the cameras and participate in familiar routines.

> [KL]: Scripted spontaneity is always what we have here. The photographers are always pushing for that real moment. Does it do a disservice to the public? Yeah, because they get a warped sense of what's going on…It definitely manifests itself… when they [tourists] come and watch the Senate in person…they're used to watching on television and on television there's a Senate camera, it's not these many cameras, it's the Senate camera that's controlled by the Senate. They can only show one image. They're very tightly controlled about what image they can show. It's mostly one Senator talking on the floor. So when you're watching on TV, you just assume that everybody else is out on the floor listening to this guy. And you come into the chamber, everyone's stunned to find out that he's talking to an empty chamber.

[WB] believes that voters would have different political views if only they knew what he witnessed at political events:

> Basically as a journalist when you go to these things, when you go to the campaigns around the country, you're so limited on what you see and what you cover, it is just a complete joke. And if the American people were in my back pocket and they saw what I saw, they would a) think this is not a democracy, this is a total joke. It's a stage show.

A longtime network photographer described an incident during which he, as the pool camera photographer, disobeyed the rules in order to expose an event's theatricality.[14]

> [GP]: I was in a hearing, it was a confirmation hearing for a Supreme Court justice…[Two Senators] came into the room and they got into an argument about what one promised the other one and that "you wasn't [*sic*] gonna do this" and "I'll be damned if I'm going to let you do this to me 'cause you promised not to do this." Well, C-SPAN wanted to cut the mikes because they were instructed to. I told them I was the pool camera—you're not cutting the mikes, I'm rolling on this, and instructed my sound person to get his mike if C-SPAN cut the microphone off. Well C-SPAN left it up and C-SPAN stopped recording. I recorded it. I called the desk, my desk editor who handles the Hill, and I told…[him] he should check this out immediately. He checked it out; it turned out to be the lead of everybody's network news broadcast. How the back room dealing goes on, but yet when the hearing started, they were like best friends. But, you know, everybody used their argument beforehand because the mikes were open. After that C-SPAN was instructed never to have any mikes open.

Such a highly scripted and ceremonial environment not only repackages events according to the needs of those controlling the situation, but results in relatively mundane "off script" moments being presented as news, as when President George W. Bush became ill at a state dinner or bumped his head on an airplane door. When I asked how such stories serve democracy, or whether the voting public would somehow suffer if not presented with news about the president bumping his head, three network photographers were unable to answer. They didn't seem to understand my question. Such an emphasis on getting an image, any image, in order to provide material for a program, runs counter to the normative journalistic function as a gatekeeper, a responsible reporter of happenings. One veteran TV photographer went so far as to say there is no gate anymore: the news is a mere conduit, an assessment that was documented by Williams and Delli Carpini (2000) in the wake of the Bill Clinton-Monica Lewinsky sex scandal.

It is true that some controls are essential for the basic functioning of governmental activity. When hundreds of camera-bodies are following the president, or when a scrum of photographers is covering a hearing, it makes sense for their activities to be organized. Further, there are situations where the photographic press has no place; even public officials deserve privacy and time out of the public eye. Yet the rules of engagement for photographers and image managers often are not rooted in privacy concerns but image concerns. The rules create a separate class of elites, possibly journalists, other officials, and those lucky enough to be physically present for an occasion—and the news audience. Blocking the video of the House of Lords at prayer does not protect the privacy of the Lords; after all, they, their staff, and all manner of tourists in the Palace of Westminster are able to witness the prayers; the news audience does not. Requiring that microphones be turned on only during those portions of a hearing that are part of the "record" delivers only the staged portions of Congressional activity and little of the deal-making, arm-twisting, and personal interaction that go into making law.

The lack of transparency about how and why events are presented supports journalistic claims to authority, but runs counter to the norm of public service. To use Krippendorff's phrase, the audience is "at the mercy" of those whose system constructs discourse with claims to realism. The result, as Stuart Hall (1973a) noted decades ago, is a system by which elite authority is reproduced and may be at the root of the general distrust of media on the part of many members of the news audience. [NZ] believes the public understands that there is a game underway:[15]

> Well I think the fact that everybody knows what a photo op is and everybody knows what a sound bite is…which basically made pretty much everybody kind of cynical, I think. I mean…even my son was like, "Oh yeah, he just said that. That's just a sound bite, Dad." I think it's something that Americans are very aware of.

Cultural scholar Jeff Jones, in his study of comic news programs, believes that part of the appeal of *The Daily Show* and its imitators is that it breaks down the *fourth wall*, or illusions of authority created by television news fakery (Jones, 2005). As video journalism gives more nonprofessionals the ability to participate in the digital public sphere, more members of the audience are able to see around that fourth wall. There are indications that in some situations, video journalism is changing the rules of engagement between appearance managers and photographic journalists, if not the game itself.

Singularity & Expansion: Changing the Rules

Many of the norms for regulating camera-bodies, with one set of rules for still cameras and another for video, are based in conventions that are quickly disintegrating. Now that high-end, digital still cameras such as the Nikon D-90 can record short video clips, such distinctions are irrelevant. Subjects report advantages and disadvantages to the currently confused climate. [KN] says his freedom to move around at sporting events is limited now that he is classified as a video-photographer. But [TH] had more than one fortuitous moment during the 2008 presidential primary campaign when she found herself able to choose whether to stand with the video-photographers or the still photographers based on which had a better vantage point for the subject, not based on the type of camera she carried. Her very small video camera allowed her access to the often closer positions set aside for still photographers. Such crossover situations are few, and the intermediaries interviewed for this project were not as concerned about how to divide stills and video photography as much as how to contend with the new approaches to storytelling.

The appearance managers who participated in this project are already contending with video journalism's two distinctive features of singularity and expansion. More journalists and nonjournalists are using technologies that not only create filmic stories but easily distribute them to the world, and as they do so, they are experimenting with form. Transitioning video journalists, especially those working for newspapers or citizen organizations, don't necessarily share television's conventional preconceptions of what a filmic news story should look like. Because the shared preconception is an image manager's source of influence, this shift is inspiring changes in their work routines.

New Technologies & the Rules of Engagement

If a shared preconception is the basis for a mutually beneficial relationship between VJs and intermediaries, what happens when the preconception changes? New approaches to narrative—by newspaper VJs reinventing filmic news or by citizens committing journalistic acts outside of the conventional boundaries of professional news—are doing just that. Until now, intermediaries could influence coverage through their understanding of the needs of TV journalists. New media forms of exhibition are creating a new game:

> [LM]: News outlets want to get a news story that…tells an important story, or that tells a story that is interesting to viewers, but they also want to be first, so those digital cameras in this day and age, you can take a video, download it to your computer, plug in your air card, and upload it to your website—all within an hour of something happening—and so everybody's using these things now and from my role as the communications director…it creates a whole new set of challenges to the extent that I have to provide content now for a whole new array of video cameras.
>
> So whereas it used to be that, um, I would get, you know, maybe two or three phone calls from somebody at the [local newspaper] during this campaign, I got eight to ten phone calls from people…because not only did I get the calls from the people writing for the print edition, but I also got the calls from people writing for the website, but also people posting video to the website. And so it creates a whole new layer of responsibilities for me and it makes it harder for the campaign.

For [LM] and [DX], the difficulty was not simply a matter of more cameras and journalists, but that some of the camera-wielding journalists wanted to tell different stories than traditional TV journalists did. One of the more unusual requests for campaign coordinator [LM] was from a *Wall Street Journal* reporter who wanted to create a web video story about romances that blossom on the campaign trail. [DX], who has decades of experience in news and in political communication, found the emerging preconceptions of a news story disconcerting:

> I just don't have as much confidence as necessary in the people doing the interview as when you have that big camera from the TV station, and the reporter in a suit or the nice dress and you say OK, I know what's the object here, I know it's going to be edited, so I also know when I'm speaking in my sound bites, and I say my sound bite three or four times, odds are pretty good that my sound bite is what's going to be on there. They're looking for a sound bite.
>
> Whereas the people with the little camera, they just kind of want to get…all the time, whatever, they like that raw footage sort of a thing, and I experienced…that when people would come in and I'd be in my office until midnight, and…I was

> thrown for a loop, 'cause a couple of times, [it was] "Oh, well I've got my camera with me and so I'm just going to get you here with you and your hat and...the potato chips that you're not supposed to be eating and all this mess that your office looks like." I'm more interested in capturing this realistic sort of mess, "You look haggard and so tell me about whatever." I always felt much more exposed by the little camera than I did with the big camera.

Intermediaries who don't work in the cutthroat world of political campaigns note a difference in video journalism's approach, but do not see it as a problem so much as an additional element in their work routine. [NX] says that these days he only knows to expect a video camera to arrive for an interview when he's working with a television station because newspaper VJs don't necessarily explain that they'll need video when negotiating for access—they simply arrive with one. [EC] makes no distinction between the photographers who carry conventional cameras and VJs using the small ones. He jokes that he hasn't noticed any difference in the way news is gathered: "You get good questions and you get stupid questions. I mean you get that no matter what, honestly. No, it hasn't changed one bit." A major market freelance PR representative, [OA], similarly sees no difference:

> Video is video. It's got to be compelling; it has to help disseminate the message in the way that you want to disseminate the message and it has to be a good visual...I don't approach anything without thinking about who the end user is and the end user is the audience.

Other intermediaries do see a difference with some of the VJs and their storytelling style, and the way those stories are associated with new forms of exhibition. [EP], for instance, sees a similarity to radio:

> It's just a little less techie, you don't have all the lights and all of that to make up, it's just a grimier, grittier, like a grittier feel to it, especially when you see it on people's websites. You'll go on [a local news website] and see some of these things up there, someone goes to a scene of an auto accident, that's the same sort of feel it's going to have, a lot closer to the ground.
>
> I've seen them done and they they're just, almost identical to doing radio interviews. You know that when you do the radio, they sit down, they put the microphone in front of you, and they push the button and you know everything you say is now live. So it's essentially the same thing, the same feeling, except for they can see you—so you obviously gotta sit up.

Yet, while [EP] knows that there's likely to be a difference in the form a VJ story takes and how it might be exhibited, he has come to consider any video camera a window to the entire world, not a tie to a television station.

He makes no differentiation between large and small cameras, or a VJ's ties to an organization. If a video camera is present at an event, [EP]'s boss, the mayor, treats it as though it were sending a signal live to the entire world. This adds stress to everyday interactions in public, but it is the essential response to the current environment. Other political intermediaries are taking a similar stance.

Corporate representative [NX] noted that he has to be more careful than ever to control his message. He says that he's worked with some video-photographers who are there only to shoot video and are not all that invested in the entire story because it will be written by another journalist. He's also encountered newspaper VJs who conduct a customary in-depth interview with a notepad, then pull out a small video camera and ask for sound bites to be repeated for a web production. With more than 20 years' experience, [NX] is comfortable with the changes, but worries about the executives he represents:

> It's easier when you're acting as the spokesperson—much harder as intermediary that's trying to prepare an executive. The people involved become uneasy. They don't know how it will play out.

[BG] has already noticed that she is interviewed differently for web-centered video journalism stories. She says that the web interviews are less conversational and require her to carry a bit more of the narrative burden—something she interprets as an opportunity to tell her company's story her way. The smaller cameras' ease of use and expanded access so far has not troubled her efforts to protect the interests of the park. She's aware that guests are bringing in video cameras and post material to *YouTube*, performing journalistic acts even though they may not be thinking of themselves as journalists at all.

> They put together home movies, if you will. They put together their own videos and load 'em up on *YouTube*, "My trip to [the park]." So we now monitor those. Granted, once it's on *YouTube* we may not actually be able to do anything directly about that, but we monitor just to see how many hits are they getting. What are the comments? Anything.
>
> *(Are they good for you?)*
>
> I think so. I see a lot of positive things…very favorable. I should say, "Visiting here is fun!"

Because the typical nonjournalist is using videos to create a particular type of story for the web—in this case, a happy travelogue story—she is able to adjust her work routines accordingly. At the same time, she knows there is a risk that someone could easily use a small video camera to create an unflattering story. Security guards at the park are instructed to look for equipment that looks professional and to alert her. She also monitors the web for mentions of her employer. Taken together, singularity of practice and expanded participation are making an impact on the source-journalist story preconception. Appearance managers may ultimately lose some control over the image. Changing technologies may inspire different regulations about how and where anyone might be able to use a camera.

Video Journalism as a New Game

The spread of video technologies to users who are not professional journalists bypasses the business-as-usual relationship between sources and journalists. No longer is there an exclusive game with mutual benefits. Citizen VJs and nonprofessionals who occasionally commit journalistic acts are free not to merely break the rules, but to invent an entirely different game. As more individuals participate in video journalism—that is, as the number of camera-bodies proliferates—it becomes much harder to regulate where and how they operate.

Recall [KN]'s desire to cover nothing that required a credential; many of the citizen journalists do not have credentials, but are able to participate in the public sphere by working where they can—what might be called "street level" newsgathering. One example of street-level video journalism came from a citizen journalist on the West Coast who interviewed people outside of an event; he did not have credentials. The well-reasoned, articulate sound bite, lasting more than 13 minutes, spread like wildfire across the internet (Carr, 2008). The citizen journalist, who has in the past volunteered with community access television but is not associated with any particular organization, communicated with me via e-mail. He shoots video when he's interested, and won't bother if the weather is too hot or too cold. In an e-mail, he wrote that one of his challenges is simply the mechanics of internet uploading:

> [UM]: For the debate vids I just walked up and down Hollywood Blvd questioning people and got a total of 2 hrs 43 mins. I wanted people to see this before the primary election so I upload the first three vids that would fit on *YouTube* without editing that night. I was tired—trust me. 100 MB and 10 minute limit sucks, plus it's slow as hell uploading on DSL. It took several hours.

From the tone with which [UM] questions the young man supporting Obama, it's evident that [UM]'s political views run counter to those gathered outside the democratic debate. Yet, he still put his subject in what turned out to be a positive spotlight:

> It is truly amazing that a little snippet has gone around the world and inspired so many people in so many different ways.
>
> Derrick is an amazing man and was perfect for interviewing in this style—of on-camera debate and letting the talking points he was prepared to speak about convey the message, and not being put off by the fast-paced, deep questioning or taking it as a personal attack.
>
> After watching this video, I see where I could have asked so many more questions and could have had a very good discussion of both of our ideas on this particular subject and come away with something workable. He is the kind of guy I would like to sit around with, in the coffee shop of the old days, and discuss the topic of the day. Knowing that in the end, "Gentlemen can always come to an agreement" [to] quote from the Tom Hanks miniseries *John Adams*.

The response to his video upload may have been a surprise to [UM], but his description of a subsequent incident reflects what leaders in the citizen journalism community advocate, namely that new technologies make it possible for greater participation in the public sphere:

> I am amazed at all the press, blog, and television coverage this little conversation on the street has generated. I was just speaking to another young man the other day and said he should get involved in politics and what's going on. His response was, "I'm not interested in politics. I'm street, pure street." My response was that he should still speak his ideas because you never know whose ears they will fall on. This video kind of proves the point.

Street-level reporting reflects the very sort of "under the skin" style of filmic journalism the BBC has tried to encourage amongst its video journalists. It avoids the theater of staged news events and seeks out characters—people who are affected by news—rather than elites protecting their stakes. By not playing the game that mutually benefits professional journalists and intermediaries, such an approach breaks down the fourth wall and equalizes members of the system. As more individuals participate in the creation and sharing of filmic news, this change shifts the larger discourse from a monologic, declarative form to one that is more dialogic, propositional, and conversational. Intermediaries will no doubt endeavor to find new ways to control the discourse according to their interests, yet the monopoly on video discourse that intermediaries once shared with television journalists is crumbling.

Summary

This chapter has examined the way the source-journalist relationship evolves in the context of video news production. A video journalist's essential need for physical access, on top of the well-known metaphorical, informational access, gives intermediaries an extra means of controlling the way stories are told. The corporeal element of video newsgathering, coupled with the cognitive impact of the visual, compound the effects of an image manager's influence. The source of power for intermediaries in their relationship with television journalists, and now video journalists, has been in a shared preconception of the story. By finding ways to assist the photographic press in its desire to gather certain elements for news stories, those elements can be shaped according to the needs of the image manager's interests. But the effects of video journalism's singularity and expansion are changing the way intermediaries work to control the images they're paid to protect.

In this chapter, I relied on interviews and observations from years of research, but it is colored by my own years in the field. As I wrote in the notes, I myself witnessed legislators committing the "grill and kiss" turnaround when the cameras were on and then turned off. I have also been held essentially captive to camera platforms and no-petting zones, unable to gather information from other angles on location. So, while I have done my best to root my descriptions of these phenomena in the present study, I must be honest about having had similar experiences during my professional life.

I am aware that I may seem to display a bias on behalf of news photographers—especially in their roles as proxies for the public—so at this point I must acknowledge their less attractive tendencies. Especially when working in large groups, photographers carrying all manner of cameras can indeed be rude, loud, and insensitive to the people they cover. Sometimes they do disrupt events when they set up microphones and place lights in a room. There is no question that a certain amount of camera regulation makes sense. My argument is not that photographers and VJs need sympathy, but that we as scholars, and the audience, need knowledge of how they work, the ontogenesis of news images, and how the circumstances surrounding their construction and the social forces that influence that construction can literally shape the way we see the world.

The process of video journalism poses unique challenges for its practitioners. It is forcing news organizations to rethink their approaches to news, and is changing the relationship between journalists and their sources. The past three chapters have detailed the ways the process itself is changing. To better understand how the changed processes affect the product, it is necessary to switch to a different form of analysis—one that involves carefully examining the content and structure the narratives themselves.

NOTES:

1. cf. (Gandy Jr., 1982)
2. Senator Edward Kennedy, who was in the Senate from 1962 to 2009.
3. An unconfirmed rumor suggests that the system in the White House started after a large group of TV photographers clustered around the desk of President Bill Clinton and spilled something or broke something in the Oval Office.
4. A 2007 research census of statehouses in the US found that a majority of state legislatures were covered either by dedicated cable coverage, public broadcasting coverage, or internet video streaming.
5. During the 2005 hearings regarding Major League Baseball and steroids, several nonmember organizations tried to sneak into the hub room to take the signal; while Senate gallery coordinators are technically in charge of preventing such infractions, in this instance, one of the project's C-SPAN informants objected, and asked them to leave.
6. Colonel Oliver North's testimony during the Iran-Contra hearings are an illustration of why the camera angle on the witness is important; at that time, cameras were larger and placed below the table's level—so they would not stand between the witness and the panel. Arthur Limon, the chief counsel for the Senate's special committee later wrote that Steven Spielberg called this the "hero's" angle. (Limon, 1998)
7. Who, in 1603, was caught in the cellar of Parliament with 36 barrels of gunpowder in an apparent attempt to overthrow the government, and was subsequently executed.
8. http://www.parliament.uk/commons/lib/beef.htm.
9. A device that allows multiple audio recorders to access a microphone signal, and provides broadcast-quality sound when a camera is physically wired in.
10. During one observational visit, ceremonial picture-taking took an entire hour at the start of the council session.
11. A term used for news coverage, as opposed to paid media (i.e., advertising).
12. Leaders of the campaign quickly apologized to the two women, calling the action by volunteers at the event "a mistake." (Rutenberg & Zeleny, 2008)
13. While my presence on observations undoubtedly always affects the observed, in this case I could sense my own effect. I introduced myself after [EU] did, and got the impression that the work leader didn't want to escalate an argument in front of a researcher—or a researcher who happened to be female. I also engaged in a short, friendly conversation with the worksite leader during the few minutes [EU] shot through the fence.
14. During my time as a professional journalist, I witnessed a similar incident in which a prominent Senator harshly grilled a witness who was a prominent businessman during the hearing when the cameras were rolling, but then, smiled and glad-handed the witnesses after the hearing when the cameras were off. This incident, and the one [GP] describes, took place in plain view in a public setting.

15. Recall also the incident described in Chapter Three in which a woman from a burnt-out apartment building volunteered to shoot stills inside her home with a cell phone, and knew that the various story elements would be edited into a story, or in her words, "cropped up."

Chapter Six:
The Product

"Only that which narrates can make us understand."

—Susan Sontag

Introduction

There is a point in every project where the researcher must answer the question, "*num curae es aliquis*?" or, more plainly, "who cares?" So far, this book has revealed the way the process of video journalism, while varying according to organizational context, is developing as a unique form of newsgathering. But aside from those who are affected by the concerns and challenges of this practice, who cares? Does this new process change what news consumers experience? This is the second question that inspired and guided my research; specifically, "How, if at all, does the product of video journalism as practiced by news organizations differ from other forms of filmic news?"

Technology's relationship with journalism has not simply granted news workers new methods by which to create the same types and styles of stories. Chapter One identified the ways new technologies have often been accompanied by changes in what is defined as news, as well as the style in which stories are told. Video journalism presents two characteristics that might be expected to change the form of its product: expanded participation and singular production. As more individuals adopt video journalism, whether as professional news workers or as citizens, how might this affect the way stories are crafted? With only one person shooting, writing, and editing a story, how might a narrative's authorship be manifest in a VJ story? These questions about structure and authorship guide the organization of this chapter.

Video Narrative Analysis

Two dimensions of narrative structure are relevant here: first, the way that video is used to construct the story itself—its use of diegesis and mimesis,[1] and the arrangement of narrative components, such as character, setting, and action; and second, authorship is of special interest here because of the nature of news—journalists present themselves as a special category of authors who purport to honestly report on witnessed happenings. This declarative mode is a matter of journalistic practice, as Zelizer has described, but it is also a discursive function. Both of these dimensions stand to be altered by the processes of video journalism in that the new technologies make it possible to show scenes differently, increasing the reliance of mimesis in a story; and in that one person—working as the shooter, writer, producer, and editor—has new options for establishing authorship and the journalistic authority that comes with it.

The analysis that follows blends three strands of scholarship that are helpful in understanding filmic narrative: Discourse Analysis, Film Rhetoric, and Narratology. Discourse analysis looks for the way various interests are reflected in the language of news and the way journalists presume to make declarative statements about a set of circumstances. The tradition of film scholarship provides a vocabulary for interpreting composition, lighting, camera angle, and other cinematic components. Film scholars also note the importance of the connections between one or more images and the way meaning might be constructed in their linkages. Finally, structural narratology provides a conceptualization for identifying various narrative components, such as character, setting, action, and conflict, as well as the various layers of authorship: known, presumed, and "visible." The complication for video journalism is that authors might be known and visible, but they might also be unknown and heard. Some video journalists believe that the smaller cameras and singular nature of their work allows them to change the typical news narrative to one that is more intimate and mimetic than distant and diegetic. This analysis attempts to clarify how this might be manifest in a filmic story. Here's how someone who trains VJs for the BBC describes it:

> [MM]: I was explaining this…in the sense of a bubble…reporters on television, it's [like] they almost stand on the outside of the bubble and say look, that's what's going on in that story. I don't want you to stand there and point and tell me that's what's going on in the bubble. As a viewer, I want to be in there, and I want to know what's happening, and the best people to tell me what's happening to the people that are in the bubble. The restrictions with news is I have to be able to get that across in 90 seconds and a lot of the time you can't get people to say it in 90 seconds, so that's when I will voice it, I will introduce a line, but most of my pieces are predominantly

> people, other people, telling the bits of the story because, "Who gives a damn who I am?"

A veteran of Video News International, who is now teaching emerging video journalists, believes that the singular nature of the work will change the way filmic news is presented:

> [CH]: I think the style is going to change. I think that the whole model not only implies but necessitates a more intimate contact with the subject matter by the video journalist. In the best of cases, this VJ will be intimately knowledgeable of the subject that he she is covering…I think this can be a much more effective means of covering issues than the typical or traditional means of using a filter—a correspondent to interpret things. I think video journalism has a potential to give viewers a… truer version of reality than the old model of tools or cameras and the message filtered through so-called correspondents.

Indeed, some practitioners and trainers strongly encourage VJs to use their smaller cameras and less imposing equipment so as to depart from the familiar conventions of television news, and create film stories that incorporate more mimesis than diegesis—to get out of the way and let stories "tell themselves," and to (in the vernacular of video-photographers) "let the story breathe." Their arguments reflect a debate within the documentary film community over the degree to which a filmmaker can let a story tell itself, a mimetic ideal considered by some to be more easily accomplished with a singular producer:

> Shooting one-person restores the possibility of kinship. The filmmaker doesn't carry on with "his people" in front of "his subjects." The dichotomy those labels reveal, in the filmmaker himself, is gone along with the crew…The filmmaker becomes another human being in the room.[2]

How does this translate into practice? At the BBC, trainers using the Rosenblum model encouraged VJs to rely on interesting "characters," people who could be interviewed and essentially sum up the story from start to finish. One resulting story from this technique turned into an unlikely lead[3] for a local newscast: an interview with the mother of an autistic child. The story revealed the difficulties faced by such parents in Britain, but this particular piece was told entirely by one mother, whose voice was accompanied by images of her home, her child, and her daily struggles to keep both under control. Another BBC VJ story that incorporated a compelling "character" was built upon one interview with a senior citizen who once worked at a local factory. The main point of this story was the demolition of the factory building, but the VJ used the sound from this one man to create the narrative.

In keeping with the tendency of journalists to look to each other for clues about what to cover, successful, character-driven stories inspired other BBC trainees to seek out other pathos-ridden situations. [EN] says the trend went to an extreme:

> It's good if you find a good character, but then there's a danger that you end up making kind of freak show television, where you're just looking out for people with strange afflictions and diseases...We went through a phase where, "Well, look at this person." People who were on death's door, who were morbidly obese or anorexic. It was real kind of freak show stuff. We don't do it so much now but we, immediately post-Rosenblum, we definitely had a period of putting weirdoes on the telly just because they were supposed to be interesting characters.

A BBC executive concurred that the point of searching for characters is not to create "victim TV," but to seek out people involved with the current events of the day whose experience is reflective of the human condition. By interviewing the people affected by the news, a story's authority can be based on individuals attesting to their own truth, rather than having it recited by an outsider.

Video stories have multiple layers of information, i.e., the sound, scripted narrative, and visuals. Consequently, the shift from diegesis to mimesis—from it is not a binary distinction, but a matter of degree. The shift might involve a change in literary voice from third person to first, or it might eliminate the spoken narrative entirely. It might involve longer shots with sound from the scene that draw a viewer in, utilizing pauses to establish a scene instead of a spoken phrase. The still photographers transitioning to video who assisted with this project tend to favor the mimetic approach, in part because it draws from their visual and technical skills, but also because they have long operated as hidden journalistic authors.

Comparing VJ Narratives

To better understand how a changed process might affect video journalism's product, I carefully examined six stories produced by the VJs portrayed in the preceding chapters: two from VJs working for television organizations, two from VJs employed by newspapers, and two stories from citizen journalists. The stories are analyzed according to the two dimensions discussed above, namely their narrative structure, and the means by which they signal authorship. In my examination of structure, I considered those linkages, as well as the nature and variety of visual scenes employed by the VJ. I looked at camera angle, composition, audio components (NATSOT, sound bites, etc.), and the use of graphic elements. I examined the way settings, characters, and actions are presented, and the editing technique used for transitions. In short, I looked for elements that might reflect differences in shooting technique that might be indicative of a single person working with a small camera. The stories in their entirety are classified according to Nichols' six-category typology (namely, Poetic, Performative, Observational, Expository, Reflexive, or Participatory), but this is just one dimension of the analysis. I have also broken down the stories and analyzed their components using a set of functional categories. These five functional categories include:

- Showing (Mimesis/Scene and Action): Imagery without language, possibly with natural sound or music
- Eliciting (Mimesis/Characters): Interview sound that displays the questioning of a journalist without the sound or appearance of the journalist
- Declaring (Diegesis, i.e., explaining and describing): Scripted narrative spoken by a VJ, using the third-person language of conventional news discourse
- Performing (combination of Mimesis and Diegesis): Visual or aural presentation by the VJ in which it is evident that he or she is actively participating in the story
- Reflecting (Diegesis): First-person language in a narrated script by the VJ that reflects an awareness of their role in the constructive process

For my analysis of authorship, I examined the stories according to these dimensions:

- How is authorship presented (heard, seen, presumed)?
- Who is presented as the author?
- What cues exist regarding visual and textual authorship?
- Does the story include reflexive cues that make the author and her process known?
- What language is used by the narrator to address the viewer?

Taken together, these parameters—looking at structure, authorship, and the way they operate in combination—allow for an analysis that is systematic yet acknowledges the complexity of filmic journalism.

I borrowed heavily from Kracauer's (1947) system to create maps of video stories that would help with this analysis. *Figure 6.1* represents a portion of one such map. To interpret it, start by reading down the column

Function	Voice	Script	Linkage	Image	Graphics	Sound under
S	Reporter	Healing hands	↔	cu hands	Added effects	Music
				face		
				feet		
				hands		
D		The art and science of a physiotherapist can work wonders.	↔	MS with physiotherapist face, pan to patient		
		But while there's no shortage of people wanting to take it up as a vocation,		WS massage		
		the chances of a job are slim		MS massage new angle (from below)		
		This is Mai		Mai walks down steps	None	
		She's currently a part-time secretary, which is fine,		Mai walks toward camera		
		but it's not what she spent the last three years training for.		Mai, new angle, walking		
E	Subject (Mai)	Um, there's about 73, 74 of us graduating this year, in the summer 2007. And as far as I know, there's one person who's got a job doing part time work down in Salisbury in a private practice so…not looking good.		Mai, interview shot; faces screen left	Lower title	
D	Reporter	The NHS pays for students to take the course at nearly 30-thousand pounds a head.		group of students	None	None

Figure 6.1: Physiotherapy jobs, runs 2:51

marked "Script." It contains the audio information that comprises the spoken narrative. The column on the left, labeled "Function," indicates the apparent narrative role that that section of the story fulfills, according to the scheme described, whether declaring, eliciting, showing, and so forth. The second column, "Voice," indicates the aural origin of the narrative, whether it is the VJ, an interviewed subject, or language recorded naturally from the scene. The column labeled "Image" describes what is seen. The columns marked "Graphics" and "Sound under" describe what kind of text or graphical information is visible and whether there is any background sound. Finally, in the center, there is a column labeled "Linkage," which indicates whether the script and image are meaningfully connected. If there is no square for the link, that means that the script and image are synchronized on the tape: you hear the speaker as she is speaking. A dark black double arrow ↔ indicates that the script is directly referring to what is shown in the image. A grey one indicates an implied connection between what is discussed and what is seen. If the Linkage column is grey, it means that there is no meaningful connection between what is said and what is shown, and the visual and aural streams of information are unrelated. The small black diamonds along the center columns ◆ indicate ten-second intervals, representing the story's temporal pacing.

For example, in *Figure 6.1*, the column marked Voice indicates that we hear the reporter speak. His words are transcribed in the column labeled Script. The words we hear provide the preliminary explanation of what we see: the healing hands of a physiotherapist. The reporter's voice guides us through most of the story using declarative language, as marked by the "D" in the column labeled Function. Reading down the column marked Image explains what we see in the story: hands of a physiotherapist, a face, a man on a table receiving a massage, and so on. The column marked Graphics indicates whether we see text or other graphical elements—alone or layered onto the video. The column marked Sound under indicates whether music or NATSOT (ambient sound from the scene, not spoken words) can be heard. In this story, the center column is often filled in with grey, indicating that the scripted words of the reporter are usually disconnected from what we see.

It is crucial, in the course of this analysis, to not forget the socially constructed nature of the process that brought forth these stories. The stakeholder networks, within which the various VJs worked, shape the way narratives are structured; how authorship and its partner, authority, are established; and how new technologies are deployed. The workplace routines for one newsroom may influence story structure more than the affordances presented by smaller, lighter cameras, or, for example, a VJ's previous experience as a still photographer (one who is accustomed to anonymity) might lead him to prefer establishing authorship by implication rather than performance.

Physiotherapy

I accompanied the reporter who produced this story for part of his shooting, and was present when he shot illustrative video (B-ROLL) of a man receiving a therapeutic massage for back pain in a physiotherapist's[4] office, and an interview with the administrator of a university physiotherapy program. He produced this story with the tape collected on the day I shadowed him, along with video shot previously. He'd been granted about three days to complete this story, so it was not a daily turnaround piece. The story's essential message is that the national health system in Britain is paying for the education of physiotherapists for whom no jobs exist.

Elements & Structure. Only twice does the script directly reference the video (indicated by the ↔ symbol), and one of those times the reference is somewhat indirect—when he opens the story by saying "healing hands." There is no reference to the woman to whom those hands belong, no explanation of who the man on the massage table is or why he's there, and no explication of the circumstances under which this video was shot. The story is built largely with images of students walking around the Northumbria University campus and, while at one point the story refers to "students," it is never made clear whether any of the students depicted is a physiotherapy student, or how these people walking around might have anything to do with the story.

The piece incorporates some special effects editing, though no "video grabs" or stills. It does, however, use a textual graphic when quoting the government's response. There is music, too, at the beginning of the piece, adding a sense of style and urgency. The music sets this story apart as something more highly produced or "special" than a day-of or spot-news item. The entire piece is written in third-person language; there is no "I" and no "you." There are very few direct linkages or references to specific shots. Finally, the video is shot quite conventionally; there are no pans, zooms, or shaky shots that call attention to the photography.

Authorship. What is most notable about this story is that the VJ never appears—not even his hands are seen holding a microphone. We only hear his disembodied voice. He does not even sign off with his name. The story itself contains no cues that the narrator is the author of the piece, though this is implied during the program by the presenter's introduction that the report is "from" a BBC journalist. The story in no way hints that the narrator was the photographer of the piece, nor is there any indication that the narrator himself personally witnessed the recorded material. There are no reflexive cues about the construction of the story; for instance, the reporter does not explain that the story was shot over the course of more than one day, that it was necessary to request access to the physical therapist's offices, and so on.

The story places nearly all of its rhetorical energy into a declarative vocal script and uses images as a somewhat disconnected background, constituting an iconic example of Nichols' expository form. While the VJ is never seen, it was presented as part of a BBC newscast in which an anchor introduced the story, implying that it was the work of the speaker-narrator. The story's primary narrative mode is declarative. The VJ presents information in a third-person, authoritative manner that presumptively states information as fact without reflexivity.

Love Canal Anniversary

As with the Physiotherapy story, I was able to observe the VJ who created the Love Canal Anniversary story on the day he produced it. Also in common with the Physiotherapy story, the Love Canal Anniversary story was part of a daily television newscast, and it was not shot entirely by the VJ—some video was gathered by a video-photographer who covered the news conference before the VJ arrived on the scene.

Elements & Structure. Of the six stories examined here, the Love Canal Anniversary story is among the shortest, running precisely two minutes. It uses short declarative sentences in the expository language typical of television news discourse. There are no visual or spoken reflexive components; this story purports to "tell it like it is" without any acknowledgment of its human-centered construction. It uses the conventions of objectivity identified long ago by Molotch and Lester (1974) in that it incorporates sound bites from representatives of two sides of an issue—in this case, the woman who led the fight to help people move away from what turned out to be a highly toxic waste site, and a man who has been involved in helping to resettle parts of the neighborhood. The VJ made a priority of tracking down this second interview, waiting nearly a half hour to reach the man, then driving nearly another hour to the man's office, all in an effort to add what journalists would call balance—or narrativists would call conflict—to the story.

Perhaps what is most remarkable about the structure of this story lies in the column marked Linkage. Note that at the start of the story, the script closely matches the visuals; there is a connection three times in a row wherein the VJ calls attention to the empty lots, the irrelevant stop sign, and so on. Later, though, visuals appear without such clear explanation. Historical video of the Love Canal neighborhood is shown with snow on the ground (the story aired in the summer); historic file footage of activist Lois Gibbs is shown with scripting that implies its history. The script ruled the story's construction, with illustrative video attached even when the connection was tenuous. The VJ had to write, track, and edit two versions of this story piece in about three hours after returning to the station.

Authorship. The Love Canal Anniversary story is an example of a typical TV news package, which is a self-contained story that is introduced by a presenter in the studio as having been authored by a TV reporter. As with the Physiotherapy story, authorship is established discursively by the organization, with an in-studio anchor-presenter introducing the reporter in the studio. There, the reporter performed an additional short introduction with video displayed for the home viewer on what's known as a "green screen," which superimposes the image of the reporter over video from the story, visually emphasizing the reporter's involvement in the story as a witness and establishing the reporter as author and authority. Nothing, however, was said about the fact that the VJ also shot part of his story and edited the piece himself. There are no reflexive or performative cues within the story, though within the story there are two shots establishing the reporter at the scene, each time as a questioner eliciting information from the interviewees. There is no indication that the VJ shot or edited any part of the story.

River Rescue

The river rescue story appeared on the website of the *Spokesman-Review*, based in Spokane, Washington. The VJ who created it is a former still photographer who is largely self-trained as a VJ and who taught at one of the workshops I observed. The story portrays the rescue of a man in a river, with attention to the work of the paramedics on the scene who had to engineer a way to fish the man out of the water and then attend to his injuries.

Elements & Structure. This story is as short as a typical TV story, running a minute-40 seconds, but the similarity ends there. The story has no reporter narration and no indication of the journalist's involvement other than the full screen credits at the very end. The voice of the story is primarily that of the rescue leader, whose sound bites were connected into a coherent order, starting with what the team found upon arrival, and how they rescued the man. Sound from the scene, such as the rushing of the water, the clanks of rescue hooks, and the ambulance engine are woven into the soundtrack in a way that brings the viewer closely into the scene—a mimetic strategy.

As with the Love Canal Anniversary story, the most significant part of the story map was in the Linkage column, with nearly all the video in the story referenced by the soundtrack. Yet, unlike the Love Canal Anniversary story, there were very few grey boxes, indicating that the connection was often indirect, such as when the rescue leader talks about the man complaining of a possible broken bone. We see the victim on the stretcher, but do not hear from him directly. The pauses in the story allow for the extended and frequent use of natural sound.

Authorship. The author of the story is identified on the website's multimedia page with a cutline and with a textual credit at the end of the story. The VJ's name is *not* on the organization's home page; the video is presented as a link with a one-sentence description. At no time is the VJ's voice heard in a script or eliciting a question. The story takes the viewer "inside the bubble," as described by [MM], in true mimetic fashion. The rescue is shown and its description elicited from a person at the scene. The journalist does not describe or vocally interpret, and there are no reflexive components. The VJ's role in editing the story is implied but not delineated by the end credit.

Chinese Earthquake Aftermath

At nearly four minutes, this VJ story from the *Washington Post*'s website runs roughly twice as long as a typical television news story. The VJ shot and edited the story alone, but was accompanied by a translator as he interviewed the parents of a little girl who was missing in the aftermath of the 2008 earthquake in China. The VJ believes that his small camera was helpful in gaining access to the parents at their home, and that a network-style crew with a large camera may easily have interfered with the emotion of the tragic interviews.

Elements & Structure. The Linkage column in the story map showed the sharpest contrast with the two TV news stories analyzed above, Physiotherapy and Love Canal Anniversary. The video and audio are frequently synchronous. There are few shots referenced vocally by the VJ, and there are very few shots that are disconnected from the audio script. The VJ in this instance had two freedoms not normally granted to daily TV journalists: first, in the amount of time he could take to produce his story, and second, in the length of time this story could run. The camera is placed at a wide variety of angles: on the ground for the father's footsteps, to the side as a group of parents argue, and from slightly above as the girls' mother speaks while seated next to a campfire at what's left of her home. The pace of this story is slower than a typical television story. The VJ added numerous pauses for background: sounds of children playing, birds singing, and the father's sad footsteps. This longer, richer format is not typical of a TV newscast, though it might run in a broadcast TV magazine program.

Authorship. The newspaper website featured this VJ in ways that are similar for one of its newspaper columnists. More than a year after the earthquake occurred, his dispatches from China remain on the website with the following introduction: "On May 12th,[5] a 7.9-magnitude quake killed 70,000 people in China's Sichuan province. This [VJ]...was on assignment in China at the time and was among the first Western journalists to reach the earthquake zone, where he filed daily panoramas and video dispatches. Click on the icons below to explore." Yet, while the website makes it clear who created the story, he is never seen. He tracked a script and is heard throughout the story, as is the translator who worked with him. All the translations are communicated to an English-speaking audience through the sound of the parents speaking Chinese and the translations of their remarks displayed at the bottom of the screen. There is one section of the story that is indirectly reflexive—when the local officials look into the camera as they try to shoo the angry parents away from the journalists—but the script does not use the words "we" or "I," nor does it explicitly describe their response. The camera simply remains in place.

Jena Six Rally

Independent citizen journalist Amani Channel worked with a friend to cover the Jena Six rally in 2007.[6] His story, which is posted as a part of an independent program on *YouTube*, called *My Urban Report*, represents the way citizen journalists appropriate those aspects of filmic structure they find useful and reject others. Channel is a former TV reporter and is an experienced video editor.[7] He posts material to *My Urban Report* when opportunities arise. The series is designed as an internet news source that presents information from the point of view of the African American community.

Elements & Structure. Nearly the entire 3-minute-45-second story uses a mimetic, observational style to show the rally to the viewer. Music from an African-style drumming group playing at the scene is layered under most of the story. The majority of the component functions can be categorized as showing and eliciting. The narrative is built upon sound bites from rally leaders, such as Al Sharpton, the father of one of the boys arrested in the controversial case, and rally participants. There are full-screen graphics to open the story and close it, and there are superimposed labeling graphics to identify each of the people interviewed. About halfway through the story, Channel makes another performative, though not reflexive, appearance and uses a colloquialism to describe the size of the media contingent, calling it "deep." The story ends with a comment from the father of the jailed boy, whose sentence ends with the phrase, "in Jena," closing the narrative with a mirror to its beginning.

Authorship. What is remarkable about Channel's Jena Six story is its mixture of performative, indirectly reflexive, elements with a primarily observational/mimetic style of presentation. The piece opens with his partner who is driving, saying, "It's Thursday, the day of the rally. This is it, we're headed to Jena." The viewer then sees and hears what Channel and his partner hear in the car: a radio report about the upcoming rally. The scene moves to a parking area where a police officer waves them through, and again, the driver comments about being allowed to pass. The two men make an effort at the top of the story to establish that they are the ones there to cover it.

The performative nature of the story is not all that unlike conventional television stories that utilize a reporter standup, although the colloquial language is unique. What is relatively unusual is for the story to open with indirectly reflexive information that reveals the process by which the citizen VJs travelled to Jena, and what their experience was like. This episode is not consciously reflective; that is, it does not exemplify Krippendorff's (1989) self-referential imperative, but it does indicate to the viewer some information about the story's ontogenesis as a human construction.

Our City, Our Voices & Gun Control

The video calling for better gun control, created by a team of participants in the *Our City, Our Voices* project, is remarkable for the way it appropriates conventional television form. The shots used in the story are head-on and framed according to conventional expository views, and the script is written as a series of third-person, fact-based statements about gun violence in Philadelphia, some of which might easily be found in a news program. Of all the stories mapped for this chapter, however, this one stood out with a unique approach to structure and its authorship strategies.

Elements & Structure. The piece runs 3 minutes, 24 seconds—longer than a conventional television news story. The story opens with African music (instrumental and vocal) under scenes of Philadelphia's City Hall. The declarative statements that start the story are a bit more openly opinionated than conventional news discourse might allow ("There should be a law," for example) but are not strident. The piece uses identifying lower-third graphics to identify those interviewed in the story, and has full screen credits at the end. The visual and technical construction of the story is technically on par with the work of beginning filmmakers. The citizen VJs used head-on shots and a variety of angles and views, but with a limited number of scenes: a few basic views of Philadelphia's City Hall, a close-up of a sign from a gun store, and shots of taxi cabs in traffic. The illustration used to discuss a specific shooting was recorded and borrowed from a TV newscast. There are few passages that could be considered mimetic, but most of the piece uses diegetic techniques.

Authorship. What is most unusual about this piece is the way authorship shifts without any explanation, yet without destroying the viewer's understanding. A female narrator is heard voicing a script at the beginning, and she is heard eliciting a question during an interview. Then, without introduction, another one of the VJs appears, speaking from the driver's seat of his taxi cab about his experiences on the streets of Philadelphia and his own fears about gun violence. It is not possible to know from the way he appears that he is also one of the VJs who created the story, nor is it clear that he was one of the questioners of the teenage boy. This knowledge was only possible by my observation of the group in action. The story ends with four people, all of whom participated in creating the video, holding a large sign that calls for an end to gun violence and chanting, "Take the guns off the streets" several times. The functional attributes of most of the components are declarative. In Nichols' typology, this story would be classified as expository, though the taxi driver appearance and the closing chant could be classified as performative. None of the appearances by the VJs, whether visual or vocal, uses discourse that directly addresses the viewer, or gives any indication of their work on the story.

Comparing Narrative Form

The foregoing analyses indicate that video journalism is indeed fostering changes in narrative form for filmic news, and those changes are correlated according to the VJ's organizational affiliation. For VJs working outside of television, video has indeed been "liberated," while stories created outside of television organizations incorporate a different structure, and establish authorship in new ways among the six stories.

The two television stories, Physiotherapy and Love Canal Anniversary, adopt the expository form of documentary with the declarative voice of a reporter. Even though they were shot in part by the same person who wrote and edited them, they appear much like any other daily television news story. They are on the shorter side, running less than three minutes. Their components are largely declarative and employ diegesis more than mimesis. They are built with the reporter's written audio track at the base, and have a number of sections without a meaningful link between audio and video.

The stories created for newspaper websites provide a very different experience for the viewer, one that is far more mimetic. Although the piece is not very long, the pace of the River Rescue story is much slower than a typical television story, with many pauses for natural sound. The pace of the Chinese Earthquake Aftermath story is also slow, and the story runs too long to run in a typical TV newscast. The linkages in these stories are far more frequent and direct in these two pieces; there are fewer disconnected passages. The stories rely more heavily on mimesis than diegesis. While authorship in these stories is largely established by the institutional context that presents them, there is little or no authorial performance. The VJ who created the River Rescue story remains entirely hidden from the viewer; and while the Chinese Earthquake Aftermath story includes a narrated script by Travis Fox, we do not ever see him. Both stories largely employ the photo journalist's traditional source of authority—the mechanical perfection of the camera.

The stories by citizen journalists are much more a bricolage of form, moving from voices that are declarative to eliciting, and mixing observational and performative modes without explanation or elaboration. They are longer than a typical TV news story, and the two examples vary considerably in the number and quality of shots. The Gun Control story uses fewer shots per minute than the others in this sample, a reflection of the difficulty for nonprofessionals in shooting and incorporating B-ROLL. What is most remarkable about these stories is the way they establish authorship. Both make use of performance in different ways. In the case of the Jena Six rally, there is a short but significant revelation of the way Amani Channel and his friend drove to the rally and were admitted into the area by police. There is no recorded script of the VJ in this piece, yet about halfway through, he makes a short appearance on camera to point out how many media outlets are on the scene. The *Our City, Our Voices* team took turns performing in the story, with one providing an expository voice track, joined midway by other members of the team in vocally eliciting questions from an interviewee, and then all together appearing on camera in their closing chant "Keep the guns off the street." This mix of a performative and observational style does not assume the traditional authoritative voice of professional journalism. Because the producers are not members of a professional community and cannot claim the authority of journalism's interpretive community, they instead must rely on their authority as witnesses. Such a style does not presume to deliver a truth, but instead mixes the authority of witnessing with that of a more personal sincerity to deliver their truth: what they see, what they think, and what they've experienced. The approach, more dialogic than pedagogic, invites the viewer to share more than learn.

Those who see video journalism and its smaller cameras and digital technologies as a way to create more intimate and mimetic stories might be encouraged by the work of the newspaper VJs presented here. Both of the newspaper VJ stories are indeed more mimetic, with strong, consistent links between soundtrack and images. They take time and use NATSOT to establish a mood for the viewer, drawing a viewer into the story more completely. Those who hope that video journalism will ease the price of entry to the video sphere in terms of skill and money might also be encouraged by the pieces from the *Our City, Our Voices* project and Amani Channel's independent online series, *My Urban Report*. The stories from these sources are longer than the typical TV story, and mix their modes between performative and expository. They borrow from TV news conventions and adapt it in ways that allow for them to establish a more personal point of view. Yet, critics who charge that video journalism is simply a cheaper way to produce conventional television stories might also feel affirmed by this analysis—the two TV stories produced by VJs are no different than typical TV stories produced by crews.

Just as the Leica® changed the way still photographers could capture life's "decisive moments," and electronic newsgathering ushered in possibilities for experiencing the world live and in real time, video journalism's singular process is indeed fostering a greater sense of intimacy in its product—but only where organizational norms allow for a change in narrative form. The stories produced by VJs working for television stations continue to reflect the temporal demands of that form. The two stories produced by newspaper VJs do seem to bring its subjects closer to the viewer, if only because the VJs themselves remain largely hidden. By incorporating multiple sound bites from the grieving father in the Chinese Earthquake Aftermath story, the viewer is able to feel the man's pain more acutely. In the River Rescue story, the VJ used natural sound and multiple pauses throughout the story to provide a sense of presence for the viewer. The sights and sounds of the rescue are presented uninterrupted by any journalistic commentary.

Video journalism's expansion to new users is manifest in the work of the citizen journalists who post their work directly to the web. Unencumbered by norms of professional journalists, citizen VJs are inventing a discourse as they go along, assembling stories with performative, observational, or expository elements as convenient. Rather than relying on the authority of their membership in an interpretive community, their stories make greater use of the authority of witnessing and personal testimony.

It is significant that the singular nature of the work does not seem to have inspired an increase in transparency or reflexivity. There are few indicators of any sort of reflexivity in any of the stories. Only the citizen journalism stories give any clue that the story's teller is also the shooter. The driver on the Jena Six rally who says, "This is it, we're headed to Jena," presents the most reflexive moment of the six stories here. For the most part, whether working for television, newspapers, or independent websites, the VJs whose work is represented here are not changing their voice because they are working alone. The TV journalists are using the same distant, third-person voice of an observer using the language of presumed "objectivity." The newspaper VJs are mixing some of that language into their stories or using no voice at all; and the citizen journalists seem to be choosing voice on a contingent basis, possibly according to what happens to be convenient.

Content Analysis

These qualitative analyses were useful for exploring stylistic differences and helped with the design of a small quantitative study. In 2011, I sampled 100 video stories from the web: half from newspaper websites and half from television station websites. (Citizen videos were not part of the sample because there is no reliable population of citizen videos from which to draw cases.) Stories were coded[8] according to narrative voice, the appearance of the journalist, the appearance of story subjects, and so on. They were carefully timed so that the narratives could be analyzed according to their diegetic and mimetic qualities.

The content analysis yielded no surprises except in the degree to which newspaper and television website stories differed. As illustrated in *Table 6.1*, television stories were far more likely (96%) to be narrated by a journalist, while newspaper videos were more apt to turn the storytelling reigns over to a subject or provide no narration at all. (In three cases, the videos were primarily narrated by an image manager, exemplifying a trend noted in the previous chapter.)

	Television N=50	Newspaper N=50
Percent of stories narrated by a journalist	96%	24%
The amount of time a journalist is heard (as a percent of the story time)	77%	17%
The amount of time a *subject* is heard (as a percent of story time)	17%	42%
Average story length (min:sec)	1:27	2:35
Average story *pacing* (seconds per shot)	11.33	49.63

Table 6.1: Narrative content analysis, 2011

Journalists could be heard 77% of the time of a television story posted to the web, while journalists were only heard 17% of the time for videos posted to newspaper websites. Note the mimetic shift for newspaper videos: subjects were heard 42% of the time in a newspaper story, while they were heard in much shorter sound bites in television station videos, averaging 17% of the time of a story. As the VJs who work for newspaper websites explained during their interviews, time is not as constricting on newspaper websites, and this is reflected in the data, with the average story time of a newspaper story at 2:35 compared with the average television story at 1:27. Finally, the pace of stories was found to be different for newspaper stories, with the average number of seconds per shot of a newspaper story at 49.63 versus 11.33 for a television story. Again, since their websites are not associated with a real-time schedule, as television newscasts are, newspaper journalists are less likely to worry about how long their shots run in a story. As their interviews in previous chapters indicate, many are still learning their way around video editing.

The content analysis wrought some observations that could not be quantified, but were revealing nonetheless. Recall the complaints from VJs at newspaper organizations that they feel ill prepared and pressured to put "anything" up as long as it's video. Some of the stories in the sample, such as a five-minute-long clip of raw scenes from a fire or a little league game, could easily be placed in that category. Complaints about television news overemphasizing crime could be bolstered (yet again) by this small study, as the television station videos included many more crime stories than on newspaper websites. Newspaper organizations tended to post many more feature stories with video. Most problematic for newspaper websites, though, was the lack of contextualizing information. Stories were posted without any indication of the date something happened—sometimes without any sort of introductory information at all. It's not possible to ascertain motive from a content analysis, of course, but the historic pattern among textual workers to treat images as fungible—merely decorative or self-explanatory—may be, at least in part, behind this treatment of videos.

Comparing Coverage for One Event: Hillary

The preceding comparison of stories from VJs working for a variety of organizations, and covering disparate events provides a sense of the stylistic range that exists for video journalism. To better highlight how the product of video journalism compares with other forms, however, it makes sense to examine the way one particular event was covered by different media. For this comparison, I attended a campaign rally for then-presidential-candidate Hillary Clinton at a central Pennsylvania community college on March 24, 2008. Pennsylvania had become a key state in the primary, so local and national media attended the event. Every manner of camera was on the scene. I arrived hours before they opened the doors to the public and did not leave until the candidate and nearly all media representatives had left. In addition to observing the way VJs, traditional crews, and print reporters covered the event as it was happening, I recorded and collected a sample of stories from an assortment of media outlets for analysis, including:

- A local newspaper VJ story
- A network television story
- A CNN story
- A *YouTube* posting
- A printed newspaper story

I used the same mapping system to analyze the video stories. For the printed version, I used the original, physical newspaper. Before analyzing these various products, however, let me offer a description of how journalists worked at the rally that day based on my observations before, during, and shortly after the rally.

Covering the Hillary Event

The *Women for Hillary* rally was scheduled days before the crucial 2008 Pennsylvania primary. The rally was widely publicized and open to the public, so I was able to attend without a ticket. I was simply asked to sign a form indicating whether I was interested in hearing more from her campaign and possibly volunteering. (I declined both.) The rally was to be held in the gymnasium of a large building on Montgomery County Community College's Blue Bell campus.

As of 9:15 a.m., there were nearly as many police officers as attendees and volunteers. The line at the gymnasium door was already forming as I approached. The building's lobby had been converted into a reception area that included security officers, and signs were hung on the doors proclaiming that by entering the area individuals were consenting to be searched. A door on the side of the building was open to media, with a parking area for live trucks and access to the gym for the cables required for live coverage. The first photographer I observed was a VJ for a local newspaper who arrived at 10:46. He did not enter the building, but instead interviewed and photographed people in line. He was shooting with both a still and video camera. Soon thereafter, about two more video-photographers arrived to record video of the people in line, one of which was a pair of media students from a nearby university. At about 11:30, I and the rest of the crowd were allowed inside the gymnasium. Other journalists had already gathered on a set of risers that took up most of the goal end of the gym's basketball court. Video cameras and still cameras were on the tops of the risers, and a set of tables was placed on the floor in front of the risers for the textual press. The stage where Clinton would speak was on the other end of the basketball court, with curtains at the back so the speakers could enter and exit to a secure area. Rally attendees filled the bleachers and the gym floor, and eventually the crowd grew too large for the gym. The remaining attendees were directed to an overflow room where they could hear, but not see, the rally.

There were minimal camera restrictions, and photographers were not required to remain in place. A variety of large and small video cameras were in use on the platform and on the floor. Very loud and upbeat music filled the gym as the crowd mingled and found seats. A small platform was set up for media up high and to the side for a cutaway view; about three photographers took advantage of this side-view platform. Just after 1:00 p.m., a busload of journalists arrived, the corps of reporters and photographers who travel with the campaign. A few minutes after they took their positions, a local, elected official started the rally.

During the rally, most photographers worked from the platforms provided by the event's image managers, which offered a full view of the stage over the heads of rally attendees. Clinton's local allies spoke for a few minutes to warm up the crowd. Clinton herself spoke for nearly a half hour. There were some technical difficulties with her microphone at the very start, which prompted her to make a joke about Republican gremlins. Around 2:00, the rally ended and video-photographers took to the floor to interview rally attendees for their reaction.

The coordination between the campaign coordinators and journalists, particularly the traveling press, reflected a shared understanding of a preconception for the story. The risers were set up for an optimal view of the candidate, and a mult-box provided for a clean recording of her speech. Journalists seemed to operate with a preconception of what was needed for the story by interviewing rally participants before and after the speech to elicit their opinions and by remaining nearly motionless during Clinton's speech.

Comparing Coverage of the Hillary Event

Echoing the observations made in previous chapters, the resulting stories reflect the media logic of their exhibiting media organizations. The *Women for Hillary* rally was only one of Clinton's campaign stops that day. She began her morning with a news conference that outlined a plan to assist families facing foreclosure. She also met with editors at the *Philadelphia Daily News*, where she clarified remarks about a 1996 visit to Bosnia that was far less dangerous than she'd once claimed. As a result, the rally was not prominent in much of the national coverage. It was overshadowed, especially by the tarmac gaffe, which was the focus of CNN's coverage the next morning. Video from the rally was incorporated into campaign-trail stories, such as the one on WPVI that evening.

Local TV Story. The local ABC affiliate, WPVI-TV,[9] sent a lone video-photographer to the rally. His video was used in a campaign summary story that evening for the 5:00 p.m. newscast. The station's campaign coverage included a short, three-second graphic and musical open and a short statement by an anchor who introduced a reporter. The reporter, David Henry, stood on the steps of the Philadelphia Art Museum with the city skyline behind him, and reported on the overall primary race between Clinton and Barack Obama. His remarks prefaced a short video package that contained the rally video at its beginning and included six shots, lasting 20 seconds. The package began with a short sound bite from Hillary Clinton asking the crowd whether they were ready to work. The package had no sound bites from those attending the rally and simply mentioned that she held a rally in the suburbs intended to mobilize her working-class base. The rest of the package covered her program for foreclosure relief and then transitioned to coverage of the Obama campaign activities that day. Obama had campaigned in Pennsylvania that day, so the package included a sound bite from an

Obama campaign volunteer. After the package aired, the program returned to the reporter live on the Art Museum steps for a summary. The program proceeded with a short voiced-over video story narrated by the anchor regarding voter registration. The component of the program devoted to both Obama and Clinton lasted about three minutes.

Network TV Story. Similarly, one network television story used video from the rally—not to focus on the rally as much as the overall campaign. CNN's coverage was dominated by the Bosnia sniper-fire gaffe, which was discussed live by a campaign reporter for nearly three minutes. Correspondent Bill Schneider appeared live early the morning after the rally from the Philadelphia Art Museum with a CNN bus decorated as the "Campaign Express" in the background. In a live conversation with a CNN anchor, Schneider devoted nearly three minutes to Clinton's misstatement, calling it "Clearly a blunder on her part," while video of the actual Bosnia arrival played twice during his report. CNN used a graphic to display Clinton's quotation from her meeting with the *Philadelphia Daily News* (shot by a photographer from a sister publication, the *Philadelphia Inquirer*), and then segued into a more general discussion of the campaign. It was during this section of the live report that some video from the rally was aired, a single shot from a camera on the floor of the gym at the rally that ran about half a minute. CNN never exhibited the video in full screen; instead, shrinking it and putting it into a graphical box to the side of the political report. The video shows a very upbeat, smiling candidate shaking hands, and appears to have been shot by photographers who were allowed inside a fenced-in area immediately beneath the stage—an indication that CNN had two cameras at the event that day: one on the platform and one on the floor. The latter is likely to have been operated by one of the network's campaign VJs whose job it was to use a smaller camera for closer, more flexible coverage.[10]

Local Newspaper Print Story. The Reporter, a local newspaper based in Lansdale, Pennsylvania, featured the Hillary rally on its front page the next day, with a still photo credited to the same VJ who covered the rally for the web. The text was written by another journalist, a staff writer whose identity is established with a newspaper byline. Unlike CNN or WPVI, *The Reporter* devoted half of its story to those attending the rally, presumably local residents and likely readers of the small newspaper. The second half of the story is devoted to Clinton's speech, and contains six direct quotations and five paraphrased statements—far more than the local television story. There is no mention of Barack Obama. The front page of the newspaper included a color photo from the rally, taken by the same journalist who was covering the event as a VJ.

Local Newspaper-Website VJ Stories. The *Philadelphia Inquirer* ran stories in the paper and on the web, the latter of which was unexpected by the Clinton campaign staff. According to campaign handler [LM], no cameras were supposed to be present for her meeting with the *Philadelphia Daily News* editorial board that day, but because the *Daily News* and *Inquirer* share the same owner and building, *Inquirer* representatives were present for the meeting, and one of them brought a small video camera, posting a portion of the meeting in which she clarified her remarks about a visit she'd made to Bosnia. Video of her making this clarification was posted to *Philly.com*, the website that represents both the *Inquirer* and *Daily News*. The video was shaky and the audio was not perfectly clear, but the organizations apparently decided that Clinton's clarification was an important enough story that the technical flaws could be forgiven.

Chris Stanley's story for *The Reporter* followed a pattern typical for a newspaper VJ, using his own voice sparingly (in this, instance with no more than a short introduction at the very beginning and a few questions that can be heard eliciting responses from people in line to see Hillary Clinton) and a heavily mimetic style. The piece can be divided into two parts: first, one that profiles the people who waited in line to see the candidate, and second, a montage of sound bites from the candidate herself, strung together and connected by bits of applause from the audience and/or music from the scene. The video story closely mirrored the printed version, written by a different person who works for *The Reporter*. Each starts with the fans, then focuses on the candidate. Neither piece, interestingly enough, contains any reaction from the crowd after Clinton's speech. This might be because of the newspaper's deadline structure (the printed version of the paper came out the next day), it might be that there was not time nor space for additional elements, or it might be that the reporters did not think to include any reaction.

A Journalistic Act. By far, the most unusual and revelatory bit of coverage for the rally came not from the conventional media organizations but from a high school student who posted a short video clip on *YouTube.* She is not a journalist—not even a journalism student—but she committed, as Lasica (2003) puts it, a "journalistic act" by recording a bit of the event and then posting it on the internet for the world to see. What is most interesting about her video is that it does not picture Hillary Clinton at all—nor does it picture the crowd or the rally room. The young woman who shot the video did not arrive on time to get a seat inside the gym where the rally took place, and so was sent to an overflow room where she and her friends could only hear the candidate. The video she posted to *YouTube* depicted the floor of that room, with audio of Clinton making her joke about Republican gremlins messing up the microphone sound. It's possible to hear laughter from the people in the room. That's it. The clip runs all of 23 seconds. Its very simple map consisted of one image and one sound clip. Here's her account of how the clip came to be and why she posted it to *YouTube*:

> We happened to be on spring break so it was a perfect opportunity to go to the rally. We didn't realize that the event would create such a huge crowd so we arrived pretty late and we got put into the overflow room. We literally missed the cut by about seven people. So in the overflow room the mood and atmosphere was a little low, we were all upset that we wouldn't be able to see Hillary give her speech. My friends and I were trying to start cheers to bring up the atmosphere so I started taking just random videos with my digital camera. It just so happened that I captured that quote about a Republican gremlin making her microphone cut out and my friends and I thought it was hilarious and [they] made me promise to put it on *YouTube* as soon as I got home. I agreed and it was definitely a very lighthearted and funny moment.

The young woman is considering pursuing a career in broadcast journalism and takes her small video camera along whenever she's at an event such as a football game, school play, or, in this case, the Hillary Clinton appearance. She believes the clip works because it captured a shared moment of humor, even though Hillary Clinton cannot be seen:

> I think it works because it's the truth; you can't manufacture a moment like that. It probably would have been better if we could have seen her face or the faces of people reacting to what she said, but you hear the mike cutting out, you hear the joke, you have all the elements that make the joke funny.

Her assessment is meaningful and reflects the work of Halbwachs (1992, 1941) and Nora (1997) on the socially constructed nature of memory. What is also significant about this video is that it worked as a testament to the student's physical witnessing of the event. The clip served as evidence that she had, indeed, been there with her friends. She did not attempt to add narration to the clip, and the caption she provided on *YouTube* was minimal. The quality of the image is poor—it's a shaky shot of the floor. Yet for her, it was meaningful enough to share with the *YouTube* audience; enough for her to go through the trouble of isolating the clip and posting it. The "story" is evidence of the way video works as a form of physical witnessing as much as storytelling and the way image's aesthetic presentation is subsumed by the story behind it.

This comparison of five stories from the same event provides another way of understanding how video journalism's process affects its product, and how singularity and expansion influence video narratives. The video story created by the local newspaper VJ is very different from the two conventional stories based on the same event in terms of its length and narrative style. The network and local television stories used video from the event to add illustration to a larger campaign story—in one case not even mentioning the event itself, but simply rolling the video while a correspondent talked more generally about the primary in Pennsylvania. The local newspaper's VJ story is more mimetic, with significantly more reliance on video from the scene as the basis for the narrative, as opposed to a reporter's narrative as the controlling foundation. The similarity between the citizen contribution and those from the previous section lies in its personal and performative nature. It didn't matter to the VJ who posted the video that it was technically problematic; what mattered to her was that it captured a moment that was personally important to her and her friends, and its authority is rooted in her direct, physical witnessing of the moment.

Summary

This chapter explored whether changes in the way video news can be created leads to differences in the product. By carefully examining stories from three types of media organizations, and by comparing stories based on a common event, it was possible to identify how video journalism stories might be unique and under what circumstances. Two dimensions of filmic narrative might be affected by changes in practice: the narrative structure of a story and the establishment of authorship. Using a mapping system adapted from Kracauer (1947) to examine each story's elements and the way they work in combination, it was possible to explore the way video journalism practice affects these dimensions. It is interesting to note that even as organizations converge on the web, the videos they post are distinctive, and tied to their organizations' originating media identity.

For television-based VJs, the narratives appear much like those created by conventional reporter-photographer crews. Newspaper VJs are inventing a style that recalls traditional documentary filmmaking—one that relies on the traditional authority of the camera's technology and having membership in the larger community of professional journalists. Nonprofessional VJs who post their work to the web are also experimenting with form, often incorporating identifiable points of view and performative elements. They derive their authority from their role as witnesses, not as members of an interpretive community. These stories, as one workshop leader proclaimed, "are not TV"—not for the difference in technology, but in form and presentation.

Do these changes reflect a utopian revolution in filmic news production, as advanced by video journalism's strongest proponents like Michael Rosenblum and his followers? Revolution may be too strong a label for what is happening. More voices, both professional and nonprofessional, are participating in the video conversation and there are changes underway. Television's grip on filmic news is weakening, but the changes in form are more subtle than extraordinary. Rather than consider this a revolution, perhaps this might be better called a sea change, with implications that might only be understood with the passage of time.

NOTES:

1. I use these terms to roughly define the continuum of showing and telling. Rhetorical scholars are far more nuanced in their use of diegesis and mimesis.
2. Joel DeMott & Jeff Kreines (as cited in David Schwartz, 1988).
3. The lead story in a newscast is the first story, and is therefore presented as the most important.
4. This is the British term; US English speakers use the phrase "physical therapist."
5. 2008.
6. The Jena Six were defendants in a racially-charged assault case in Jena, Louisiana, involving racial slurs. Thousands of people protested the sentences imposed on the young men, all African Americans.
7. Though there is one apparent editing error in the piece: when we hear one person's voice but see a different person's face for less than a second.
8. Two coders worked according to a standard, and conferred over questionable decisions to ensure reliability. A subset of the sample was double-coded to test for reliability using Krippendorff's alpha, which was calculated with an SPSS macro program designed by Andrew F. Hayes (Hayes & Krippendorff, 2007). Nominal variables exceeded .80 and ordinal variables exceeded .90.
9. I was employed by WPVI from 1989 to 2003.
10. Personal communication, CNN political producer.

Chapter 7: Conclusion

> *"If I could tell the story in words, I wouldn't need to lug around a camera."*
>
> *—Lewis Hine*

Introduction

Early in this book, I asked: "In the end, is there anything truly 'special' about video journalism?" The answer is a qualified yes. Its process poses new challenges and concerns, and its product, in some organizational contexts, is indeed distinct.

In less than a generation, the weight of a video camera has gone from about 35 pounds to about five pounds—the difference between a large bag of cat litter to a typical-sized bag of flour. In that same time, the price of a camera and edit system has gone from the equivalent of a mortgage to a living room set. One more significant change has unfolded: transmitting a video story is now possible for nearly anyone with access to broadband internet. Together, these developments make it possible for just one person to create and transmit video stories, something inconceivable a generation ago. The nature of a job that has always involved the body has changed considerably in that one person can more easily do the work, and far more individuals can become video camera-bodies. These two attributes, what I named singularity and expansion, made a difference at many levels, both in process and product.

Throughout this book, I have argued that video journalism cannot be adequately understood without attending to the role of the body—not the "social body" of society, nor the "king's body" that represents the state. No, here, the conception of the body has been quite literal: the sweaty, kneeling, camera-carrying, stair-climbing, elbow-bumping bodies of the men and women who work as VJs—camera-bodies. This conception of the body, along with the understanding that news images are human-made artifacts that decontextualize scenes of the physical world with technology and recontextualize those scenes discursively, helped shape the method by which I sought to answer what is unique (if anything) about video journalism's process and product.

Video Journalism's Process

It is clear that video journalism is developing as a distinct form of newsgathering according to the needs and norms of varied news organizations. The smaller camera is changing the relationship between journalist and source, but it not necessarily changing practices in the domain of conventional television news. The singularity of practice is considered a travesty in some organizations and a form of liberation in others. Video journalism's expansion to new users is inspiring innovation—not by those who have experience with filmic news gathering, but by those who have never dealt with video before.

The singularity of the process and its physical demands affect video journalists in a number of very practical ways, but more importantly in terms of story choice. Many VJs, especially those asked to produce a story a day, are concerned that they are able to produce only easy one-stop feature stories—at the expense of more serious, hard, or investigative news. For organizations, singularity means that one person might be able to do the work of three people, but a number of managers observed that they cannot always do it as quickly as those three people. Most of the managers I interviewed saw video journalism as a valuable element in a "mix" of approaches, but not something that could be relied on exclusively. Finally, singularity and its daily pressures work in favor of appearance managers, who can control the nature of a story by granting or denying access to photographic locations.

The second distinctive feature of video journalism, expansion, is having its own impact on news discourse. The power to witness with a camera is now in the hands of far more people than ever before, and that power is sure to test the unevenness with which professional journalists have often made the claim. Video cameras, operated by multitudes of new camera-bodies, have simply made coverage of certain events possible. Cell-phone footage from the Virginia Tech massacre in 2007 and the subway bombings in London in 2005 simply could not have happened within normal news production practices, which quite logically can only cover the aftermath of events unless a news crew also happens to be in the "wrong" place at the "right" time. The 2009 Green Revolution in Iran also was covered via nonprofessionals in Iran with cell phone cameras and access to a social networking site. Conventional news organizations were sent scrambling to devise appropriate ways to inspect such material for authenticity, and use it on the air. The implications are both heady and frightening for the professional. Video is no longer the sole province of moneyed organizations and skilled professionals. Consequently, control of the story is not in the hands of a few gatekeepers, with its discourse defined by an elite, interpretive community. It is, instead, more of a conversation—sometimes cerebral, sometimes contentious, and sometimes obtuse, as many *YouTube* videos indicate—but it is certainly no longer a sole proprietorship.

The spread to new users provides a counterbalance to the increase in power for appearance managers. As more professionals and nonprofessionals carry cameras, it is harder to control photographic access. It becomes nearly impossible to tell professional from blogger from tourist, something that wreaks havoc on business as usual. Nonprofessionals may have stronger ties to their conceptualized audience than to intermediaries. They may be unwilling or unable to work according to the conventional rules of engagement between intermediaries and journalists. Their street-level reporting injects a new strand of discourse into the public conversation.

Video Journalism's Product

Sociologies of journalism are more valuable if they reveal the connection between human interaction and the news, and this project was designed with that premise in mind. Video journalism does constitute a new way of gathering news, with unique practices that vary according to a journalist's affiliating organization and purpose. The question that matters for the audience, however, is whether changed practices yield changed products. Does the work of a VJ, incorporating the body as a witness to physical reality, make a difference? While this book does not incorporate an audience response study, questions regarding the product as delivered to the audience are perhaps the most critical—what's the use of understanding video journalism, after all, if it has no impact on public discourse?

A careful analysis of VJ stories indicated that yes, a new form of filmic news is developing in some domains. Interestingly, the changes in equipment alone do not seem to be connected to the development of these new forms, though the singular nature of the practice is having some impact. Here, the adoption of video journalism by new users seems to be the more influential of the two trajectories.

VJ stories produced for television news programs are nearly indistinguishable from TV stories produced conventionally, with specialist reporters and video-photographers working as a team. The stories I analyzed use the declarative language and expository style associated with television news. These stories are built upon a script voiced by a reporter, and video is added to illustrate that script. The linkages between language and image—that is, the connections between what we see and what we hear—are often tenuous or missing entirely. In keeping with the presumptions of contemporary journalism, the authority of the story rests in what the reporter declares to be true. The VJ stories created for newspaper websites, however, are in large part more observational. One of the stories uses no scripted narrative at all, another uses only two sentences, and the third uses scripted narrative but to a lesser degree than the TV news counterparts. The stories posted to the web by nonprofessionals represent the most experimental forms in this strategic sample, incorporating expository, performative, observational, and other narrative forms—sometimes within the same piece.

The differences between the narrative styles chosen by VJs in these three domains are related to the sources of authority for each. The expository television news stories draw authority from the interpretive community that produced them—journalists. They presume to declare objective facts unreflexively. The more observational newspaper videos draw authority from the camera's technical perfection, allowing the viewer to experience the story as a second-order witness without any revelations about the first-order witness, the VJ who made myriad idiosyncratic choices in the process of creating a story. The nonprofessional VJs, however, could not draw from the authority of an interpretive community. Instead, they interspersed their stories with performative and reflexive moments that transparently establish their role as direct witnesses to events. Given professional journalism's propensity to claim the authority of witnessing unevenly, these citizen accounts provide a refreshing, albeit sometimes clumsy, subjective counter-balance to the typical news narrative.

What of the complaint by specialist journalists, particularly those in television news, that video journalism stories are of a poorer quality? Some subjects insisted to me that it was possible to detect visual differences between conventional and small cameras. In viewing the stories online, this difference is not readily apparent, and the trade literature indicates that viewers are similarly indifferent. More important are the complaints by specialists that quality is diminished when one person works alone. This complaint may have more weight, though not necessarily in terms of photo-graphic or technical quality. There are indeed variations in skill evident between VJs. Some of the stories used more creative angles, made better use of sound, and incorporated more sophisticated editing techniques than others. This was not tied to singular working practice but photographic experience.

The greatest disparity in quality seems to be rooted in the preconceptualization stage for some of the one-man-band stories. VJs who work for television organizations, and must deliver a package a day complain every day that they are unable to contend with heavier, hard-news materials, and spend more of their time covering easy, one-location feature stories. This contradicts what some of the managers interviewed for this project perceived as a positive characteristic of video journalism. Managers who favor singular production see that VJs are more easily deployed, and better able to cover spot news, especially when two or three are sent to cover multiple angles of a hard-news story. That may well be. But based on the interviews and observations of the television VJs who participated in this project, their day-to-day experience seems one of a constant struggle to be taken seriously, not only in terms of their technical skills but the types of stories they cover.

In contrast, the VJs at newspapers (at this stage, admittedly, still largely a self-selected group) report being relatively happy with the product they're delivering. The notion that "video has been liberated" was echoed by many of the newspaper website VJs, whether still photographers who've transitioned to multimedia or text-based reporters who wanted to add video to their repertoire. Because their work is not tied to a real-time program, their stories can be as long or as short as they deem necessary. Also, because video is so new to newspaper practice, they are often organizational pioneers, inventing their formats as they go along, sometimes with minimal oversight. Finally, for many of the former still photographers, the freedom to *not* appear on camera, or use their recorded voice in narration seems a great relief. The observational form allows them to maintain the anonymity of practice that they apparently were drawn to as part of the original job.

It is at the margins of what constitutes filmic news where some of the most compelling cases can be made that video journalism is changing public discourse. Video on *YouTube* that shows hardwood flooring while Hillary Clinton made a joke is not something television stations would normally broadcast, but the young woman who posted it found it meaningful and memorable. Is this news? One might answer, why not? As Schudson (Schudson, 2001, 2003), Barnhurst (Barnhurst & Nerone, 2001), and others have pointed out, the form of news is malleable. Tuchman (1978) found that one of America's influential social shifts, the women's movement of the late sixties and early seventies, was largely ignored by mainstream media because the meetings and events for feminist activists occurred outside the routine times and locations for newsgathering. Yet in 2009, the *New York*

Times ran a front page story on whether or not The White House was as "family friendly" to its employees as it aspired to be (Swarns, 2009). Later that same month, the *Washington Post* ran a story on the front page of its feature section about a *YouTube* video of a heartwarmingly offbeat wedding procession (Kaufman, 2009). Such stories would have been unthinkable in 1970. While video journalism may not be changing narrative in clear-cut, dramatic ways, it may well change the way filmic news is created and defined in the years to come.

Subjects Respond

In keeping with Krippendorff's (1989) proposal that the subjects of our research have the right to a say in their representation, I sent drafts of chapters from this book to about two dozen of my subjects inviting their feedback and comments. Some of them took the time to respond. Some of them were simply grateful for the opportunity to see how they were represented. For instance, [BG], an image manager, wrote:

> Fascinating topic…I took a look at the comments. They sound about right. I appreciate the way you have presented the material and identified locations in very general terms, not by actual name. I appreciate the opportunity to look the comments over.

A VJ who allowed me to follow her while she shot a story found the accounts of other VJs to be a validation:

> [LT]: I particularly enjoyed reading about other people's accounts…There are so many things that other people said about the one-man band experience that ring true—whether you are in the Bronx, England, or the Midwest.

[LT] has since moved to a larger market and no longer shoots for herself. She does not miss the ownership that comes with working alone, and now that she no longer answers to a shop that employs only one-man bands, she was a bit more candid about her assessment of video journalism:

> I know the one-man band shops really save on money—and some people might even prefer being able to have complete ownership of their piece—not me. I think more often than not, the product suffers.

[NC] was pleased to see some of her everyday aggravations appear in Chapter Four:

> I absolutely loved the time you spent on doors!!! Such a huge part of our day that the "average" person doesn't think about. Photographers usually have reporters to open doors. MMJ's do it alone. Love it.

One comment from [NC] caused me to adjust the way I represented her decision to not interview the librarian, as described in Chapter Three, in order to emphasize her organization's expectations:

> Not that it matters now, but I know that if I brought back the interview with the librarian, the news managers would not have been happy. That's another thing about being a MMJ…I always feel like I'm competing with reporter/photographer teams and that my content needs to be just as "hard" as theirs…One of the biggest shocks to me when I got into this business is the sheer lack of reporting that goes on sometimes…It's sad because creative writing and telling stories is why I got into the business. I've now realized that shooting my own stuff has made it very difficult to find a new job. First and foremost, the stories I have, for the most part, are fluffy.

One of my subjects thought it unfortunate that I only focused on video journalism in the United States and England:

> [DH]: I wonder if you had included India, who has actually not suffered much of the economic problems of the rest of the world, if it wouldn't have made a much different picture. Do they have VJs or do they typically have one-man bands or two-person crews? What about a place like Japan, where consumer technology is light years ahead of America…?

[HT] was satisfied with my characterization of television news organizations:

> Once published, if anyone ever asked me why/how I became a VJ…I would refer them to your work. It really tells all of what happened/is happening to TV news right now in this country.

[KN] was surprised that he was in the minority when it came to feeling snubbed while carrying a small camera but did not argue with my findings in that regard. As a longtime still photographer, he was also pleased to see some of his daily challenges and complaints in print:

> I have never previously seen anybody articulate the truth that many have historically viewed photography as culturally lower than text…Your detailed attention to all the new jobs—audio editing for some, visual grammar for others—was enriching. Video journalism's "double whammy" definition was a slam dunk too. Every little detail, from opening doors with hands full, to driving while managing multiple devices, added to a complete portrait. (By the way, I have 180'd on my use of mobile devices while driving. Never again. Education works.)

At the BBC, [MM] corrected me on a point regarding a health and safety directive. She also enjoyed reading about the American VJ experience. [DT] noticed that I'd mentioned his image of Hillary Clinton that was published on the front page of the paper. As is often the case when photographers talk about their work, he not only told me the image was the result of a "frame grab" (a still image taken from video), but identified the specific make and model of the camera he used to make it. Finally, a former TV news director who helped with my research, but did not participate as a subject, provided me with the most validating assessment of all:

> You nailed it. I might quibble with you on some points, but overall you explained the process extremely well. The irony, of course, is the VJ project is likely doomed in traditional broadcast settings. Too much resistance from news folks and unrealistic corporate expectations on cost-savings.
>
> Newspapers have a different motivation…survival. Unfortunately, management does not have a decent handle on when and how to use and promote video news coverage. While there are exceptions, most newspaper web sites require multiple link-through to get to video stories. This effectively kills the experiment.
>
> Fact remains that the future for Video Journalism is through non-traditional outlets. You described the possibilities.

Not all future readers will agree with my analysis and may find fault with my conclusions. There is comfort, though, in the knowledge that my subjects thus far have not found significant errors or faults in the approach this book has taken.

Parting Thoughts

I must admit: when I started this research, I'd hoped that video journalism would develop according to the utopian vision promoted by its most enthusiastic supporters, that its stories would feel more intimate, that news organizations would present a wider range of stories, and that the use of smaller cameras would provide easier access and less reliance on pseudo-events. For the most part, this utopia remains a distant vision. In fact, I observed some trends that run counter to journalistic norms, and should be cause for concern: a tendency to produce many more features than hard news, to opt for easy single-location stories, and a stronger, not weakened, reliance on appearance managers for help in producing a story. As video journalism continues to develop, news professionals must continue to be vigilant about their ideals if the public sphere is to be adequately nourished.

Writing this has felt a bit like a race. Since the summer of 2007 when I started this project in earnest, the BBC has changed the way it trains VJs for its Nations & Regions. Three of my informants have left their jobs to teach (two of them in higher education). The photo department at a major newspaper I visited was merged with another department in the company. Nearly every week brought another announcement of layoffs and closings in newsrooms around the United States.

I have been frequently asked by my informants, other journalists, and scholars what I "think" of video journalism now that I've observed it in so many domains. Do I personally see it as a cheap way of doing the same thing? Or a new method for doing something better? My stand remains neutral: video journalism itself is a tool like any other. A hammer cannot be good or bad, and neither can the small cameras that have helped spread this new form through newsrooms around the world. A primary complaint that has been leveled against video journalism is that it's "all about cost-cutting." That may be partly true. But when an industry is shrinking, and jobs are disappearing, cutting costs is not necessarily evil, especially when it makes hyper-local coverage possible for areas that might not otherwise be served with electronic news.

Throughout my research, I was reminded of the parallel difficulties of journalism that claims to be truthful and ethnography that claims to be scientific. Ethnographic inquiry is inherently messy. A certain kind of detachment is absolutely necessary in order to provide a scholarly perspective, one that informs theoretical inquiry and helps us to understand why things are as they are. Just as important is the need to make comparisons between what people say and what they do, which is why the data for this book is drawn from both interviews and eight notebooks filled with observational notes. Rather than pretend that my observations are objective, I instead have attempted to be transparent and overt in my perspective, not one of a scientific objectivist, but of a former professional turned scholar who has the luxury of taking not an objectivist or bird's-eye view, but a larger and long-range view of video journalism and its impact on newsgathering. I spent hours and days with my subjects during which we talked about their work, about journalism generally, about their personal ambitions, and about what they would like to see happen in the new media environment. I made friends. How does one treat friends as data? Only ethnography could present this sort of dilemma.

My goal was to shed light on the human-centered process that is video journalism, on the skills it requires, the challenges its practitioners face, and the way this affects what we see on our television and computer screens.

When I first embarked on this project, I posted a question on TV-Spy's *The Watercooler* about KRON's VJ transition. One of the responses to my questions was a warning: "Danger MaryABock Danger" headlined my anonymous responder, "Imagine a room of rabid animals all snarling at each other. This topic brings out the beast in those waiting around for it to come up again."[1] Perhaps because of my own journalistic background, this was my enticement to dive in—not turn back.

As I was finishing the project, I lamented to one of my subjects that what passed as journalism in contemporary local TV news was breaking my heart. He wrote back: "RE: State of TV News: Please, my new friend, don't despair. It's a transition. You are a part of it. You ARE making a difference with the questions you ask."

I was grateful for the encouragement, but I fear that he was only partly correct. Asking questions is only the very beginning. The reward, if one exists, is in the answers—clear, detailed, verifiable answers. Moreover, the general distrust journalists tend to harbor for the academics who study them is surely an impediment to this project "making a difference." What I hope is that I have at least provided a clear and detailed examination of video journalism: what it is, how it works, and most importantly, what it might be.

NOTES:

1. Posting Apr 9, 2007 4:20 PM EST, www.TVspy.com.

References

Aho, J. (2002). *The orifice as sacrificial site: Culture, organization and the body*. Hawthorne, NY: Aldine De Gruyter.

Aitken, I. (Ed.). (1998). *The documentary film movement: An anthology*. Edinburgh: Edinburgh University Press.

Altheide, D. L. (1987). The format of TV network news. In J. Vidal-Beneyto & P. Dahlgren (Eds.), *The focused screen* (pp. 139–180). Strasbourg, France: AMELA/Council of Europe.

Altheide, D. L., & Snow, R. P. (1979). *Media logic*. Beverly Hills, CA: Sage.

Ananny, M., & Stohecker, C. (2002, December). *Sustained, open dialogue with citizen photojournalism*. Paper presented at the Development by Design Conference, Bangalore, India.

Archebald, R. (1986). *Camera as prosthesis*. (Unpublished master's thesis). University of Pennsylvania, Philadelphia, PA.

Associated Press. (2008, August 15). Gannett is cutting 1,000 newspaper jobs. Retrieved from http://www.clip&copy.com.

———. (2009, August 5). New journalists roam world in search of stories. *New York Times*. Retrieved from http://www.nytimes.com.

Baddeley, W. H. (1973). *The technique of documentary film production* (3rd ed.). New York: Hastings House.

Bantz, C. R., McCorkle, S., & Baade, R. (1980). The news factory. *Communication Research, 7*(1), 45–68.

Barnhurst, K. G. (1994). *Seeing the newspaper*. New York: St. Martin's Press.

Barnhurst, K. G., & Nerone, J. (2001). *The form of news*. New York: The Guilford Press.

Barnouw, E. (1974). *Documentary: A history of the non-fiction film* (1983 ed.). Oxford: Oxford University Press.

Barsam, R. M. (1973). *Nonfiction film: A critical history*. Bloomington: Indiana University Press.

Bauers, S. (2007, March 21). Science gets an eyeful: A web-cam death match, 40 floors up. *Philadelphia Inquirer*, p. A01.

Becker, K. (2003). Photojournalism and the tabloid press. In L. Wells (Ed.), *The photography reader* (pp. 291–308). London: Routledge.

Bell, D. (1995). Woodstock: From vision to symbolic reality. In M. Tobias (Ed.), *The search for reality: The art of documentary filmmaking* (pp. 65–85). Studio City, CA: Michael Wiese Productions.

Bennett, W. L. (1996). *News: The politics of illusion*. White Plains, NY: Longman Publishing.

Berger, P., & Luckmann, T. (1967). *The social construction of reality: A treatise in the sociology of knowledge*. New York: Random House.

Berkowitz, D. (1990). Refining the gatekeeping metaphor for local television news. *Journal of Broadcasting & Electronic Media, 34*(1), 55–68.

Bird, S. E., & Dardenne, R. W. (1988). Myth, chronicle and story: Exploring the narrative qualities of news. In: D. Berkowitz (Ed.), *Social meanings of news* (pp. 333–350). Thousand Oaks, CA: Sage.

Bissell, K. L. (2000). A return to "Mr. Gates": Photography and objectivity. *Newspaper Research Journal, 21*(3), 81–93.

Blair, N. (2009, October 3). CNN launches 1.99 iPhone app. *USA Today Technology Live*. Retrieved from http://www.USAToday.com.

Bliss, E. J. (1991). *Now the news: The story of broadcast journalism*. New York: Columbia University Press.

Bock, M. A. (2008). Together in the scrum: Practicing news photography for print, television and broadband. *Visual Communication Quarterly, 15*(3), 169–179.

———. (2009). Who's minding the gate? Pool feeds, video subsidies and political imagery. *International Journal of Press & Politics 14*(2) 257–278.

Boczkowski, P. J. (2004). *Digitizing the news: Innovation in online newspapers*. Cambridge, MA: MIT Press.

———. (2009). Technology, monitoring, and imitation in contemporary news work. *Communication, Culture and Critique, 2*(1), 39–59.

Boorstin, D. (1961). *The image: A guide to pseudo-events in America*. New York: Harper & Row.

Bourdieu, P. (1980). *The logic of practice* (R. Nice, trans.). Stanford, CA: Stanford University Press.

———. (1993). *The field of cultural production*. New York: Columbia University Press.

———. (2003). The political field, the social science field, and the journalistic field. In R. Benson & E. Neveu (Eds.), *Bourdieu, the Frankfurt School, and cultural studies: On some misunderstandings* (pp. 29–47). Cambridge, UK: Polity Press.

Bourdieu, P., & Wacquant, L. J. D. (1992). *An invitation to reflexive sociology*. Chicago: University of Chicago Press.

Boyd, A. (1993). *Broadcast journalism: Techniques of radio and TV news* (2nd ed.). Oxford: Focal Press.

Boyer, D. (2005). The corporeality of expertise. *Ethnos, 70*(2), 243–266.

Brecheen-Kirkton, K. (1981). A strategy for the interpretation of press photographs. *Journal of Communication Inquiry, 7*, 65–72.

Broadcast. (2001, October 22). Trade secrets...VJs. *Broadcast*. Retrieved from http://www.broadcastnow.co.uk/news/multi-platform/news/tradesecretsvjs/1184264.article.

Burriss, L., & Burriss, K. G. (2008). Gender differences related to co-orientation discrepancy in NASA space photography. *Visual Communication Quarterly, 15*(4), 258–265.

Cablevision. (2009, May 7). *Cablevision Systems Corporation reports first quarter 2009 results*. Bethpage, NY: Retrieved from http://www.cablevision.com.

Campbell, C. A., formerly with the *Newark Star Ledger*, as quoted in the *New York Times*, June 1, 2009, p. B1.

Caranicas, P. (2007, October). NY-1 at 15—newsgathering: The cable channel that helped change the face of broadcasting. *TVB: Television Broadcast*, 18–21.

Carey, J. W. (1989). *Communication as culture: Essays on media and society*. Boston: Unwin Hyman.

Carlebach, M. L. (1997). *American photojournalism comes of age*. Washington, DC: Smithsonian Institution.

Carr, D. (2007, December 10). Muckraking pays, just not in profit. *New York Times*. Retrieved from http://www.nytimes.com.

———. (2008, March 17). More than a sound bite, this clip has some teeth. *New York Times*. Retrieved from http://www.nytimes.com.

———. (2009, June 1). Cast out, but still reporting. *New York Times*, p. B1.

Cartier-Bresson, H. (1952). *The decisive moment*. New York: Simon & Schuster.

Chatman, S. (1978). *Story and discourse: Narrative structure in fiction and film.* Ithaca, NY: Cornell University Press.

———. (1990). *Coming to terms: The rhetoric of narrative in fiction and film.* Ithaca, NY: Cornell University Press.

Churchill, S. (2009, April 23). AT&T reports dramatic growth of WiFi. [Web blog post] Retrieved from http://www.dailywireless.org.

Clarke, G. (1997). *The photograph.* Oxford: Oxford University Press.

Coffman, E. (2009). Documentary and collaboration: Placing the camera in the community. *Journal of Film and Video, 61*(1), 62–78.

Cohen, N. (2009, July 13). How the media wrestle with the web. *New York Times.* Retrieved from http://www.nytimes.com.

Cook, T. E. (2005). *Governing the news: The news media as a political institution.* Chicago: University of Chicago Press.

Cookman, C. (1985). *A Voice is born: The founding and early years of the National Press Photographers Association under the leadership of Joseph Costa.* Durham, NC: National Press Photographers Association.

Corner, J. (1999). *Critical ideas in television studies.* Oxford: Clarendon Press.

Cregan, K. (2006). *The sociology of the body: Mapping the abstraction of embodiment.* London: Sage.

Cumings, B. (1992). *War and television.* London: Verso.

Dahlgren, P. (1987). Tuning in the news: TV journalism and the process of ideation In J. Vidal-Beneyto & P. Dahlgren (Eds.), *The focused screen* (pp. 1–90). Strasbourg, France: Amela, Council of Europe.

Delli Carpini, M. X., Cook, F. L., & Jacobs, L. R. (2004). Public deliberation, discursive participation and citizen engagement: A review of the empirical literature. *Annual Review of Political Science, 7,* 315–344.

de Sola Pool, I. (1983). *The technologies of freedom.* Cambridge, MA: Belknap Press.

Deuze, M. (2004). What is multimedia journalism? *Journalism Studies, 5*(2), 139–152.

Deuze, M., & Platon, S. (2003). Indymedia journalism. *Journalism, 4*(3), 336–355.

Dewey, J. (1934). *Art as experience.* New York: The Penguin Group.

Douglas, M. (2002). *Purity and danger: An analysis of concept of pollution and taboo.* London: Routledge.

Dupagne, M., & Garrison, B. (2006). The meaning and influence of convergence: A qualitative study of newsroom work at the Tampa News Center. *Journalism Studies, 7*(2), 237–255.

Eastlake, L. E. (1980). Photography. In A. Trachtenberg (Ed.), *Classic essays on photography* (pp. 39–68). New Haven, CT: Leete's Island Books. (Original work published 1857)

Edmunds, R. (2008, April 13). 2,400 newsroom jobs lost: Biggest dip in 30 years. *Poynter Online.* Retrieved from http://www.poynteronline.org.

Elias, N. (1978). *The civilizing process* (Vol. 1, *The history of manners*). New York: Pantheon Books.

Ellis, J. (1992). *Seeing things: Television in the age of uncertainty.* London: I.B. Tauris.

Epstein, E. J. (1973). *News from nowhere: Television and the news.* New York: Random House.

Fang, I. (1972). *Television news* (2nd ed.). New York: Hastings House.

Farhi, P. (2008, December 12). WUSA moves to one-person news crews. *Washington Post,* p. C1.

Flint, J., & James, M. (2009, November 12). Current TV to shift from video format. *Los Angeles Times*. Retrieved from http://www.LAtimes.com.

Foucault, M. (1977). What is an author? (D. F. Bouchard & S. Simon, trans.). In D. F. Bouchard (Ed.), *Language, counter-memory, practice: Selected essays and interviews* (pp. 113–138). Ithaca, NY: Cornell University Press.

———. (2001). Panopticism. In J. Evans & S. Hall (Eds.), *Visual culture: The reader* (pp. 61–71). London: Sage.

Gandy Jr., O. H. (1982). *Beyond agenda setting: Information subsidies and public policy*. Norwood, NJ: Ablex.

Gans, H. (1979, 2004). *Deciding what's news: A study of CBS Evening News, NBC Nightly News, Newsweek and Time, 25th anniversary edition*. New York: Pantheon Books.

Gergen, K. J., & Gergen, M. (1991). Toward reflexive methodologies. In F. Steier (Ed.), *Research and reflexivity* (pp. 76–95). Thousand Oaks, CA: Sage.

Gibson, J. J. (1979). The theory of affordances. *The ecological approach to visual perception*. Boston: Houghton Mifflin.

Gitlin, T. (1980). *The whole world is watching: Mass media in the making and unmaking of the new left*. Berkeley: University of California Press.

Glaister, D. (2007, May 12). US website recruits news reporters living in India—Journalists cover council meetings via internet. *The Guardian*. Retrieved from http://www.guardian.co.uk.

Gordon, R. (2003). The meaning and implications of convergence. In K. Kawamoto (Ed.), *Digital journalism: Emerging media and the changing horizons of journalism* (pp. 57–74). Lanham, MD: Rowman & Littlefield.

Gorenstein, D. (2008). *New Hampshire political travel guide*. Concord: New Hampshire Public Radio. Retrieved from http://www.npr.org.

Graulich, H. (2007, September 15). A photographer's legacy tarnished. *News Photographer*. Retrieved from http://www.nppa.org.

Gyimah, D. D. (2007). *About David Dunkley Gyimah*. [Web Log Post] Retrieved from http://viewmag.blogspot.com/2007/03/video-journalist-decree.htm.

Halbwachs, M. (1992). *On collective memory* (L. Coser, trans.). Chicago: University of Chicago Press. (Original work published 1941)

Hall, S. (1973a). The determination of news photographs. In S. Cohen & J. Young (Eds.), *The manufacture of news* (pp. 176–190). London: Constable.

———. (1973b). *Encoding and decoding in the television discourse*. Unpublished manuscript, University of Birmingham, Birmingham, UK.

Hampe, B. (1997). *Making documentary films and reality videos: A practical guide to planning, filming and editing documentaries*. New York: Henry Holt & Company.

Hancock, P., & Tyler, M. (2000). Working bodies. In P. Hancock, B. Hughes, E. Jagger, R. Russell, E. Tulle-Winton, & M. Tyler (Eds.), *The body, culture and society: An introduction* (pp. 86–100). Buckingham, UK: Open University Press.

Harmon, M. D., & White, C. (2001). How television news programs use video news releases. *Public Relations Review*, *27*(2), 213–222.

Harris International (2007, June 11). *TV network news top source of news and information today*. Rochester, NY: Harris Interactive. Retrieved from http://www.harrisinteractive.com/harris_poll/index.asp?PID=768.

Hartley, J. (1982). *Understanding news*. London: Metheun.

———. (1992). *The politics of pictures: The creation of the public in the age of popular media*. London: Routledge.

Hayes, A. F., & Krippendorff, K. (2007). Answering the call for a standard reliability measure for coding data. *Communication Methods and Measures, 1*, 77–89.

Helmers, M., & Hill, C. A. (2004). Introduction. In M. Helmers & C. A. Hill (Eds.), *Defining visual rhetorics* (pp. 1–24). Mahwah, NJ: Erlbaum.

Henderson, L. (1988). Access and consent in public photography. In L. Wells (Ed.). *The photography reader* (pp. 275–287). London: Routledge.

Herman, L., & Vervaeck, B. (2005). *Handbook of narrative analysis.* Lincoln: University of Nebraska Press.

Hill, C. A., & Helmers, M. H. (2004). *Defining visual rhetorics.* Mahwah, NJ: Erlbaum.

Horrigan, J. (2008, July 2). Home Broadband 2008. Pew Internet and American Life Project. Washington D.C.: Pew Foundation. Retrieved from http://www.pewinternet.org/Reports/2008/Home-Broadband-2008.aspx.

Horton, B. (2001). *The Associated Press guide to photojournalism* (2nd ed.). New York: McGraw Hill.

Huxford, J. (2001). Beyond the referential: Uses of visual symbolism in the press. *Journalism, 2*(1), 45–71.

Jarl, S. (1998). A manifest on the subject of documentaries. In Tobias (Ed.), *The search for reality: The art of documentary filmmaking* (pp. 149–153). Studio City, CA: Michael Wise Productions.

Johnson, M. (1987). *The body in the mind: The bodily basis of meaning, imagination and reason.* Chicago: University of Chicago Press.

Jones, J. (2005). *Entertaining politics: New political televison and civic culture.* Lanham, MA: Rowman & Littlefield.

Kaniss, P. (1991). *Making local news.* Chicago: University of Chicago Press.

Kaufman, S. (2009, July 25). Going to the Chapel & We're Gonna Get Jiggy. *Washington Post*, p. CO1.

King, K. (2008). Journalism as conversation. *Neiman Reports, 62*(4) 11–13.

Kochberg, S. (Ed.) (2002). *Introduction to documentary production.* London: Wallflower Press.

Kracauer, S. (1947). *From Caligari to Hitler: A psychological history of the German film.* Princeton: Princeton University Press.

Krippendorff, K. (1989). On the ethics of constructing communication. In B. Dervin, L. Greenberg, B. J. O'Keefe & E. Wartella (Eds.), *Rethinking communication: Paradigm issues* (Vol. 1, pp. 66–96). Newbury Park, CA: Sage.

———. (1993a). Major metaphors of communication and some constructivist reflections on their use. *Cybernetics and Human Knowing, 2*(1), 3–25.

———. (1993b). The past of communication's hoped-for-future. *Journal of Communication, 43*(3), 34–44.

———. (2003). The dialogical reality of meaning. *American Journal of Semiotics, 19*(1–4), 19–36.

———. (2006). *The semantic turn: A new foundation for design.* Boca Raton, FL: Taylor & Francis.

———. (2009). A constructivist critique of semiotics. In F. Bermejo (Ed.), *On communicating: Otherness, meaning and information.* New York: Routledge.

Lakoff, G., & Johnson, M. (1980). *Metaphors we live by.* Chicago: University of Chicago Press.

———. (1999). Philosophy in the flesh: The embodied mind and its challenge to western thought. New York: Basic Books.

Lang, T. (2004). The longer view. *Columbia Journalism Review*, campaigndesk blog. Retrieved from http://www.campaigndesk.org/archives/000988.asp.

Lasica, J. D. (2003). Random acts of journalism. *Media Musings: Charting the rise of open, democratic, grassroots media*. Retrieved from http://www.newmediamusings.com/2003/03/random_acts_of_.html.

Leica Corporation. (n.d.). Leica Corporation history. Retrieved from http://en.leica-camera.com/culture/history/oskar_barnack/.

Levine, L. W. (1988). *Highbrow/lowbrow: The emergence of cultural hierachy in America*. Cambridge, MA: Harvard University Press.

Lewis, C. D. (1984). *Reporting for television*. New York: Columbia University Press.

Limon, A. (1998). *Lawyer: A life of counsel and controversy*. New York: Public Affairs.

Lindekugel, D. M. (1994). *Shooters: TV news photographers and their work*. Westport, CT: Praeger.

Linell, P. (1998). Discourse across boundaries: On recontextualizations and the blending of voices in professional discourse. *Text, 18*(2), 143–157.

Livingston, S., & Bennett, L. W. (2007). Gatekeeping, indexing and live-event news: Is technology altering the construction of news? *Political Communication, 20*(4), 363–380.

Lutz, C. A., & Collins, J. L. (1993). *Reading National Geographic*. Chicago: University of Chicago Press.

Martin, S. E. (1998). How news gets from paper to its online counterpart. *Newspaper Research Journal, 19*(2), 64–73.

Martyn, P. H. (2009). The mojo in the third millenium. *Journalism Practice, 3*(2), 196–215.

Marvin, C. (2004). The body of the text: Literacy's corporeal constant. *Quarterly Journal of Speech, 80*(2), 129–149.

———. (2006). Communication as embodiment. In G. J. Shepherd, J. Saint John & T. Striphas (Eds.), *Communication as...Perspectives on theory* (pp. 67–74). Thousand Oaks, CA: Sage.

Massing, M. (2009). Out of focus: How indie dogma undercuts the documentary. *Columbia Journalism Review, 46*(6), 41–44.

Mayeux, P. E. (1991). *Broadcast news: Writing and reporting*. Dubuque, IA: William. C. Brown.

McEnteer, J. (2006). *Shooting the truth: The rise of American political documentaries*. Westport, CT: Praeger.

McManus, J. (1994). *Market-driven journalism: Let the citizen beware?* Thousand Oaks, CA: Sage.

Medoff, N. J., Fink, E. J., & Tanquary, T. (2007). *Portable video*. Boston: Focal Press.

Messaris, P. (1994). *Visual literacy: Image, mind & reality*. Boulder: Westview Press.

———. (1997). *Visual persuasion: The role of images in advertising*. Thousand Oaks, CA: Sage.

———. (2001). The role of images in framing news stories. In S. D. Reese, O. H. Gandy Jr. & A. E. Grant (Eds.), *Framing public life: Perspectives on media and our understanding of the social world* (pp. 215–226). Mahwah, NJ: Erlbaum.

Messaris, P., & Moriarty, S. (2005). Visual literacy theory. In K. Smith, S. Moriarty, G. Barbatsis & K. Kenney (Eds.), *Handbook of visual communication* (pp. 481–502). Mahwah, NJ: Erlbaum.

Moeller, S. D. (1989). *Shooting war: Photography and the American experience of combat*. New York: Basic Books.

Molotch, H., & Lester, M. (1974). News as purposive behaviour: On the strategic use of routine events, accidents and scandals. *American Sociological Review*, *39*, 101–112.

Morris, J. G. (2002). *Get the picture: A personal history of photojournalism*. Chicago: University of Chicago Press.

Morrow, K. (2007). The birth of photojournalism. *Civil War Times*, *46*(7), 40–46.

Mulvey, L. (1975). Visual pleasure and narrative cinema. *Screen*, *16*(3).

Murray, M. (2006). Best of photojournalism 2007: TV contest rule changes and additions. *NPPA News and Events*. Retrieved from http://www.nppa.org/news_and_events /news/2006/11/2007_tv_bop_rules.html.

Nason, D. (2008, May 7). Making money: Pre-roll, post-roll and the ads in between. Arlington, VA: Newspaper Association of America. Retrieved from http://www.naa.org.

National Press Photographers Association. (2005). *History*. Retrieved from http://www.nppa.org/about_us/history.html.

National Press Photographers Association. (n.d.). *NPPA code of ethics*. Retrieved from http://www.nppa.org/professional_development/business_practices/ethics.html.

National Press Photographers Association. (2008, May 29). *NPPA board adopts $1.5M budget, elects new officers, does not change name*. Retrieved from http://www.nppa.org.

Neveu, E. (2005). Bourdieu, the Frankfurt School, and cultural studies: On some misunderstandings. In R. Benson & E. Neveu (Eds.), *Bourdieu and the journalistic field* (pp. 195–213). Cambridge, UK: Polity.

New York Times. (1995, April 7). *The media business: Times Company to buy a video stake*. Retrieved from http://www.nytimes.com.

Newton, J. H. (2001). *The burden of visual truth: The role of photojournalism in mediating reality*. Mahwah, NJ: Erlbaum.

———. (2006). Influences of digital imaging on the concept of photographic truth. In P. Messaris & L. Humphreys (Eds.), *Digital media: Transformations in human communication* (pp. 3–14). New York: Peter Lang.

Nichols, B. (1991). *Representing reality: Issues and concepts in documentary*. Bloomington: Indiana University Press.

———. (2001). *Introduction to documentary*. Bloomington: Indiana University Press.

Nora, P. (Ed.) (1997). *Realms of memory: Rethinking the French past* (Vol. 1). New York: Columbia University Press.

Ourand, J. P. (2004, March 8). C-SPAN proves the value of a nickel. *Cable 360 Net*. Retrieved from http://www.cable360.net/programming/shows/C-Span-Proves-the-Value-of-a-Nickel_15695.html.

Parr, B. (2005). Things I wish I'd known before I became a citizen journalist. *Neiman Reports*, *59*(4), 29–31.

Peters, J. D. (2001). Witnessing. *Media, Culture & Society*, *23*(6), 707–723.

Pew Research Center. (2009, March 12). *Many would shrug if their local newspaper closed*. Pew Research Center for the People and the Press. Washington, DC: Pew Foundation. Retrieved from http://www.people-press.org/2009/03/12/many-would-shrug-if-their-local-newspaper-closed/.

———. (2011). *The state of the news media 2011*. Washington DC: Pew Research Center's Project for Excellence in Journalism. Retrieved from http://stateofthemedia.org/.

Quart, A. (2008). Flickring out. *Columbia Journalism Review*, *47*(2), 14–17.

Reed, C. (2009, August. 24). Journalists recent work examined before embeds. *Stars and Stripes, Mideast Edition*. Retrieved from http://www.stripes.com.

Rentschler, C. A. (2004). Witnessing: US citizenship and the vicarious experience of suffering. *Media, Culture & Society*, *26*, 296.

Rosenberg, K. (2010, April 26). A man who stopped time to set it in motion again. *New York Times*. Retrieved from http://www.nytimes.com.

Rosenblum, M. (n.d.). *Who we are*. Retrieved from http://www.rosenblumtv.com/about/michael-bio/.

Rosenblum, N. (1997). *A world history of photography* (3rd ed.). New York: Abbeville Press Publishers.

Rosenthal, P. (2008, July 13). TV, papers crossing paths in future of news. *Chicago Tribune*. Retrieved from http://chicagotribune.com.

Rothstein, A. (1956). *Photojournalism*. New York: American Photographic Book Publishing.

Russell, R. (2006, April 12). KRON's last gasp: How a once-proud San Francisco television station became ground zero in the nation's most controversial experiment in local TV news. *SFWeekly*. Retrieved from http://www.sfweekly.com/2006-04-12/news/kron-s-last-gasp/.

Rutenberg, J., & Zeleny, J. (2008, June 19). Obama's campaign tightens control of image and access. *New York Times*. Retrieved from http://www.nytimes.com.

Saba, J. (2008, March 28). Newspapers face biggest ad revenue plunge in more than 50 years. *Editor & Publisher*. Retrieved from http://www.freepress.net/node/38006.

Samuels, D. (2008, April). Shooting Brittany. *The Atlantic Monthly*, *301*(3), 36–51.

Sass, E. (2008, November 12). Trad media hit harder than past recessions. *Media Post*. Retrieved from http://www.mediapost.com.

———. (2009, March 17). Newspapers expand digital platforms. *Media Daily News*. Retrieved from http://www.mediapost.com.

———. (2010a, March 26). Red ink: Newspapers fell 23.7% in 4Q. *Media Daily News*. Retrieved from http://www.mediapost.com.

———. (2010b). Video views surge on newspaper sites: Advertisers take notice. *MediaPost*. Retrieved from http://mediapost.com.

Scannell, P. (2004). What reality has misfortune? *Media, Culture & Society*, *26*(4), 573–584.

Scharf, A. (1974). *Art and photography*. Baltimore: Penguin.

Schatzki, T. (1996). *Social practices: A Wittgensteinian approach to human activity and the social*. Cambridge: Cambridge University Press.

Schram, M. (1987). *The great American video game*. New York: William Morrow & Company.

Schudson, M. (1978). *Discovering the news: A social history of American newspapers*. New York: Basic Books.

———. (2001). The objectivity norm in American journalism. *Journalism, 2*(2), 149–170.

———. (2003). *The sociology of news*. New York: Norton.

Schwartz, David. (1988). *Documentary meets the avant-garde*, Independent America: New Film 1978–1988. Astoria, NY: American Museum of the Moving Image.

Schwartz, Dona. (1992). To tell the truth: Codes of objectivity in journalism. *Communication*, *13*(2), 95–109.

———. (1999). Objective representation: Photographs as facts. In B. Brennen & H. Hardt (Eds.), *Picturing the past* (pp. 158–181). Urbana: University of Illinois Press.

Searle, J. R. (1969). *Speech acts: An essay in the philosophy of language*. Cambridge: Cambridge University Press.

———. (1995). *The construction of social reality*. New York: The Free Press.

Sekula, A. (1984). On the invention of photographic meaning. *Photography Against the Grain*. Halifax, Nova Scotia: Press of the Nova Scotia College of Art and Design.

———. (1986, Winter). The body and the archive. *October*, *39*, 3–64.

Shoemaker, P. (1991). *Gatekeeping*. Thousand Oaks, CA: Sage.

Sigal, L. (1973). *Reporters & officials: The organization and politics of newsmaking*. Lexington, MA: D.C. Heath & Co.

Singer, J. B. (2003). Who are these guys? *Journalism*, *4*(2), 139–163.

———. (2009). Ethnography. *Journalism and Mass Communication Quarterly*, *86*(1), 191–198.

Slattery, K. L., Hakanen, E. A., & Doremus, M. E. (1996). The expression of localism: Local TV news coverage in the new video marketplace. *Journal of Broadcasting and Electronic Media*, *40*(3), 403–413.

Smith, B. (2003). John Searle: From speech acts to social reality. In B. Smith (Ed.), *John Searle* (pp. 1–33). Cambridge: Cambridge University Press.

Sontag, S. (2003). *Regarding the pain of others*. New York: Farrar, Staus and Giroux.

———. (2004, May 23). Regarding the torture of others. *New York Times Magazine*. Retrieved from http://www.nytimes.com.

Spratt, M., Peterson, A., & Lagos, T. (2005). Of photographs and flags: Uses and perceptions of an iconic image before and after September 11th. *Popular Communication: The International Journal of Media and Culture*, *3*(2), 117–136.

Stam, R. (2000a). The author. In R. Stam & T. Miller (Eds.), *Film and theory: An anthology* (pp. 1–7). Malden, MA: Blackwell.

———. (2000b). Television news and its spectator. In R. Stam & T. Miller (Eds.), *Film and theory: An anthology* (pp. 361–380). Malden, MA: Blackwell.

Stelter, B., & Carter, B. (2010, February 23). ABC News to cut hundreds of staff. *New York Times*, p. B5.

Sterne, J. (2003). Bourdieu, technique, and society. *Cultural Studies*, *17*(3), 367–389.

Strentz, H. (1977). *News reporters and news sources: What happens before the story is written.* Ames: Iowa State University Press.

Swarns, R. L. (2009, July 4). 'Family Friendly' White House Proves Less So for Many Aides. *New York Times*, p. A1.

Swartz, D. (1997). *Culture and power: The sociology of Pierre Bourdieu*. Chicago: University of Chicago Press.

Tagg, J. (1999). Evidence, truth and order: A means of surveillance. In S. Hall & J. Evans (Eds.), *Visual culture: The reader* (pp. 244–273). Thousand Oaks, CA: Sage.

Taylor, J. (1998). *Body horror*. Manchester: Manchester University Press.

Tompkins, A. (2009). WTSP-TV uses Skype to broadcast live shot. *Poynter Online: Al's Morning Meeting*. Retrieved from www.poynteronline.org.

Tuchman, G. (1972). Objectivity as strategic ritual: An examination of newsmen's notions of objectivity. *American Journal of Sociology*, *77*(4), 660–679.

———. (1978). *Making news: A study in the construction of reality*. London: The Free Press.

Turner, B. (1984). *The body & society*. Oxford: Blackwell.

Turow, J. (2003). *Media today* (2nd ed.). Boston: Houghton Mifflin.

Vaughn, D. (1995). The man with the movie camera. In L. Jacobs (Ed.), *The documentary tradition: From Nanook to Woodstock* (pp. 53–59). New York: Hopkinson and Blake.

Vidal-Beneyto, J., & Dahlgren, P. (Eds.). (1987). *The focused screen*. Strasbourg, France: Amela/Council of Europe.

Weaver, D., & Wilhoit, G. C. (1986). *The American journalist.* Bloomington: University of Indiana Press.

Webster's New Collegiate Dictionary. (1977). Springfield, MA: G. & C. Merriam.

Wertheimer, D. (2007, October). One is the loneliest number. *Press Photographer, 62*(10), 16.

Weynand, D. (2007). *Apple Pro training series: Final Cut Pro Six.* Berkeley, CA: Peachpit Press.

Williams, B., & Delli Carpini, M. X. (2000). Unchained reaction: The collapse of media gatekeeping and the Clinton-Lewinsky scandal. *Journalism, 1*(1), 61–85.

Yaschur, C. (2011, May). *More with less: Factors influencing photojournalists' changing roles and job satisfaction.* Paper presented at the International Communication Association Conference, Boston.

———. (2012). Photojournalists Enjoy Web Work, Additional Autonomy. *Newspaper Research Journal. 33*(1), 71–85.

Zelizer, B. (1990a). *Covering the body: The Kennedy assassination and the establishment of journalistic authority.* Chicago: University of Chicago Press.

———. (1990b). Where is the author in American TV news? On the construction and presentation of proximity, authorship and journalistic authority. *Semiotica, 80*(1), 37.

———. (1993). Journalists as interpretive communities. *Critical Studies in Mass Communication, 10*(1993), 219–237.

———. (1995). Journalism's "last stand": Wirephoto and the discourse of resistance. *Journal of Communication, 45*(2), 78–92.

———. (1998). *Remembering to forget: Holocaust memory through the camera's eye.* Chicago: University of Chicago Press.

———. (2004). When facts, truth and reality are god-terms: On journalism's uneasy place in cultural studies. *Communication and Critical/Cultural Studies, 1*(1), 100–119.

———. (2005). Journalism through the camera's eye. In S. Allen (Ed.), *Journalism: Critical issues.* (pp. 167–176). New York: Open University Press.

———. (2006). What's untransportable about the transport of photographic images? *Popular Communication, 4*(1), 3–20.

———. (2007). On "having been there": Eyewitnessing as a journalistic key word. *Critical Studies in Media Communication, 24*(5), 408–428.

Index

Mass Communication and Journalism

Lee B. Becker, *General Editor*

The Mass Communication and Journalism series focuses on broad issues in mass communication, giving particular attention to those in which journalism is prominent. Volumes in the series examine the product of the full range of media organizations as well as individuals engaged in various types of communication activities.

Each commissioned book deals in depth with a selected topic, raises new issues about that topic, and provides a fuller understanding of it through the new evidence provided. The series contains both single-authored and edited works. For more information and submissions, please contact:

Lee B. Becker, Series Editor | *lbbecker@uga.edu*
Mary Savigar, Acquisitions Editor | *mary.savigar@plang.com*

To order other books in this series, please contact our Customer Service Department at:

(800) 770-LANG (within the U.S.)
(212) 647-7706 (outside the U.S.)
(212) 647-7707 FAX

Or browse online by series at www.peterlang.com